The Shenandoah Valley Campaign of 1862

MILITARY CAMPAIGNS OF THE CIVIL WAR

EDITED BY

GARY W. GALLAGHER

The Shenandoah Valley
Campaign of 1862

The University of North Carolina Press

Chapel Hill and London

Designed by Heidi Perov

Set in Monotype Baskerville

by Keystone Typesetting, Inc.

Manufactured in the United States of America

The paper in this book meets the guidelines for permanence
and durability of the Committee on Production Guidelines for
Book Longevity of the Council on Library Resources.

LIBRARY OF CONGRESS CATALOGING-IN-PUBLICATION DATA

The Shenandoah Valley Campaign of 1862 /

edited by Gary W. Gallagher.

p. cm. — (Military campaigns of the Civil War)

Includes bibliographical references and index.

ISBN 0-8078-2786-x (alk. paper)

1. Shenandoah Valley Campaign, 1862.

I. Gallagher, Gary W. II. Series.

E473.7.S54 2003

973.7'32—dc21

2002013374

07 06 05 04 03   5 4 3 2 1

For Barbara J. Wright,
whose many kindnesses I can never repay

CONTENTS

Introduction

ix

The French artist Charles Hoffbauer painted a series of imposing murals depicting the seasons of the Confederacy. Completed in the years following World War I, the four works fill a large gallery at the Virginia Historical Society in Richmond. For *Spring*, Hoffbauer chose as his subject Stonewall Jackson in the Shenandoah Valley. The painting pulses with energy, conveying a sense of optimism and potential in the incipient southern republic. Under the eye of Jackson, who sits sternly astride "Little Sorrel" on rising ground beside what is probably the Valley Turnpike, the leading figures in a long line of infantry march past the viewer. The soldiers strain under a pace that tells on their faces. One of them raises an arm in a gesture of respect for his commander, as does a mounted officer, whose horse, with flared nostrils and open mouth, also suggests extreme effort. Most of the infantrymen focus resolutely ahead, their long strides carrying them through the beautiful Valley countryside, past wounded comrades, and into Civil War history as Jackson's fabled "Foot Cavalry." Hoffbauer's sweeping image ascribes a heroic spirit to Jackson and his Army of the Valley—a spirit that captivated Confederates in 1862 and has fascinated students of the Civil War ever since.[1]

Events in the Valley between March and early June 1862 took on fabulous proportions over the years. It is important to keep in mind, however, that they functioned at the time as a secondary dimension of military affairs in an Eastern Theater dominated by Maj. Gen. George B. McClellan's offensive against Richmond. The scale of combat in the Seven Days battles, which marked the bloody climax of McClellan's effort to capture the Confederate capital, dwarfed that in the half-dozen engagements fought in the Valley between Jackson and his various Federal opponents. Nearly twice as many men fell on June 27 at Gaines's Mill, costliest of the Seven Days, as in all of Jackson's battles in the Shenandoah combined.[2] The strategic stakes were also much higher at Richmond. Gen. Robert E. Lee's victory over McClellan

Spring, by Charles Hoffbauer. Virginia Historical Society.

profoundly affected the course of the war, an impact beyond the power of the much smaller forces that contended for superiority in the Valley.[3]

Yet Jackson's Valley campaign fully merits the intense scrutiny it has received, both because timing gave it psychological importance out of proportion to the number of men involved and because it circumscribed McClellan's ability to draw reinforcements from other parts of Virginia. Jackson operated in the Valley during a period of Confederate military failure and plummeting national morale. During the first five months of 1862, Union armies took control of huge sections of the western and Trans-Mississippi Confederacy, including the invaluable port of New Orleans. In the East, McClellan's Army of the Potomac was closing in on Richmond. The Confederate people searched in vain for inspiriting news from the battlefield, even as they hotly debated the constitutionality and necessity of a national conscription act passed in mid-April. None of the Confederacy's senior generals seemed poised to lead the way toward southern independence. Gen. Albert Sidney Johnston, once widely heralded across the South, had been killed at Shiloh on April 6. Gen. P. G. T. Beauregard, the "Hero of Sumter" and co-victor with Gen. Joseph E. Johnston at the battle of First Manassas, had added no luster to his record since transferring to the Tennessee-Mississippi arena in early 1862. Joseph Johnston had retreated with the Confederacy's largest army from northern Virginia to the Peninsula without a major battle, and he showed little predilection for the type of aggressive generalship favored by the Confederate populace. The Seven Days campaign would reveal Robert E. Lee, who took charge of Richmond's defending troops after Johnston was wounded on May 31, to be the general best suited to meet the Confederacy's needs, but in the spring of 1862 he served behind a desk in Richmond as Jefferson Davis's primary military adviser. This grim Confederate picture changed when Jackson, on the strength of his victories in the Valley, shot into national prominence. Displaying resourcefulness, unbending purpose, and a penchant for speed and audacity, he earned the adoration of his people and eclipsed in popularity all other Confederate generals.

A few words about the Valley's geography and logistical and strategic significance will provide a useful context for discussion of the 1862 campaign.[4] The Shenandoah cuts a fertile, rolling slash between Virginia's piedmont and the rugged mountains of the state's antebellum western regions. A landscape of breathtaking beauty and agricultural bounty, it extends from the Potomac River to beyond Lexington in Rockbridge County. With the Blue Ridge Mountains on the east and the more imposing Alleghenies to the west, the Valley runs southwest to northeast and drops gently in its course to meet the Potomac. The forks of the Shenandoah River thus flow south to north (or southwest to northeast), which means that an individual traveling to the Potomac goes "down the Valley"—an odd circumstance in a world where north is almost always "up." Between Strasburg and Harrisonburg, Massanutten Mountain divides the Valley. West of Massanutten, in the Valley proper, the North Fork of the Shenandoah River meanders toward the Potomac, while to the east the South Fork runs through the Luray (or Page) Valley on its journey to join the North Fork at Front Royal. The lower Valley, as the northern portion is known, includes the broad expanse between Williamsport on the Potomac and Strasburg, as well as the land west of Massanutten Mountain as far south as Woodstock. A secondary valley parallels the northeastern flank of the Shenandoah, nestling between the Blue Ridge and the modest bulk of the Bull Run Mountains.

The logistical value of the Valley during the war scarcely can be overstated. Its agricultural riches promised sustenance for Confederate forces in Virginia. The most important wheat growing area of the entire Upper South through most of the antebellum period, it also led Virginia in production of other grains and cattle and contributed substantial quantities of leather, wood products, woolen textiles, and whisky. No rail system served the entire Valley, but three lines provided links to northern and eastern Virginia. The Virginia Central crossed the Blue Ridge near Waynesboro and ran to Staunton, the largest rail depot in the Valley, and thence to Covington; the Manassas Gap Railroad connected Mount Jackson, Strasburg, and Front Royal to Manassas Junction via Thoroughfare Gap in the Bull Run Mountains; and the Winchester and Potomac Railroad, a spur of the mighty Baltimore & Ohio (B&O), penetrated the lower Valley from Harpers Ferry to Winchester. Supplementing these railroads as an artery for the movement of logistical goods and armies was the macadamized Valley Turnpike, which provided all-weather service between Staunton and Martinsburg.

The Valley also loomed large as a strategic avenue whence either side could mount a threat to the western flanks of Washington and Richmond. All of the Valley below Strasburg lay north of the U.S. capital. A Confederate army marching down the Valley, screened by cavalry in the gaps of the Blue Ridge, might easily cross the Potomac and descend on the right rear of Washington. The B&O was vulnerable to Confederate attack where it dipped south of the Potomac between Harpers Ferry and Martinsburg. Moreover, any Federal advance through north-central Virginia along the Orange & Alexandria Railroad would present an open right flank to Confederates lurking behind the passes in the Blue Ridge. Similarly, Federals moving up the Valley could cut the rail lines to eastern Virginia, thereby disrupting the flow of supplies to the soldiers defending Richmond, while at the same time placing in jeopardy the left flank of any southern army between the Occoquan and the Rappahannock-Rapidan River line.

The 1862 Valley campaign had its origins in Robert E. Lee's desire to limit the size of the Union threat against Richmond. By early May, McClellan's main force numbered roughly 100,000 and was progressing through Yorktown and Williamsburg up the Peninsula. Near Fredericksburg, just fifty miles north of Richmond, another 40,000 Federals under Maj. Gen. Irvin McDowell were poised to assist in crushing Johnston's army. Farther to the north and west, Maj. Gen. Nathaniel P. Banks led 20,000 Yankees in the lower Shenandoah Valley, and Maj. Gen. John C. Frémont headed about 8,000 in the Allegheny Mountains. Lee proposed reinforcing Jackson with Maj. Gen. Richard S. Ewell's division, bringing Confederate strength in the Valley to about 17,500, after which he wanted Jackson to engage Banks and Frémont in such a way as to preclude their joining either McDowell or McClellan.[5] Jackson had taken an initial step toward this end with an offensive movement in late March that resulted in the battle of First Kernstown. A Confederate tactical defeat, First Kernstown nonetheless had persuaded the Federals to hold Banks and Frémont in the Valley, which in turn set up Jackson's subsequent success.

The outline of the campaign can be sketched quickly. Jackson took part of his command westward from Staunton, united with a small force under Brig. Gen. Edward "Alleghany" Johnson, and struck an advance element of Frémont's army under Brig. Gen. Robert H. Milroy at McDowell on May 8. With these Federals falling back through the rugged terrain of the Alleghenies after an inconclusive engagement, Jackson returned to the Valley and marched northward toward New Market while Ewell's division paralleled his movement to the east in the Luray Valley. Traversing Massanutten Mountain at New Market Gap, the only passage across that forbidding barrier along its fifty-mile length, Jackson joined Ewell in the Luray Valley. The Army of the Valley then hastened toward Front Royal, captured a Federal garrison there on May 23, defeated Banks's army in the battle of First Winchester on May 25, and over the next several days pursued retreating Federals to the Potomac River.

A minor irritant to the Union before his appearance at Front Royal, Jackson posed a much greater potential threat when he reached the Potomac frontier. But he also had placed himself in a difficult position, far from supporting Confederates and subject to pressure from several directions. Abraham Lincoln recognized Jackson's vulnerability and pressed for a three-pronged offensive designed to bring Federal forces together south of Jackson's army, isolating it in the lower Valley, where it could be destroyed or captured. Frémont would march east out of the Alleghenies, one of McDowell's divisions under Brig. Gen. James Shields would proceed west through Front Royal toward Strasburg, and Banks, who had crossed to the Maryland side of the Potomac, would return to Virginia and harass the Confederate rear. Jackson recognized his predicament and responded by driving his men to the limit. Beginning on May 30, the Confederates marched southward, much of the time through a driving rain, beating their opponents to Strasburg on June 1 and continuing up the Valley to the far end of the Massanutten Range near Harrisonburg. There Jackson stopped to face his pursuers, defeating Frémont at Cross Keys on June 8 and Shields at Port Republic on June 9. Following these twin defeats, Frémont withdrew northward down the Valley proper while Shields retreated down the Luray Valley, and Jackson soon joined Lee's army outside Richmond.

Jackson's string of victories provided enormous emotional sustenance for Confederates long denied good news from their military forces. In terms of effect, *what* had happened at these engagements counted for less than *when* it had happened. It mattered little that the battles—McDowell, Front Royal, and Cross Keys might better be described as skirmishes—had been minor affairs with relatively few casualties. A pair of civilian diarists exhibited the heartfelt satisfaction many Confederates experienced upon learning that one of their generals had crafted stirring victories. Catherine Ann Devereux Edmondston, a North Carolinian whose immensely informative journal sheds light on myriad facets of the war, recorded on May 29 that "Jackson has had another splendid success in the Valley & has completely routed Banks at Front Royal & driven him into and through Winchester which we now hold. . . . This victory has cheered our army before Richmond greatly. God grant that it may have correspondingly depressed our enemies." On June 9 a woman living in Richmond voiced feelings typical of many southerners who read about Cross Keys and Port Republic. "General Jackson is performing prodigies of valor in the Valley," she observed; "he has met the forces of Fremont and Shields, and *whipped them in detail*." She added three days later that Confederates were "more successful in Virginia than elsewhere"—success that had come when desperately needed because the "whole Mississippi River, except Vicksburg and its environs, is now in the hands of the enemy, and . . . Memphis has fallen!"[6]

Newspapers across the Confederacy prophesied that Jackson's victories would yield rich dividends and lauded his style of leadership. A few quotations will suggest the tenor of this editorial coverage. The *Charleston Courier* ventured an assessment shortly after the battle of First Winchester, expressing confidence that Jackson would "follow up the good work he has commenced" with movements calculated "to make Lincoln tremble in his capital." Two days after the victory at Port Republic, the *Richmond Dispatch* crowed that news from the Valley augured ill for both Lincoln and McClellan: "The success of glorious 'Stonewall' in the Valley cannot fail to raise a high old panic among the functionaries of Washington and divert, in a measure, the plans of McClellan opposite Richmond. The result of these splendid victories is too evident to need comment. . . . [They] are as surely aids in the defence of Richmond as any along the line of the Chickahominy."[7]

A number of newspapers, sharing their readers' impatience with retreats or inactivity, celebrated Jackson's offensive-minded generalship. Shortly before Cross Keys and Port Republic, the *Lancaster (S.C.) Ledger* observed that "all tongues are now ready to speak the praises of this victorious hero, who exhibits and applies the spur, while other Generals seem inclined to apply the spade. . . . We anticipate and utter the wishes and expectations of all readers when we nominate him for the first vacancy to be filled by promotion." A correspondent for the *Savannah Republican*, quoted in the *Charleston Mercury*, similarly approved of Jackson's aggressiveness and hoped it would have a salutary effect on commanders elsewhere. "The country need not be surprised if the bold movement of Stonewall Jackson upon the Potomac should be imitated in the West," noted this man: "Whether it will be on the east or west side of the Mississippi, or both, I shall not undertake to say." Another correspondent, identified only as "S." in the *Richmond Whig*, offered a panegyric to the rebel commander. Cross Keys and Port Republic ranked "among the most brilliant—if not the most brilliant"—battles of the war, averred the enthusiastic "S.": "Jackson and his army, in one month, have routed Milroy— annihilated Banks—discomfited Fremont, and overthrown Shields! Was there ever such a series of victories won by an inferior force by dauntless courage and consummate generalship?"[8]

Apart from boosting morale among the Confederate people, Jackson also had accomplished Lee's strategic goals. Not only did Banks remain far from Richmond, but McDowell's troops at Fredericksburg also were withheld from McClellan, who complained vociferously about a lack of reinforcements. "Little Mac's" whining, in the past typically composed of equal parts wind and petulance, for once had merit. When the military moment of truth came at Richmond toward the end of June, the Confederates benefited immeasurably from the absence of McDowell's divisions. Military analysts through subsequent decades fully appreciated what Jackson had accomplished, using his campaign in the Valley as a case study in how to frustrate a series of opponents through rapid movement, deception, and a willingness to take risks.

It takes nothing away from Jackson's achievement to note that his campaign did not create a pervasive sense of alarm on the northern home front. This phenomenon deserves some emphasis because many accounts have gone beyond Jackson's obvious accomplishments to make extravagant claims about his impact in May and June 1862. The northern press reported Banks's retreat after Winchester and conceded that Jackson's advance toward the Potomac created brief consternation in Washington, but few editors labeled the Confederate presence in the lower Valley a serious threat. The *New York Evening Post*'s correspondent, for example, filed a story on May 26 that appeared under the heading "The Panic At The Capital. Its Causelessness Exposed." A day later the *Albany (N.Y.) Atlas and Argus* observed that "the sudden dash of the Rebels upon Banks' division, created a momentary apprehension in the public mind, that they seriously intended a formidable movement against Washington through Maryland." In fact, continued the article perceptively, Jackson's goal almost certainly was to prevent "reinforcement of McClellan, by engaging the attention of Banks' and McDowell's divisions upon the safety of Washington." Admitting a grudging admiration for Jackson's ability, as did a number of other northern papers, the *Atlas and Argus* nevertheless doubted that his march "toward the Potomac will accomplish more than to cover the retreat of [Jefferson] Davis's forces in a southerly direction." On May 27 Philadelphia's *Daily Evening Bulletin* acknowledged that news of Banks's retreat "went through the sensitive nerves of the country like a sharp pain," but the paper went on to depreciate the extent of real damage: "We have no idea, however, that it can make any special difference in the great result." One day later the *Daily Evening Bulletin* reprimanded politicians who, it claimed, initially had magnified the danger before reversing course to assure the public "that Washington was not in the slightest danger."[9]

Several themes recurred in northern press coverage once Jackson began his withdrawal from the lower Valley. Most editors interpreted the Confederate march from Harpers Ferry through Winchester and Strasburg and on toward Harrisonburg as evidence of Federal success. In New York the *Tribune*'s headlines on June 3 announced, "Jackson's Force Overtaken. He Declined Battle and Ran Away. Occupation of Strasburg." The *Times* weighed in the next day: "Department of the Shenandoah. Highly Important Movements Against the Enemy. Encounter of Gen. Fremont with Jackson's Rear Guard. Defeat of the Rebels and Capture of Prisoners and Cannon." Readers of the *Chicago Tribune* opened their papers on June 2 to learn, "From Gen. Banks' Department. The Federals Rout the Rebels in Turn. Skedaddle No. 2 From Front Royal. Gen. Banks Regaining Lost Ground. Our Forces Drive

The Rebels After A Brisk Battle."[10] Several newspapers also highlighted the death of Brig. Gen. Turner Ashby, who commanded Jackson's cavalry and fell mortally wounded near Harrisonburg on June 6, and many praised the generalship of Banks, Frémont, and to a lesser degree, Shields and McDowell.[11]

Summaries of the campaign typically dwelled not on the magnitude of Jackson's threat but on the lost opportunity to destroy his army during its trek from Harpers Ferry to Harrisonburg. In contrast to their southern counterparts, northern editors treated Cross Keys and Port Republic as Federal victories or, alternatively, as Confederate holding actions designed to permit the fleeing Jackson's safe exit from the Valley. In the latter vein, the *Boston Daily Advertiser* opined that of "all the escapes which Jackson has made in the valley of Virginia, the most narrow was probably that which he effected at Port Republic. . . . Fremont pursuing Jackson hotly had fought him on Sunday at Cross Keys, . . . and Jackson severely handled then had resumed his flight, intending to cross the Shenandoah at Port Republic, and thus escape from the valley." The *New York Tribune* adopted a somewhat dismissive tone toward the rebels in its reckoning of the campaign: " 'Stonewall Jackson,' with what is left of his army, has evidently escaped from the Valley over the Blue Ridge. . . . His retreat has evinced good qualities—strength of arm and fleetness of foot." Jackson's command probably should have been "caught between Shields and Frémont and dispersed," but the moment passed after Port Republic. "Jackson's raid down the Valley and race out of it are among the most stirring episodes of the War," summed up the *Tribune*. "We presume he is now beyond successful pursuit."[12]

The 1862 Valley campaign invites examination from a number of perspectives. For this eighth volume of Military Campaigns of the Civil War, contributors wrote essays that illuminate various dimensions of the subject. Readers new to the series should keep in mind that its titles never have sought to provide comprehensive tactical or strategic narratives that give all the major commanders their full measure of attention. Anyone seeking such an overview should read the revised edition of Robert G. Tanner's *Stonewall in the Valley: Thomas J. "Stonewall" Jackson's Shenandoah Valley Campaign, Spring 1862* (Mechanicsburg, Pa.: Stackpole, 1996), which, as its title suggests, focuses more on the Confederate than on the Federal side of the story. As with earlier volumes in the series, these essays collectively engage famous leaders and events, explore the impact of military operations on civilians, and discuss how participants remembered the campaign. Also as in the past, the contributors sometimes disagree with one another's conclusions, in this instance on such questions as the role of Lincoln, the quality of Union military leadership, and the impact of the campaign on people in the North. Veteran readers of the series will note an unusual imbalance between Union and Confederate topics. The predominance of the latter stemmed from various factors, including changes in the roster of authors, and does not presage a long-term editorial emphasis.

The opening essay, one of two on predominantly Union topics, follows the campaign from Abraham Lincoln's perspective. Among the more durable misconceptions about Jackson's campaign is that Lincoln panicked in the wake of the battles of Front Royal and First Winchester. A number of authors have argued that the president, fearing for the safety of the national capital, decided that General McClellan might have to abandon his offensive against Richmond in order to protect Washington. This essay challenges the portrait of an unnerved Lincoln, suggesting that he kept his head and used Jackson's success in an attempt to coax McClellan into a more aggressive stance on the Peninsula. Beyond hoping for more decisive action at Richmond, Lincoln also sought to coordinate the efforts of Banks, Frémont, and McDowell to deal a fatal blow to Jackson in the lower Valley.

Jackson began the campaign with a reputation based largely on his role at the battle of First Manassas. Although generally admired and blessed with one of the best sobriquets in American military history, he did not rank alongside more famous Confederate generals such as the Johnstons and P. G. T. Beauregard. Robert K. Krick's essay explores how the final month of Jackson's campaign in the Valley catapulted him into national prominence. Krick takes pains to demonstrate that the Valley campaign, rather than postwar Lost Cause mythmakers, produced the "Mighty Stonewall" so familiar to students of the Civil War. Krick draws on contemporary writings by soldiers and civilians, newspaper accounts, and various other sources to clinch his point that by mid-June 1862 the taciturn Virginian had become a towering figure in both the Confederacy and the United States.

In stark contrast to Jackson, the principal Federal generals in the Valley campaign have been criticized, or even ridiculed, by innumerable historians and other writers. Banks, Frémont, Shields, Milroy, and McDowell appear as clumsy foils to the brilliant Stonewall, bumbling their way through a comedy of errors and frustrating Lincoln in the process. William J. Miller reminds readers that the Federal commanders operated within a strategic framework that lacked a firm directing hand, contended with enormous logistical difficulties, and in some instances acquitted themselves quite well. Always judicious in his conclusions, Miller detects no martial genius in any of these men. But he does force a reconsideration of many comfortable assumptions about Jackson and his opponents.

In the fourth essay, Jonathan M. Berkey shifts the spotlight from armies and generals to civilians. Historical literature most often uses the 1864 campaigns of Philip H. Sheridan and William Tecumseh Sherman, in the Shenandoah Valley and Georgia, respectively, to discuss the impact of military operations on civilians. Berkey demonstrates that residents of the Valley also experienced enormous dislocation in 1862. He explores material loss and social disruption, giving full attention to Federal activities, internal dissent among Confederates, and the importance of race and gender as factors in the volatile intersection of military and civilian affairs. Berkey's essay underscores the need to remember that in the Valley in 1862, as in all Civil War campaigns, Union and Confederate armies did not confront each other in a vacuum.

No military unit experienced more dramatic successes and failures during the Valley campaign than the 12th Georgia Infantry. The 12th received praise from many quarters for its steadfast performance at the battle of McDowell, where it was badly cut up. Just three weeks later the regiment suffered a debacle at Front Royal that spawned severe criticism of its officers and men. Keith S. Bohannon's essay analyzes the 12th's service in the Valley with an eye toward how it was evaluated during the war and remembered in the postwar era. Both wartime newspaper coverage in Georgia and veterans' reminiscences, shows Bohannon, presented highly selective accounts that reveal the problematical quality of historical evidence.

Peter Carmichael's essay on Turner Ashby also examines how contemporaries tailored their descriptions of events and leaders to suit political and psychological needs. A complex man with populist tendencies and a mixed record as a Confederate officer, Ashby died in action during a skirmish near Harrisonburg on June 6. Newspapers and eulogists turned him into an archetypal cavalier who possessed a devout Christian faith, a well-developed sense of honor, and an aristocratic mien. This retrospective image of Ashby, though deeply flawed, supported the notion that the South's slaveholding civilization had produced chivalric leaders superior in character to their Yankee opponents.

Brig. Gen. Charles S. Winder, a Marylander from an aristocratic background not unlike that attributed to Ashby, commanded the famous Stonewall Brigade throughout most of the Valley campaign. Winder graduated from West Point in the class of 1850 and spent his entire adult life as a soldier, dying at age thirty-two on the battlefield at Cedar Mountain just two months after the end of Jackson's operations in the Shenandoah. Robert E. L. Krick exploited a mass of material at the National Archives and an array of other sources to offer the first substantial biographical sketch of his subject. Winder emerges as a thorough professional with a stern approach to command that impressed Stonewall Jackson but alienated many soldiers in the ranks. Some of Winder's subordinates also questioned his harsher actions, but other comrades believed that his martial talent would have carried him to a position of much greater responsibility. Although Krick avoids hyperbolic claims, he pronounces Winder a gifted young officer with a Confederate record unsurpassed by any other man from Maryland.

Winder's predecessor at the head of the Stonewall Brigade had been Brig. Gen. Richard Brooke Garnett. At the battle of Kernstown on March 23, 1862, Garnett ordered a withdrawal of his regiments that infuriated Jackson. Virtually everyone who knew anything about the battle believed Garnett had acted prudently, but Jackson relieved him of command and pressed formal charges. In the final essay, A. Cash Koeniger uses the Garnett case as a focal point in assessing Jackson's predilection for arresting officers. Koeniger paints an unlovely picture of a martinet whose inability to handle problems with subordinates almost certainly rendered him incapable of assuming command of a major army. Stonewall had reached his ideal level of leadership—where his clumsy managerial style caused unnecessary friction but could not seriously compromise the Confederate war effort.

Readers concerned with historical chronology should note that this volume of Military Campaigns of the Civil War best compliments *The Richmond Campaign of 1862: The Peninsula and the Seven Days*, which was published in 2000. The introduction to *The Richmond Campaign* predicted that the series would next cover the 1862 Valley campaign and then move on to Second Bull Run (Manassas). In fact, the book on Second Bull Run has been deferred for at least a year or two, replaced by one on the 1864 Valley campaign. Plans beyond these two titles are uncertain, though eventually there should be at least a dozen and perhaps fifteen books in the series.

I have thanked Keith Bohannon, Peter Carmichael, Bob Krick, R. E. L. Krick, and Bill Miller for stalwart work on earlier volumes in this series. I renew those thanks and add grateful appreciation to Jonathan Berkey and Cash Koeniger for their essays and to George F. Skoch for his continuing work as our cartographer. I also thank my friends at the University of North Carolina Press for waiting so patiently to receive this installment in the series. Finally, I am pleased to express my warmest gratitude to Robert C. Ritchie and the staff at the Henry E. Huntington Library in San Marino, California, where I performed all of the editorial work for this book. I cannot imagine a better or more beautiful place to pursue scholarly endeavors than the Huntington.

NOTES

1. For a useful discussion of the murals, see William M. S. Rasmussen, "Making the Confederate Murals: Studies by Charles Hoffbauer," *Virginia Magazine of History and Biography* 101 (July 1993): 433–56. *Spring* is reproduced in color in *Decoying the Yanks: Jackson's Valley Campaign*, by Champ Clark and the Editors of Time-Life Books (Alexandria, Va.: Time-Life Books, 1984), 96–97.

2. More than 8,000 Confederates and nearly 7,000 Federals fell at Gaines's Mill. Casualties for battles in the 1862 Valley campaign break down as follows: Kernstown (March 23), 590 U.S. and 720 C.S.; McDowell (May 8), 250 U.S. and 500 C.S.; Front Royal (May 23), 900 U.S. and 50 C.S.; First Winchester (May 25), 2,019 U.S. and 400 C.S.; Cross Keys (June 8), 685 U.S. and 690 C.S.; Port Republic (June 9), 1,000 U.S. and 800 C.S.—total, just fewer than 5,500 U.S. (more than half of whom were captured) and just more than 2,750 C.S.

3. For an overview of the military and political impact of the 1862 campaign for Richmond, see Gary W. Gallagher, "A Civil War Watershed: The 1862 Richmond Campaign in Perspective," in *The Richmond Campaign of 1862: The Peninsula and the Seven Days*, ed. Gary W. Gallagher (Chapel Hill: University of North Carolina Press, 2000), 3–27.

4. The following three paragraphs, with some alteration, are taken from Gary W. Gallagher, "The Shenandoah Valley in 1864," in *Struggle for the Shenandoah: Essays on the 1864 Valley Campaign*, ed. Gary W. Gallagher (Kent, Ohio: Kent State University Press, 1991), 1–3. Rather than present the same information in a paraphrased form, it seemed more reasonable to use the original text.

5. For examples of Lee's correspondence with Jackson in May 1862, see Robert E. Lee,

The Wartime Papers of R. E. Lee, ed. Clifford Dowdey and Louis H. Manarin (Boston: Little, Brown, 1961), 162–63, 174–75.

6. Catherine Ann Devereux Edmondston, *"Journal of a Secesh Lady": The Diary of Catherine Ann Devereux Edmondston, 1860–1866*, ed. Beth Gilbert Crabtree and James W. Patton (Raleigh: North Carolina Division of Archives and History, 1979), 184; [Judith W. McGuire], *Diary of a Southern Refugee during the War* (1867; reprint, Lincoln: University of Nebraska Press, 1995), 120–21.

7. *Charleston Courier*, May 31, 1862 (quoting the *Lynchburg Republican*); *Richmond Dispatch*, June 11, 1862.

8. *Lancaster (S.C.) Ledger*, June 4, 1862; *Charleston Mercury*, June 12, 1862; *Richmond Whig*, June 16, 1862. For other representative accounts, see *Southern Recorder* (Milledgeville, Ga.), June 17, 1862; *Lynchburg Daily Virginian*, June 13, 1862; *Weekly Raleigh (N.C.) Register*, June 11, 1862.

9. *New York Evening Post*, May 28, 1862 (quoting a dispatch filed from Washington on May 26 by the "Regular Correspondent of the Evening Post"); *Albany (N.Y.) Atlas and Argus*, May 27, 1862; *Philadelphia Daily Evening Bulletin*, May 27, 28, 1862. See also *Atlas and Argus*, May 28, 1862; *Chicago Tribune*, May 28, 1862; *New York Times*, May 26, 1862. The politician most often criticized for exhibiting panic was Secretary of War Edwin M. Stanton.

10. *New York Tribune*, June 3, 1862; *New York Times*, June 4, 1862; *Chicago Tribune*, June 2, 1862. See also *Albany (N.Y.) Evening Journal*, May 31, June 3, 7, 1862; *New York Herald*, June 4, 1862; *Philadelphia Daily Evening Bulletin*, June 3, 1862.

11. The absence of harsh criticism of the Federal generals is quite striking—especially so because innumerable historians and other writers later savaged them. For representative assessments, see *Albany (N.Y.) Evening Journal*, May 27, 1862 (Banks); *New York Herald*, June 12, 1862 (Frémont); *New York Tribune*, June 2, 13 (Banks), 20 (Frémont); *Philadelphia Daily Evening Bulletin*, May 27 (Banks), June 11 (Frémont), 1862. In contrast, the *Daily Evening Bulletin* of May 28, 1862, was quite hard on McDowell.

12. *Boston Daily Advertiser*, June 14, 1862; *New York Tribune*, June 13, 1862.

The Shenandoah Valley Campaign of 1862

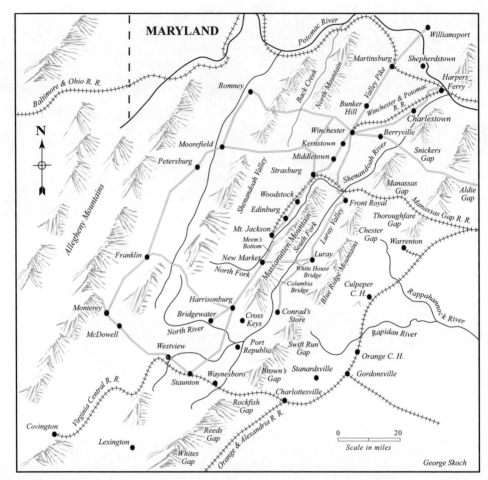

MARYLAND

Baltimore & Ohio R. R.

Potomac River

Williamsport

Martinsburg

Shepherdstown

Romney

Back Creek

North Mountain

Valley Pike

Bunker
Hill

Harpers
Ferry

Winchester & Potomac
R. R.

Charlestown

N

Moorefield

Winchester

Berryville

Petersburg

Kernstown

Snickers
Gap

Middletown

Shenandoah River

Strasburg

Shenandoah Valley

Woodstock

Manassas
Gap

Aldie
Gap

Edinburg

Front Royal

Manassas Gap R. R.

Allegheny Mountains

Mt. Jackson

Meem's
Bottom

Massanutten Mountain
South Fork

Luray Valley

Thoroughfare
Gap

Chester
Gap

Warrenton

Franklin

New Market

North Fork

Luray

White House
Bridge

Blue Ridge Mountains

Rappahannock River

Columbia
Bridge

Culpeper
C. H.

Monterey

Harrisonburg

Conrad's
Store

Bridgewater

Cross
Keys

Rapidan River

McDowell

North River

Port
Republic

Swift Run
Gap

Orange C. H.

Westview

Brown's
Gap

Stanardsville

Gordonsville

Virginia Central R. R.

Waynesboro

Staunton

Charlottesville

Covington

Rockfish
Gap

Orange & Alexandria R. R.

Reeds
Gap

Lexington

Whites
Gap

0   20

Scale in miles

George Skoch

The Shenandoah Valley

GARY W. GALLAGHER

You Must Either Attack Richmond or Give Up the Job and Come to the Defence of Washington

ABRAHAM LINCOLN AND THE 1862

SHENANDOAH VALLEY CAMPAIGN

Abraham Lincoln reacted admirably to Maj. Gen. Thomas J. "Stonewall" Jackson's famous Shenandoah Valley campaign of May and June 1862. Far from panicking when Jackson advanced toward the Potomac River during the last week of May, Lincoln used the rebel threat in an effort to force Maj. Gen. George B. McClellan to attack the Confederate army protecting Richmond. He manifested a sound grasp of Union and Confederate strategy, an understanding of his generals' personalities, and a resolute determination to prod—almost to will—his commanders to act in such a way as to forge victories outside Richmond and in the Shenandoah Valley.

As discussed in the Introduction, Lincoln dealt with Jackson's movements within a strategic picture that during the first five months of 1862 witnessed a string of fabulous Union successes. In the Western Theater, U.S. forces captured Forts Henry and Donelson, won the battle of Shiloh, and took control of Nashville, much of Middle Tennessee, New Orleans, and the upper and lower reaches of the Mississippi River. A huge army under Maj. Gen. Henry W. Halleck was closing in on Corinth, a vital rail center in northern Mississippi, by the end of May. In the Trans-Mississippi arena, the battle of Pea Ridge on March 7–8 ensured unquestioned Union control of Missouri and opened the way for further operations into Arkansas.

The Eastern Theater offered an equally dismal picture for the Confederacy. Although historians too often read backward from Union defeat during the Seven Days battles to paint a problematical situation in the East during the spring and early summer, it is more useful to focus on the northern successes preceding that failure. McClellan's Army of the Potomac, the republic's largest military force, took Yorktown on May 3 and Williamsburg three days later. Confederates evacuated Norfolk on May 9, scuttling the CSS *Virginia* on May 11 as they fell back up the Peninsula toward Richmond. The loss of the *Virginia*, a powerful ironclad that had raised southern hopes for an end to the blockade just two months earlier, proved especially devastating for many Confederates. By May 23 McClellan's host had come within a few miles of Richmond. Other important Union forces under Maj. Gens. Irvin McDowell, Nathaniel P. Banks, and John C. Frémont stood at Fredericksburg, in the Shenandoah Valley, and in western Virginia, respectively. In short, prospects for U.S. military victory scarcely could have been better as the end of May approached.

The first heartening news for the Confederacy during this period came from Stonewall Jackson in the Shenandoah Valley. Few episodes of the Civil War are more dramatically charged than Jackson's operations in May and early June 1862. They reenergized the Confederate home front and catapulted Jackson to national and international fame.[1]

Jackson's effort in the Valley ordinarily is seen as one of the greatest military campaigns in U.S. history. Most writers have pronounced it a fantastic operation carried out against long odds that immobilized thousands of Union soldiers and sent tremors through the North. Abraham Lincoln often appears as a sort of foil to Jackson's cunning generalship in the Valley. The more rhapsodic portrayals cast Stonewall as a master manipulator who not only flummoxed Frémont, Banks, and other Federal generals but also scared Lincoln into issuing a series of misguided presidential directives. Lincoln at first joined Secretary of War Edwin M. Stanton and other top Republicans in thinking only of Washington's safety, goes a common argument, wringing his hands in frustration and massing troops to deal with Jackson. Only later, his fear having abated, did Lincoln try to orchestrate a pursuit of the wily Confederate general.

Although most historians know that Lincoln quickly turned his thoughts to striking the Confederate Army of the Valley while it maneuvered near Harpers Ferry, a common perception persists that he exhibited at least a

Abraham Lincoln assumed a contemplative pose in this photograph taken about the time of the 1862 Shenandoah Valley campaign. Library of Congress.

momentary panic in the wake of Jackson's victory over Banks at Winchester. Lincoln's response in the summer of 1864 to the presence of another Confederate army in the Shenandoah lends credence to such a view. In July 1864, just as in the spring of 1862, Federal operations against Richmond dominated news from the battlefront in Virginia. But as Ulysses S. Grant settled into a siege of Petersburg that ultimately would yield success at Richmond, Robert E. Lee detached Jubal A. Early's Second Corps to operate in the Valley. Early cleared Federals from the Shenandoah and crossed the Potomac River onto U.S. soil. He then won the battle of the Monocacy, fought just south of Frederick, Maryland, on July 9, and marched to the outskirts of the U.S. capital. Lincoln experienced a brief spell of pronounced anxiety as Early's force drew near. Urging Grant to leave sufficient strength at Petersburg "to retain your hold," the president hoped his general would shift the remainder of the Army of the Potomac to Washington and "make a vigorous effort to destroy the enemie's force in this vicinity." Grant prudently pointed out that Early's movements did not warrant such a drastic response, and a hodgepodge of northern units ultimately turned back the Confederates.[2]

Did Lincoln's reaction to Stonewall Jackson anticipate his behavior in a superficially comparable situation in July 1864?[3] The crucial document on this point is the president's communication to George B. McClellan on May 25. Lincoln stated that the "enemy is moving North in sufficient force to drive Banks before him . . . [and] is also threatening Leesburgh and [Brig. Gen. John W.] Geary on the Manassas Gap Rail Road from north and south." Although the precise size and object of the Confederate threat remained unknown to political and military leaders in Washington, the president described it as "a general and concerted one, such as could not be if he was acting upon the purpose of a very desperate defence of Richmond. I think the time is near when you must either attack Richmond or give up the job and come to the defence of Washington. Let me hear from you instantly."[4]

Many historians have seen in this letter a jittery Lincoln suggesting that McClellan might have to abandon his campaign against Richmond in order to save Washington. A few examples will suggest the tenor of many accounts. In his biography of Lincoln, David Herbert Donald remarked that Banks's defeat caused many northerners to fear "Jackson might cross the Potomac and threaten Washington itself." The president "at one point believed the Confederates were planning to take the national capital" and warned McClellan he might have to leave the Peninsula. Stephen B. Oates, in an earlier biography of Lincoln, described how, on May 24–25, Washington received "shattering news from the Shenandoah Valley, where rebel columns under Stonewall Jackson were on a rampage." With Stanton's support, wrote Oates, Lincoln responded by ordering McDowell to guard Washington and telling McClellan that he might have to return to the capital. Robert G. Tanner's history of the 1862 Valley campaign, which remains the standard on the topic, argues that Lincoln kept his head very well as news from the lower Valley arrived in Washington on May 23–24. But reports about Banks's defeat at Winchester wrought a dramatic change. The president "did apprehend a catastrophe, at least on the afternoon and evening of May 25," and when he wrote to McClellan that day, "fear and frustration marked every word" of his message.[5]

Jackson's biographers often have sketched an even more nervous Lincoln. Just as McClellan closed in on Richmond with the prospect of reinforcement by McDowell, observed Byron Farwell in language typical of many other biographies, news of Banks's reverse at Winchester derailed northern plans: "To the utter dismay of McClellan and McDowell, Lincoln, alarmed by reports from the Shenandoah, changed everything in a twinkling." British author G. F. R. Henderson, whose 1898 biography of Jackson has wielded more influence than any other, employed very dramatic language. "Terror had taken possession of the nation," he observed regarding northern reaction to news from the Valley, and "Lincoln and Stanton were electrified even more effectually than Banks." More recently, James I. Robertson Jr., author of the most detailed modern biography, maintained that the "sudden appearance of Jackson in the lower valley, followed by the rout of Banks's command, shocked the Federal government" and prompted Lincoln to tell McClellan that he might have to abort the advance against Richmond. "For the next couple of days," asserted Robertson, "alarm replaced shock in the Northern capital. The Lincoln administration overreacted."[6]

Some participants and observers rendered similar verdicts at the time. Charles W. Trueheart, a soldier in Jackson's command, sent a strongly upbeat account to his father on July 4, 1862. After the victory at Winchester, averred Trueheart, "we marched to the Ferry to make a demonstration at crossing into Md., and going towards Washington. And it had the desired effect. Yankeedom trembled in its boots. Lincoln immediately called on the Yankee Govs. to send on the State Militia to protect the 'Capitol.' " Behind the lines in the North, New Yorker George Templeton Strong recorded in his diary on

May 25 that "these are critical hours. The rebels are pressing Banks in great force, and he has fallen back from Winchester on Harper's Ferry." Just the day before, Strong had been quite optimistic: "That Richmond is in a frenzy and fury and desperation, even as a nest of hornets invaded by unfriendly fumes of brimstone, seems certain." But the latest word from the Valley convinced him that Jackson sought to "annihilate Banks, and then make a rush for Baltimore."[7]

Confederate movements after the victories at Front Royal and Winchester sent ripples of alarm through much of official Washington. No one reacted more precipitately than Secretary of War Stanton, who on May 24 ill-advisedly requested that northern governors "organize and forward immediately all the volunteer and militia force in your state" to deal with Jackson. The War Department also assumed temporary "military possession" of northern railroads to expedite the movement of troops to meet the crisis. From the capital on May 26, Secretary of the Treasury Salmon P. Chase said Jackson's force had "endangered Harpers Ferry & even Washington, & menaced Maryland." "To repel it & if possible capture or destroy the invaders became a prime necessity," remarked Chase: "To this end two of McDowells divisions were ordered to the support of Banks & Fremont." Senator Charles Sumner of Massachusetts, narrating events on the afternoon of May 25, recorded that Senators Lyman Trumbull of Illinois and James Wilson Grimes of Iowa "told us the news—that Banks was flying—that Washington was menaced." After dinner that night, Sumner spent time with Lincoln and a group of advisers that included Stanton, Chase, Secretary of State William Henry Seward, and several generals. He described a Lincoln clearly unhappy about the behavior of Banks's command but not so obviously fearful about the capital's safety. "I addressed myself at once to the Presdt.," noted Sumner, "& from his lips learned what had occurred—he described it vividly—& said among other things that Banks's men were running & flinging away their arms, routed and demoralized."[8]

McClellan answered Lincoln by telegraph at 5:00 P.M. on May 25. Thinking first of himself as usual, "Little Mac" insisted—correctly as it turned out—that the object of Jackson's movement "is probably to prevent reinforcements being sent to me." He alluded to information gathered from observation balloons, Confederate deserters, and slaves who had fled to Union lines—all of which indicated that most of the rebel army remained at Richmond. The most important part of McClellan's message reported that "the time is very

Lincoln's initial response to rebel movements in the lower Shenandoah Valley had more to do with George B. McClellan, who conveyed a sense of determined authority in this early-war view, than with Stonewall Jackson's possible threat to the U.S. capital. National Archives.

near when I shall attack Richmond." Two Union corps had crossed the Chickahominy River and reached a point within six miles of Richmond, and the rest of the army stood ready to cross as soon as engineers completed bridges. McClellan thus promised the major Union offensive on the Richmond front that Lincoln desperately desired.[9]

That desire had ripened during months of frustrating relations with McClellan. By late May 1862, McClellan had been in command of the Army of the Potomac for about eight months and had yet to fight a big battle. He consistently had asked for more men, more animals, more guns, more supplies—more of everything—before he could attack. Lincoln had lost patience with this behavior, and he seized upon Jackson's movement toward the Potomac as a pretext to force McClellan to take the offensive or risk abandonment of his cherished movement toward Richmond. That threat was implicit in the message he sent McClellan on May 25, and McClellan's response probably signaled to Lincoln that the threat had served its purpose (McClellan's telegram claimed that he had planned the offensive before Lincoln's message came to hand). To reiterate, the May 25 correspondence should not be construed as evidence of panic on Lincoln's part growing out of fear for the safety of Washington, but as an effort to get McClellan to apply offensive pressure against the rebel force defending Richmond.

Lincoln's instructions to Generals Frémont and McDowell on May 24 support this interpretation. They also demonstrate that Lincoln hoped to inaugurate an offensive against Jackson from the outset rather than take defensive measures to save Washington.

Lincoln received word from Frémont on May 24 of Jackson's attack at Front Royal the preceding day. That engagement had cost the Union about 1,000 prisoners and isolated Banks in the lower Valley. "General Banks informs me this morning of an attack by [the] enemy," wrote Frémont. "This is probably by Jackson, who marched in that direction some days since. [Maj. Gen. Richard S.] Ewell's force with him. General Banks says he should be reenforced immediately." Lincoln ordered Frémont to march southeastward toward Harrisonburg in an effort to cut Jackson off: "The exposed condition of General Banks makes his immediate relief a point of paramount importance. You are therefore directed by the President to move against Jackson at Harrisonburg and operate against the enemy in such a way as to relieve Banks." In a telegram sent late that afternoon, Frémont promised to "move as ordered & operate against the Enemy in such way as to afford prompt relief to genl Banks." That evening the president thanked Frémont for his rapid response but believed it necessary to emphasize the need for immediate implementation of the presidential order: "Much—perhaps all—depends upon the celerity with which you can execute it. Put the utmost speed into it. Do not lose a minute."[10]

At 5:00 P.M. on May 24, Lincoln ordered Irvin McDowell to contribute 20,000 men to the effort against Jackson. McClellan had hoped McDowell's 40,000 men, massed near Fredericksburg, would soon swell the ranks of the Union force at Richmond. On May 23 Lincoln and Stanton had visited McDowell's force at Fredericksburg and agreed that it would advance toward Richmond three days hence. Jackson's appearance in the lower Valley prompted Lincoln's new instructions to McDowell: "Gen Fremont has been ordered by Telegraph to move from Franklin on Harrisonburg to relieve Gen Banks and capture or destroy Jackson & Ewell's force. You are instructed laying aside for the present the movement on Richmond to put twenty thousand men (20000) in motion at once for the Shenandoah moving on the line or in advance of the line of the Manassas Gap R Road. Your object will be to capture the forces of Jackson & Ewell." McDowell acknowledged receipt of the order and said it was "in process of execution." But he also manifested his disappointment by declaring, "This is a crushing blow to us."[11]

Lincoln's orders to McDowell conveyed a decidedly offensive message. If fear for Washington's safety stood paramount, McDowell could have marched directly toward the city to bolster its defenses. The destruction of Jackson's army, not the protection of the capital, dominated Lincoln's thinking. Anticipating that McDowell might balk at pressing the action without cooperation from Banks and Frémont, Lincoln stipulated that "it is believed that the force with which you move will be sufficient to accomplish the object alone." Lincoln understood that both McDowell and McClellan preferred that the old orders be carried out. He probably blanched when McDowell, after stating that he obeyed Lincoln's orders immediately, listed a number of obstacles to success. "I beg to say," observed the rotund general, "that cooperation between General Frémont and myself to cut Jackson and Ewell there is not to be counted upon, even if it is not a practical impossibility. Next, that I am entirely beyond helping distance of General Banks; no celerity or vigor will avail so far as he is concerned." Moreover, it would take "a week or ten days" to shift his soldiers to the Valley by a route that afforded ample food and forage, "and by that time the enemy will have retired." But McDowell also stated that he would send Brig. Gen. James Shields's division toward Strasburg along the route of the Manassas Gap Railroad. "I have ordered General Shields to commence the movement by to-morrow morning," Mc-Dowell assured Lincoln, and a "second division will follow in the afternoon." Lincoln chose to focus on the positive elements in McDowell's communications. "I am highly gratified by your alacrity in obeying my order," he wrote after receiving the general's initial response: "The change was as painful to me as it can possibly be to you or to any one. Every thing now depends upon the celerity and vigor of your movement."[12]

Lincoln knew Secretary of the Treasury Salmon P. Chase, who maintained close ties with McDowell, preferred that the latter's command not be diverted from a march to reinforce McClellan. He knew as well that McDowell hoped to discuss the campaign with Chase on the evening of May 24 and took time to tell his cabinet officer that he hoped the new deployments would yield an offensive success. "It now appears that Banks got safely in to Winchester last night," the president explained to Chase, "and is, this morning, retreating to Harper's Ferry. . . . I think it not improbable that Ewell[,] Jackson and [Brig. Gen. Edward 'Alleghany'] Johnson, are pouring through the gap they made day-before yesterday at Front Royal, making a dash Northward. It will be a very valuable, and very honorable service for Gen. McDowell to cut them off. I hope he will put all possible energy and speed into the effort."[13]

Lincoln took these aggressive steps despite alarmist messages about the size and intentions of the Confederate forces in the lower Valley from Banks, Geary, and other Federal commanders. Stationed along the Manassas Gap Railroad, Geary behaved almost hysterically. He exaggerated Confederate numbers, claimed the rebels had moved well east of the Blue Ridge Mountains, and otherwise complicated Lincoln's effort to grasp the nature of Jackson's movements. In a single message sent on the afternoon of May 25 from White Plains, a hamlet located on the railroad between the Blue Ridge and the Bull Run Mountains, Geary claimed that rebels were moving from Front Royal toward Ashby's Gap, whence they intended to continue on to Leesburg, "there to seize the fortifications and maintain a position in that section." The Confederates numbered 7,000 or 8,000 and likely enjoyed support from "large forces at Front Royal," continued Geary, and held "full possession of the country between Front Royal and Ashby's Gap between the mountains and the river." Moreover, contrabands had told Geary of hearing their secessionist masters read family letters "stating that 10,000 cavalry are about

Irvin McDowell, whose portly figure and tall cap occasioned considerable wartime comment, with General McClellan. Francis Trevelyan Miller, ed., *The Photographic History of the Civil War*, 10 vols. (New York: Review of Reviews, 1911), 1:307.

passing through this valley from the direction of Warrenton." An earlier message from Geary had led the president, who probably doubted the general's veracity, to seek information from Gen. Rufus Saxton at Harpers Ferry. Geary claimed that Jackson's main force had crossed Ashby's Gap and was en route to Centreville. Lincoln suspected it remained in the lower Valley. "Please inform us, if possible," he told Saxton, "what has become of the force which pursued Banks yesterday."[14]

Over the next several days, Lincoln sought unsuccessfully to coordinate the efforts of McDowell and Frémont. On May 26 he asked McDowell, who remained at Falmouth, just up the Rappahannock from Fredericksburg, "Should not the remainder of your force except sufficient to hold the point at Frederick'sburg, move this way—to Manassas junction, or to Alexandria? As commander of this Department, should you not be here? I ask these questions." The next day he telegraphed Frémont. "I see you are at Moorefield [due west of Strasburg]," stated the exasperated president. "You were expressly ordered to march to Harrisonburg. What does this mean?" A testy Frémont replied, through Stanton at 6:00 A.M. on May 28, that his troops suffered from short rations and were in no condition to undertake more marching. The general also assumed he had discretion to follow a line of march that seemed most appropriate, but if ordered to do so, he would literally follow Lincoln's directions. On Lincoln's instructions, Stanton telegraphed three more times on May 28, urging Frémont to "move against the enemy." In replying to one of these messages from Washington, Frémont stated that the "President's order will be obeyed accordingly."[15]

On May 28 Lincoln exchanged messages with McClellan. The latter reported a victory by Union corps commander Maj. Gen. Fitz John Porter near Richmond and clearly wanted more men. "There is no doubt that the enemy are concentrating everything on Richmond," claimed McClellan, who then lectured his commander in chief about priorities: "It is the policy and duty of the Government to send me by water all the well-drilled troops available. I am confident that Washington is in no danger." Lincoln promised to do what he could but reminded McClellan of dangers at other points. Conflicting reports about the size and disposition of Jackson's forces had reached Washington from different Union commanders. Some sources placed the rebels east of the Blue Ridge, others raised alarms about Confederate movements west of the Blue Ridge, and still others indicated that rebel reinforcements were marching from north of Richmond to reinforce Jackson. "I am painfully impressed with the importance of the struggle before you," stated Lincoln, choosing words that reflected his discomfiture with McClellan's failure to deliver a telling blow against the enemy at Richmond, "and I shall aid you in all I can consistently with my view of due regard to all points."[16]

On the Shenandoah front, Lincoln grew impatient with the absence of strong movements by either McDowell or Frémont. "You say Gen. Geary's scouts report that they find no enemy this side of the Blue Ridge," he commented sarcastically to McDowell at 4:00 P.M. on May 28. "Neither do I. Have *they* been *to* the Blue Ridge looking for them?" Later that day another message, sent by Lincoln through Stanton, went to McDowell: "There is very little doubt that Jackson's force is between Winchester and Charlestown. His troops were too much fatigued to pursue Banks. A large body of rebel cavalry is near Charlestown now. Jackson and Ewell were near Bunker Hill yesterday at noon. Of this there is no doubt." McDowell answered this last message at 7:20 P.M. Regarding the positions of Jackson and Ewell, McDowell replied, "I beg leave to report that I am pushing Generals Shields and [E. O. C.] Ord upon Front Royal with all expedition possible."[17]

Perhaps the most famous of Lincoln's messages during the Valley campaign also carried a date of May 28. Impatient with his commanders in the Valley, and utterly convinced that Jackson occupied a precarious position far from possible reinforcements, he wrote to McDowell. "I think the evidence now preponderates that Ewell and Jackson are still about Winchester," commented the president. "Assuming this, it is, for you a question of legs. Put in all the speed you can. I have told Fremont as much, and directed him to drive at them as fast as possible." The president could not resist getting in a dig at Frémont. "By the way," he told McDowell, "I suppose you know, Fremont has got up to Moorefield, instead of going to Harrisonburg." McDowell responded in a message received in Washington at 11:18 P.M. "I beg to assure you," he said, "that I am doing everything which legs and steam are capable of to hurry forward matters in this quarter." "I shall be deficient in wagons when I get out of the way of the railroad for transporting supplies," McDowell added by way of preparing Lincoln for further bad news, "but shall push on nevertheless."[18]

May 29 and 30 brought further frustration to Lincoln. Reports left no doubt that Jackson had reached Harpers Ferry. Lincoln reasoned that while positioned there, at the northern end of the Shenandoah Valley, the Confederates should have offered easy pickings for the converging columns of Mc-

Dowell, moving from the east toward Front Royal and Strasburg, and Fré-
mont, located west of Strasburg in the vicinity of Moorefield. Banks lay at
Williamsport, whence he also could join the effort. At noon on May 29,
Lincoln wrote Banks (virtually the same message also went to Frémont and
McDowell): "Gen McDowell's advance should & probably will be at or near
Front Royal at 12. m to-morrow. Gen. Fremont will be at or near Strasburg as
soon. Please watch the enemy closely, and follow & harass and detain him, if
he attempts to retire." Here Lincoln sought yet again to wring an aggressive
performance out of one of his generals. It was not enough that Jackson
retreated; Lincoln wanted Banks to engage him in such a manner as to allow
Frémont and McDowell to cut off his route southward up the Valley. Once
isolated north of Strasburg and Front Royal, Jackson might be vulnerable to
a decisive Union blow.[19]

Banks answered Lincoln at 3:30 P.M., employing a tone frequently adopted
by his fellow Union commanders engaged in the Valley drama. "My command is much disabled," he said, "but we will do what we can to carry out
your views." McDowell weighed in with his own somewhat gloomy report,
received in Washington at 5:45 P.M., that General Shields faced problems with
the railroad in Thoroughfare Gap. Shields first estimated that repairs might
take twenty-four hours, but McDowell sent him "the President's telegram and
he reports he will make such arrangements that will enable him to be in Front
Royal before 12 o'clock m. to-morrow, with his other two brigades within 4
miles of the town by the same hour." Mustering what for him amounted to
unbridled sanguinity, McDowell closed with the observation that "everything
seems to be getting along well now, notwithstanding this morning's trouble."[20]

John C. Frémont offered nothing to offset Lincoln's doubts about Banks
and McDowell. A telegram sent by Frémont on May 30 from Moorefield,
which arrived in Washington at 11:30 A.M., raised the specter of 30,000
to 60,000 rebels under Jackson near Winchester. Long accustomed to Mc-
Clellan's grotesque overestimates of Confederate strength, Lincoln tersely,
and accurately, replied that the number "cannot be more than 20,000, probably not more than 15,000." Frémont's location bothered the president at least
as much as his projection of numbers. "Where is your force?" Lincoln inquired sharply. "It ought this minute to be near Strasburg. Answer at once."
Lincoln sent another communication to Frémont at 9:30 P.M. With a message
in hand that indicated Jackson was near Harpers Ferry, Lincoln tried to
summon optimism in pressing Frémont to hurry. "I send you a despatch just

Northern press coverage of the Valley campaign often suggested, almost always erroneously, that U.S. forces were pursuing Jackson vigorously. This engraving depicted Banks's command recrossing the Potomac River to attack the retreating rebels. *Frank Leslie's Illustrated Newspaper*, July 5, 1862.

received from Gen. Saxton at Harper's Ferry," stated the president. "It seems the game is before you. Have sent a copy to Gen. McDowell." Informed by Frémont soon thereafter that a "heavy storm of rain most of yesterday and all last night" had left the roads in terrible condition, Lincoln could not have hoped for a rapid advance to sever Jackson's line of march up the Valley.[21]

Could McDowell retrieve the situation? "I somewhat apprehend that Frémont's force, in its present condition, may not be quite strong enough in case it comes in collision with the enemy," Lincoln had written at midmorning on May 30. "For this additional reason, I wish you to push forward your column as rapidly as possible." It is difficult to imagine the president's believing McDowell would surge boldly ahead—though he took the time to let his general know that he expected him to do all possible to bring Jackson to bay.[22]

Lincoln summed up the situation in the lower Valley on the morning of May 31. He continued to envision a Union pincers, with Frémont and Shields leading the principal Federal forces, that would close off Stonewall Jackson's escape route through Strasburg to the upper reaches of the Valley. Writing to General McClellan, he commented that a "circle whose circumference shall pass through Harper's Ferry, Front-Royal, and Strasburg, and whose center shall be a little North East of Winchester" almost certainly contained the

Confederate forces commanded by Jackson, Richard Ewell, and Edward Johnson. Shields had led McDowell's advance into Front Royal the preceding morning, capturing a number of Confederates and saving the bridge over the Shenandoah River. Frémont's troops should reach Strasburg by late afternoon on May 31, and Banks, "at Williamsport, with his old force, and his new force at Harper's Ferry," would press Jackson toward the pincers. Shields had passed along a "rumor of still an additional force of the enemy . . . having entered the valley of Virginia," noted the president, who rather casually added that "this last may or may not be true." The tenor of this letter to McClellan summons an image of Lincoln as still hopeful of grand results in the Shenandoah but weary of dealing with officers who seemed incapable of executing the requisite offensive movements.[23]

There is no need to analyze the correspondence between Lincoln and his generals over the next few days to support this essay's basic point. Throughout this period in late May, Lincoln strove to get offensives in the lower Valley and outside Richmond. He failed in both instances. Jackson avoided a prospective Union trap, beating both Frémont and Shields to Strasburg and then proceeding up the Valley. The redoubtable rebel general put the finishing touches on his Shenandoah campaign with twin victories over parts of Frémont's and Shields's forces at the battles of Cross Keys and Port Republic on June 8 and 9. For his part, McClellan repulsed Confederate attacks in the battle of Seven Pines or Fair Oaks on May 31 and June 1 but launched no aggressive movement of his own. When "Little Mac" reported on June 18 that intelligence suggested a deployment of 10,000 to 15,000 Confederate troops from Richmond to reinforce Jackson in the Valley, Lincoln immediately pressed his cautious general to attack. "If this is true," the president pointed out, "it is as good as a reinforcement to you of an equal force. I could better dispose of things if I could know about what day you can attack Richmond, and would be glad to be informed, if you think you can inform me with safety."[24]

A date for Union attacks never arrived, and within two weeks McClellan had suffered a major defeat at the Seven Days. He had withstood Lincoln's untiring efforts to coax a forward-moving victory from him. So also had the collection of generals who commanded in the Valley during May and early June 1862.

Lincoln had done all that was possible from his post in Washington. Never really unnerved by Jackson's movements, he had tried to exploit Jackson's presence in the lower Valley to prod McClellan into action at Richmond. He sought at the same time to concentrate Frémont and McDowell's forces to smash Stonewall's little army.[25] Lincoln probably underestimated the logistical obstacles that confronted Federal generals in the Valley. Indeed, several northern newspapers evinced considerable sympathy for the harried officers in this regard. For example, Philadelphia's *Daily Evening Bulletin* asserted that Frémont did very well in his ultimately unsuccessful pursuit of Jackson. "He has moved his large army, through a very difficult country, a distance of over one hundred miles," stated the paper. "He has had bridges to rebuild over swollen streams, and has had to drag his artillery over bad roads, made worse than ever by the heavy rains." Yet the president reasonably could wonder why Jackson seemed so much better able to contend with some of the geographical and climatic challenges that hamstrung his own generals.[26]

As he contemplated failure in the Valley and outside Richmond, Lincoln must have entertained thoughts similar to those expressed by his attorney general when it still seemed possible to capture or destroy Jackson's force. "It is shamefully true that the enemy's officers are vastly superior to ours in boldness, enterprise and skill, while our troops almost constantly beat theirs, with any thing like equal numbers and a fair field," wrote Edward Bates in his diary on June 4, 1862. "If our Genls. now allow Jackson to escape, they ought to lose the public confidence, for obvious lack of enterprise and action."[27]

A request from Frémont for reinforcements a few days after Jackson's victories at Cross Keys and Port Republic elicited a pointed reckoning from the commander in chief. Lincoln doubted Frémont's suggestion that Jackson had been reinforced from Richmond. "He is much more likely to go to Richmond than Richmond is to come to him," stated the president, though neither course seemed "very likely." Although wrong in the last portion of this analysis, Lincoln went on to describe exactly what had been transpiring in the Valley. "I think Jackson's game—his assigned work—now is to magnify the accounts of his numbers and reports of his movements," he remarked, "and thus by constant alarms keep three or four times as many of our troops away from Richmond as his own force amounts to." Jackson's movements assisted "his friends at Richmond three or four times as much as if he were there," concluded Lincoln. "Our game is not to allow this." The Federal "game" in the Shenandoah Valley had failed by the time Lincoln lectured Frémont, though the latter, seemingly oblivious to the strategic realities of the recent operations, would persist in demands for additional troops.[28]

On the evening of May 25, George B. McClellan wrote his wife about Lincoln's suggestion that the Army of the Potomac should attack or be withdrawn to Washington. Lincoln was "terribly scared about Washington," observed McClellan, "& talks about the necessity of my returning in order to save it! Heaven save a country governed by such counsels! . . . It is perfectly sickening to deal with such people. . . . I get more sick of them every day—for every day brings with it only additional proofs of their hypocrisy, knavery & folly—." "Well, well, I ought not to write this way," added a Little Mac obviously pleased with himself, "for they may be right & I entirely wrong, so I will drop the subject."[29] Although McClellan did not mean these last words, Lincoln *had* been right in his handling of Union military forces in response to Jackson's movements. It was a crisis that showed how far the president had come in just more than a year as commander in chief.

NOTES

1. As noted in the Introduction, the most convenient overview of the 1862 Valley campaign is Robert G. Tanner, *Stonewall in the Valley: Thomas J. "Stonewall" Jackson's Shenandoah Valley Campaign, Spring 1862* (Garden City, N.Y.: Doubleday, 1976; rev. ed., Mechanicsburg, Pa.: Stackpole, 1996). An older but still useful study is William Allan, *History of the Campaign of Gen. T. J. (Stonewall) Jackson in the Shenandoah Valley of Virginia. From November 4, 1861, to June 17, 1862* (1880; reprint, Dayton, Ohio: Morningside, 1987). Both books focus on Confederate movements and leadership. There is need of a full-scale, evenhanded, scholarly treatment of the campaign.

2. For Lincoln's communication to Grant, see Abraham Lincoln, *The Collected Works of Abraham Lincoln*, ed. Roy P. Basler, 9 vols. (New Brunswick, N.J.: Rutgers University Press, 1953), 7:437. On Early's raid, see Frank E. Vandiver, *Jubal's Raid: General Early's Famous Attack on Washington in 1864* (New York: McGraw-Hill, 1960); Benjamin Franklin Cooling, *Jubal Early's Raid on Washington, 1864* (Baltimore: Nautical and Aviation Publishing, 1989).

3. Lincoln's relationships with Grant and McClellan, which grew largely out of the two generals' vastly different approaches to winning the war, made the circumstances in May 1862 and July 1864 very different. The last thing Lincoln needed to worry about in 1864 was prodding Grant into aggressive action.

4. Lincoln, *Collected Works*, 5:235–36.

5. David Herbert Donald, *Lincoln* (New York: Simon and Schuster, 1995), 355; Stephen B. Oates, *With Malice toward None: The Life of Abraham Lincoln* (New York: Harper and Row, 1977), 301; Tanner, *Stonewall in the Valley*, 238–44 (quotation on 244).

6. Byron Farwell, *Stonewall: A Biography of General Thomas J. Jackson* (New York: Norton,

1992), 298; G. F. R. Henderson, *Stonewall Jackson and the American Civil War* (2 vols., 1898; 1-vol. reprint, New York: David McKay, 1961), 263; James I. Robertson Jr., *Stonewall Jackson: The Man, the Soldier, the Legend* (New York: Macmillan, 1997), 412. Some authors who have written about Jackson describe a more muted response in Washington to the events of May 23–25, 1862. For example, in *The Destructive War: William Tecumseh Sherman, Stonewall Jackson, and the Americans* (New York: Knopf, 1991), 42, Charles Royster observed, "Southerners liked to believe that Jackson's advance to the Potomac had caused panic in the North and thrown fear into Lincoln and Secretary of War Stanton. This greatly overstated the case. Nevertheless, the name of Stonewall Jackson thereafter carried vivid associations."

7. Edward B. Williams, ed., *Rebel Brothers: The Civil War Letters of the Truehearts* (College Station: Texas A&M University Press, 1995), 60–61; George Templeton Strong, *The Diary of George Templeton Strong: The Civil War, 1860–1865*, ed. Allan Nevins and Milton Halsey Thomas (New York: Macmillan, 1952), 227.

8. Benjamin P. Thomas and Harold M. Hyman, *Stanton: The Life and Times of Lincoln's Secretary of War* (New York: Knopf, 1962), 196; Champ Clark and the Editors of Time-Life Books, *Decoying the Yanks: Jackson's Valley Campaign* (Alexandria, Va.: Time-Life Books, 1984), 146; U.S. War Department, *The War of the Rebellion: A Compilation of the Official Records of the Union and Confederate Armies*, 127 vols., index, and atlas (Washington, D.C.: GPO, 1880–1901), ser. 3, 2:68–69 (hereafter cited as *OR*; all future references are to ser. 1); Salmon P. Chase, *The Salmon P. Chase Papers*, ed. John Niven and others, 5 vols. (Kent, Ohio: Kent State University Press, 1993–98), 3:204; Charles Sumner, *The Selected Letters of Charles Sumner*, ed. Beverly Wilson Palmer, 2 vols. (Boston: Northeastern University Press, 1990), 2:116. Although Chase's letter was dated May 24, the editors note that its content suggests it "was probably written on or about Monday, May 26." Lincoln's description of Banks's men probably derived from messages he had received that afternoon from Gen. Rufus Saxton at Harpers Ferry, one of which read in part, "There is a panic, and so few troops here I am satisfied that it is not best to send troops to Winchester, as it is now in the possession of the enemy." Three hours later Saxton telegraphed, "General Banks' column too much frightened to give a clear account of affairs. They represent his rout as complete" (*OR* 12[1]:628).

9. George B. McClellan, *The Civil War Papers of George B. McClellan: Selected Correspondence, 1860–1865*, ed. Stephen W. Sears (New York: Ticknor and Fields, 1989), 276.

10. Lincoln, *Collected Works*, 5:230–31; *OR* 12(1):642–43.

11. Lincoln, *Collected Works*, 5:232–33; Chase, *Papers*, 1:345; *OR* 12(3):220.

12. Lincoln, *Collected Works*, 5:232–33; *OR* 12(3):220–21.

13. Lincoln, *Collected Works*, 5:233, 234–35.

14. On the welter of information reaching Lincoln, see ibid., 234–40, and for the full text of Geary's message on May 25, see *OR* 12(3):241. See also John White Geary, *A Politician Goes to War: The Civil War Letters of John White Geary*, ed. William Alan Blair and Bell I. Wiley (University Park: Pennsylvania State University Press, 1995), 45–47. Geary

wallowed in self-pity as the campaign unfolded, imagining himself grossly outnumbered by the enemy and badly treated by his superiors in Washington. "You need not expect any thing good or glorious from me," he wrote his wife in McClellanesque language on June 9, 1862; "if attacked I cannot defend myself against 500 men at any one point, and defeat must surely follow. If I could I would resign and go home, but that will not do, for it would only gratify a few inveterate political enemies and do myself harm. Come what may, happen what will, I am determined to stand it out: every thing must have an end. They are jealous and fearful of me" (Geary, *Politician Goes to War*, 46–47).

15. Lincoln, *Collected Works*, 5:240, 243. Lincoln was not alone in envisioning a coordinated effort to trap Jackson in the lower Valley. As early as May 26 the *New York Times* remarked, "We do not, in fact, see by what strategy on his own part, or by what blunder less than supernatural on ours, Jackson is to escape swift destruction by his adventurous pursuit of Banks if, he continues it beyond Winchester." A hundred miles from "his proper base of operations," Jackson confronted "a powerful enemy on each flank and in his rear. Frémont from the West, and McDowell from the East, can by a rapid movement throw a force into his rear sufficient to cut him off completely, and compel his surrender."

16. Lincoln, *Collected Works*, 5:240, 243–47; McClellan, *Civil War Papers*, 277. McClellan's letter dated May 28 was addressed to Stanton, but the general certainly knew that its contents would reach the president very quickly.

17. Lincoln, *Collected Works*, 5:246; *OR* 12(3):269.

18. Lincoln, *Collected Works*, 5:246; *OR* 12(3):270.

19. Lincoln, *Collected Works*, 5:247–48.

20. *OR* 12(1):533; 12(3):277.

21. Lincoln, *Collected Works*, 5:250–52; *OR* 12(1):648–49. Toward the end of June 1862 Salmon P. Chase dictated an account of his response to events in the Valley that suggested he did not share Lincoln's manifest exasperation when Frémont failed to beat Jackson to Strasburg in late May. "Meantime, Frémont, observing the spirit though not the letter of his Orders, had marched to Moorefield & thence to Wardensville a few miles distant fr. Strasbg.—his directions being to occupy Strasb. & cut off the retreat of Jackson by that road," stated Chase. "Unfortunately Frémont did not reach Strasbg. until Jackson, defeated by Saxton on Friday in his attack upon Harper's-F., & being apprised no doubt of the movements in his rear, had passed thro. Strasbg. on his retreat down the valley" (Chase, *Papers*, 1:346).

22. Lincoln, *Collected Works*, 5:251–52.

23. Ibid., 254.

24. Ibid., 276.

25. In an effort to reassure Irvin McDowell, Secretary Chase perhaps exaggerated the degree to which Lincoln excused the general's inability to mount a rapid pursuit of Jackson through the Luray Valley following Stonewall's escape through Strasburg on June 1. "I hope you do not misconceive me so far as to think the President remained dissatisfied with your action after he saw the reasons of it," Chase wrote McDowell on

June 6. "The limited information I have seen enables me to form an opinion Shields would probably have reached New Market as soon as Jackson, but for the swollen state of the Shenandoah. The march at all events was in the right direction." Chase went on to encourage McDowell to "move forward . . . towards Charlottesville & Lynchburgh." Such a "course would be most acceptable both to the President and the Secretary [of War]; I believe your movements would be crowned with brilliant results and that your name would become a household word in patriot homes" (Chase, *Papers*, 3:208–9). In the end, as Chase probably suspected would be the case, Charlottesville and Lynchburg remained safe, and patriot homes chose other commanders for enshrinement in a Union pantheon of military heroes.

26. *Philadelphia Daily Evening Bulletin*, June 11, 1862. On June 13, 1862, the *New York Tribune* similarly enumerated some of the difficulties Frémont had faced. It described how Jackson had "pushed up the Valley, and passed Strasburg just in time to elude Fremont, who, with a force considerably smaller than his own, and just about as hungry and weary, was there descending the main ridge of the Alleghenies, which he had crossed by forced marches from Franklin and Moorfield."

27. Edward Bates, *The Diary of Edward Bates, 1859–1866*, ed. Howard K. Beale (1930; reprint, New York: Da Capo, 1971), 261.

28. Lincoln, *Collected Works*, 5:271. On June 16, in a communication that revealed the degree to which the president had given up on coaxing an offensive movement out of Frémont, Lincoln sought to put an end to the general's solicitations: "I have not the power now to fill up your corps to thirtyfive thousand. I am not demanding of you to do the work of thirtyfive thousand. I am only asking of you to stand cautiously on the defensive, get your force in order, and give such protection as you can to the valley of the Shenandoah, and to Western Virginia" (ibid., 274).

29. McClellan, *Civil War Papers*, 275.

ROBERT K. KRICK

The Metamorphosis in
Stonewall Jackson's Public Image

Was there even a remote chance that in April 1862 Thomas J. Jackson might have served as the text for a northern soap advertisement? Certainly not. Yet within a few months, based primarily on Jackson's peripatetic operations in Virginia's Shenandoah Valley, even Yankees were employing the southerner's fame as a sort of cultural icon. Pyles O.K. Soap claimed in the *American Phrenological Journal and Life Illustrated* that fall, presumably with tongue firmly in cheek, that "Stonewall" fancied their product. "In the field," the advertiser professed to know, "Stonewall Jackson nabs it, and sighs for more." Ironically, phrenology in fact was one of Thomas Jackson's eccentric minor enthusiasms. Pyles O.K. Soap almost surely was not. In the aftermath of Jackson's 1862 Shenandoah Valley campaign, however, New York advertising executives knew their market.[1]

When General Jackson launched his epic Valley venture, he had no significant popular cachet. Published mention of the Valley often poked fun at (and at times exaggerated) the general's eccentricities, when it commented on him at all. Thirty-three days worked an absolute revolution in the perceptions of the Confederate populace. Between May 8, when the battle of McDowell signaled the start of Jackson's offensive, and June 9, when the battle of Port

Republic wrote a climax to the campaign, Thomas J. Jackson became the "Mighty Stonewall" whose visage has remained so well known ever after.

Stonewall Jackson of course had distinguished company on the catapult to fame. A few months later R. E. Lee began a similar metamorphosis. Lee's emergence, however, followed a more modest trajectory up the y-axis of the graph of public opinion. Jackson's progress emitted a whistle of decidedly different timbre than that marking Lee's rise to prominence, on the order of a calliope as against a pipe organ.

Jackson had earned his famous nom de guerre at the battle of First Manassas in July 1861, but he had found no opportunity for distinction for many months thereafter. Joseph E. Johnston and George B. McClellan both cheerfully indulged in a *sitzkrieg* that consumed the rest of the summer and fall of the war's first year. Southern aspirations in the Western Theater fell prey to reverse after reverse, but Virginia remained static. As a result, Jackson remained a bright footnote to the first big battle in the East—but nothing more than that.

The opening scenes of the Stonewall tenure in the Shenandoah Valley did not lend themselves to legend building. His tiny force, optimistically if quaintly denominated the Army of the Monongahela for a time, first launched an ill-starred winter venture. Icy roads, wintry blasts, rampant illness, and short rations made the January 1862 expedition to Romney by way of the Potomac a nightmare for the troops. A Virginian major who had been among the army commander's students at Virginia Military Institute wrote back to the superintendent at the institute, without any discernible awe for his former professor, that conditions were "horrible . . . mud six inches deep in the tents." Jackson's stern notions of duty included neither tolerance for discomforts nor leeway for nonmilitary concerns. The general's medical director, Dr. Hunter Holmes McGuire, pleaded in vain for permission to attend to a popular young Winchester woman before moving his operations to Romney. The sick girl recovered, but with lingering health problems. Such single-mindedness would win campaigns to come, but it did not add gloss to a popular image not yet rooted in great victories. Only after Jackson's "brilliant campaign in the Valley," a soldier from Rockingham County noted in June, did the line troops forgive him "the trip over into Romney which led them at the time to believe him quite lunatic."[2]

Many, perhaps most, officers in the Valley army shared that premature

Stonewall Jackson at Winchester, Virginia, in November 1862, taken during the first of his two wartime photographic sittings. Mary Anna Jackson considered this the best likeness of her husband. National Archives.

judgment. The out-of-channels rebellion, launched by two of Jackson's rank-ing subordinates straight to the secretary of war, that grew out of the Romney expedition has been frequently described. What is not widely reported is the extent to which the revolt had support among regimental commanders. Gen. William W. Loring, a querulous fellow of no particular talent, fomented the mutiny, abetted by William B. Taliaferro; the inept and meddlesome secretary of war, Judah P. Benjamin, believed and encouraged the malcontents, as did the equally underinformed Jefferson Davis. (Taliaferro, ironically, did not hesitate to bask dishonestly in the reflected glow of Jackson's subsequent fame and produced an adulatory chapter for Mrs. Jackson's book about her husband long after the war.) The original document, however, also includes the signatures of Col. Samuel V. Fulkerson of the 37th Virginia and of the commanders of the 3rd Arkansas, the 1st Georgia, and the 23rd Virginia. Jackson obviously never saw the grumbling letter, because Fulkerson remained "a great favorite" with him. When the colonel died at the head of his regiment a few months later, Jackson cried at the news.[3]

By June 1862 it would have been unthinkable for a broad cross section of division, brigade, and regimental commanders to assail Jackson out of command channels. Had they done so, no one would have been receptive, even at the wailing walls in the Richmond bureaucratic hothouses. The very existence of the Romney rebellion speaks volumes about Jackson's lack of stature early in 1862. The potential results of Jackson's efforts in the direction of Romney and Hancock that winter, had they been uninterrupted by callow grumblers and bureaucrats, cannot be known. It is interesting to note, however, that Jackson told a subordinate colonel (and sometime brother-in-law) that he had harbored some grandiose plans, intending "to cross at Hancock & penetrate far into Pa."[4]

Turner Ashby, whose dashing exploits made him into something of a cult hero, genuinely believed that Jackson was entirely incompetent. He told a friend in the Confederate Congress that despite getting no aid from Jackson, "for the last two months I have saved the army . . . from being utterly destroyed." Stonewall, Ashby assured the politician, "cannot appreciate the condition of his Army and its daily diminution." Ashby's comprehensive indifference to administrative and disciplinary matters had in fact created much of the very problem he decried. Correspondence to the cavalryman from the secretary of war reminding him of his responsibilities had no effect.[5] Ashby and his friends blamed Jackson for understanding what they could not themselves see: mid-19th-century warfare was infinitely more than a medieval jousting tournament. Ashby lived barely long enough to have the chance to see clearly the defects of his position, but there is no record of his having come to recognize the fact—and little likelihood that he ever would have.

Ashby and others were bemused by General Jackson's painfully businesslike persona, his intensely pietistic worldview, his array of eccentricities, and his single-minded crusades. They doubtless heard of Jackson's letter in late February to his (and Ashby's) friend Congressman A. R. Boteler insisting that the South's distilleries be closed and their copper tubing confiscated.[6] Such a notion was, it hardly needs to be said, well outside the southern mainstream.

Even so, the general was not entirely without supporters at that early stage of the campaign. Virginia's Governor John Letcher, a fellow Lexington resident, played a key role in backing down Davis and Benjamin after the Romney rebellion. A Winchester newspaper savagely attacked the desk commandos in Richmond and the "croakers" and "fault-finders" in the army. When order was restored, one soldier of the 27th Virginia, part of Jackson's own old Stonewall Brigade, wrote with some exaggeration on February 10 that "everyone is rejoicing" over Jackson's political victory: "He is beloved by all." Distaste for a bewildered central government probably contributed to that sympathetic view. The fame that lurked just around the corner of course would yield much more support by hindsight for the Jackson of those early days than even the most diligent observer could have uncovered at the time. The aged woman who boasted at her eighty-fifth birthday celebration that she personally handed Stonewall Jackson "a slice of bread well buttered" as he marched between Paw Paw and Romney was remembering a brief close encounter with a legend, not with a hard-working frontier soldier.[7]

The campaign in Virginia's Valley built to a towering crescendo in public consciousness during the thirty-three days from McDowell to Port Republic. The resulting tumult surrounding Jackson's legend never waned. Press attention first became riveted on events in the Valley with a resounding thump as a result of the Confederate victories at Front Royal and Winchester on May 23 and 25. Southern editors trumpeted the success and polished it for all it was worth, and more besides. A Fredericksburg woman calmly accepted rumors of a victory by "Jackson (God bless him)" but rejected like tales about Confederate success near Richmond. On May 28, news of the strike northward had reached Georgia, and the *Columbus Daily Enquirer* exulted, "Jackson is imparting new life to the Confederate cause by his brilliant successes and his rapid advances. . . . He is boldly and vigorously driving the enemy before him and routing them wherever he catches them." Twelve days later, as Port Republic was being fought far to the north, the same paper hymned Stonewall's "policy and design to advance boldly and expeditiously, and every reported movement of his heretofore, though startling, has been confirmed. In reference to his movements, even fast-flying rumor has not been able to get ahead of him." Good news had been in miserly supply throughout the South for nearly a year; now it spread joyously, rapidly, far and wide—with Stonewall Jackson invariably depicted rampant astride the tide.[8]

Six days after the battle of Port Republic, a Georgian in Robert Toombs's brigade wrote home: "The news of the gallant achievements of Stonewall Jackson was most enthusiastically received by the army here, and our commanders here, when compared with Jackson's rapidity of action, are quite unpleasantly commented upon by the rank and file in the line. Jackson is the only General on our side who is fast ascending the ladder of military fame."

Anyone compared to Toombs looked like a meteoric military genius, to be sure, but emphatic accolades similar to those of the Georgian's letter extended across the entire Confederate army. A member of the 11th Virginia, not then (nor ever) under Jackson, longed for the chance to serve with the new hero: "He is the man. . . . I wish we had the whole army filled with Jacksons, and the Yankees would soon be shipped from our soil."[9] Modern critics can cavil at will about Jackson's flaws, but Confederates carrying muskets in June 1862 entertained few doubts about the general's merit.

Literally thousands of contemporary accolades to Jackson from southern pens survive and make the same point to redundancy. These few supply the flavor of innumerable others in the same vein: "He is doing more for our cause than any other one man" (55th Virginia, June 14); "If all of our Generals was like Jackson this war would not last long. He is without a doubt the best General in our army" (15th Alabama, June 13); "implicit confidence . . . admiration for him" (4th Virginia, June 14); "none more brilliant" (a different member of the 4th Virginia, June 10); "Jackson is perfectly idolized by this army" (6th Louisiana, June 14); "We have become quite famous" (Charlottesville Artillery, June 12); "Genl Jackson (My earthly God)" (1st Maryland Infantry, May, undated).[10]

It has become popular in the anti-Confederate writing now so much in vogue to claim, or at least pretend, that defeated southerners created a farcical postwar myth in which they pretended that their wartime leaders meant far more to them during the conflict than actually had been the case. The Myth of the Lost Cause soothes and lulls postmodernists who know for sure that no one could really have been all that patriotic in times of stress and turmoil—a visceral reaction in many instances to the personal tendencies of modern observers. Late-life Confederate memoirists unquestionably viewed their youthful adventures with selective hindsight (to precisely the same degree as did victorious Federals [was there a Myth of the Won Cause afoot?], and as do Arnhem and Angaur survivors). When contemporary writings by those same Confederate memoirists exist, they generally reveal identical devotion and even jingoism. Most reaction to Jackson by the end of the Valley campaign, whether literally accurate or not (and the naysayers can nibble at that more subjective question as they wish), waxed frantically positive in June 1862 in full foreshadowing of the Jacksonian enthusiasms of 1892.

An example of war-dated zeal exhibited by a postwar memoirist was expressed by Capt. James Cooper Nisbet of the 21st Georgia, who fought through the Valley under Jackson. In a later book Nisbet bewailed Jackson's absence at Gettysburg as decisive and lauded the dead hero for "the greatest generalship of the war. . . . He seemed never to tire. . . . The very demon of energy . . . ." In 1862, from the Valley, Nisbet wrote home in the grip of a contemporary passion at least as pronounced as the spirit of his postwar memoir, describing his reaction to "our glorious leader": "Like old Frederick the Great, [Jackson] fights to win, and will win or die. At the same time, he is very considerate of the lives . . . of his men. He makes his fights at the right time and in the right place. He shares the fate of the men. . . . We are ready, for we all feel that what he does is all right. His soldiers all love the old fighting cock."[11] Precisely those sentiments, expressed after the war by a veteran, would draw scorn from many modern academicians as being contrived and dishonest.

At least as significant as Jackson's apotheosis in southern eyes was the new clout that his name carried among his enemies. Federals who had never heard of Thomas J. Jackson in March feared him mightily by June. The New York lieutenant who praised Jackson as "a man of decided genius" in a June 12 letter, and admitted that "very few in our army are fit to compete with him," was expressing a widely held concern—and forecasting future events in a classic bit of self-fulfilling prophecy. When another Federal, captured in June near Richmond, learned that Jackson was on hand, he exploded, "Is that devil here?" The erstwhile Yankee had heard just hours earlier that Jackson had been destroyed—at the same time that a South Carolinian defending Richmond was certain that Stonewall had crossed the Potomac to reach Washington. A Hoosier referred to Stonewall as "this great leader" and admitted that he "outgeneralled all our commanders." Another New Yorker wondered in print, with obvious chagrin, whether his side could find "a general who is as dashy and plucky as this Stonewall Jackson." If they heard of the case, southerners must have been amused by the court-martial of a Unionist quartermaster named Simms who was brought to trial for treasonable language. This traitorous fiend had been overheard uttering the craven lie, "Stonewall Jackson had whipped the US in every battle." "I'm sorry to say," a Pennsylvanian wrote, "I have frequently heard our men . . . talk as though they believed [Jackson] could not be whipped. In fact he . . . got to be what might be called a bugaboo." Northerners of far higher station than poor Simms trembled at Jackson's feats. The French ambassador to Washington, for instance, described "a real panic" on the morning after he had accompanied Abraham Lincoln on a trip to Fredericksburg in late May. "Confidence reigned here some days ago . . . [but now] Washington is thought to be threatened," Monsieur Mercier wrote.[12]

Perceptions of Jackson among his high-ranking subordinates underwent a parallel, if reversed, metamorphosis during the spring of 1862. The relentlessly businesslike Jackson never would be anything remotely like a popular man, but the dawning awareness that he carried victory on his banners gradually relieved uncertainty that had raged among commissioned officers in the Valley army. Quarrelsome and selfish individuals found nothing more to admire in the Jackson of mid-June than in the rigid general of mid-April; patriots could recognize a military utensil invaluable to their country's survival.

Despite his late-life prose bouquets offered to Jackson's widow, presumably written with crossed fingers, William B. Taliaferro typified the former category of officers. Richard Taylor and Richard S. Ewell belonged to the latter class. During the decade after the war, Dick Taylor wrote some of the most deliciously drawn prose descriptions of Jackson in the Valley. The well-born Louisianan compared Stonewall to James Wolfe, Horatio Nelson, and Henry Havelock for "his place in the hearts of English-speaking peoples." During the opening phases of the Valley campaign, however, Taylor had gone to Richmond to implore his brother-in-law, President Jefferson Davis, to relieve "this damned old crazy fool," Stonewall Jackson. The staff officer who reported on Taylor's anti-Jackson mission concluded that this interlude was a typically human reaction: "When we ordinary mortals can't comprehend a genius we get even with him by calling him crazy."[13]

Dick Ewell, himself an eccentric of heroic proportions, certainly thought during early May that Jackson was a certifiable lunatic. On May 13 Ewell called his superior "that enthusiastic fanatic" and insisted that the Valley army had "no head . . . at all, though there is room for one or two." Ewell railed to a subordinate officer, himself no Jacksonian acolyte, that the army commander was "as crazy as a March hare . . . a crazy man." Soon thereafter the disgruntled general denominated orders from Jackson "damn foolishness." Ewell's road-to-Damascus conversion experience unfolded en route to Port Republic. Less than four weeks after his "enthusiastic fanatic" letter, the general manfully admitted that he had misjudged Jackson. "Do you remember," Ewell demanded of Col. Thomas T. Munford, "when I called [Jackson] an old woman? Well, I take it all back." Success in the Valley redrew Stonewall Jackson's image at every level.[14]

Brig. Gen. Charles S. Winder suited Jackson perfectly well, but Jackson did not much suit Winder. "Jackson is insane," he told his diary on June 5, with the campaign's successful conclusion in sight; two days later, "disgusted with Jackson"; on May 8, "requesting to leave his command." Winder never got away. He died in battle two months after that last plaintive entry.[15]

The subordinate with the most reason to dislike and mistrust Jackson that spring was Brig. Gen. Richard Brooke Garnett, whom Stonewall threw into arrest in the aftermath of the battle of Kernstown. The colonels in Garnett's brigade unflinchingly and without exception supported their chief in the jousting that ensued in preparation for a court-martial. Active operations interrupted the court in August 1862, and it never reconvened—perhaps because Jackson clearly was losing. Dr. Douglas Southall Freeman, as he was writing his classic *Lee's Lieutenants*, said in a private letter, "I never could understand why [Jackson] persecuted . . . Dick Garnett."[16] Garnett's arrest removed him from close proximity to the Shenandoah campaign, but it is easy to imagine his amazement, from afar, at the striking success of his inflexible bête noir.

Even the triumphant climax of the Valley campaign did not entirely disabuse Jackson's subordinate officers of their notions about the army's commander. In mid-June four generals refought the campaign in private and concluded that their chief had been inordinately fortunate in escaping from the tenuous limb onto which he had flung his advance elements at Harpers Ferry. The uneasy Winder and the usually feisty Isaac R. Trimble, joined apparently by Taliaferro and Taylor, agreed unanimously "that Jackson could not continue to take such risks without at some time meeting with a great disaster." They were wrong as well as slow in figuring out their miscalculation. One of Jackson's staff mused that subordinate generals and colo-nels had from the start "doubted his ability to manage a larger command [than a brigade]. . . . They feared the government had exchanged a first-class Brigadier for a common-place Major General." Such judgments died a lin-gering death in the world of stars and wreaths, though not in the eye of the South at large.[17]

The foot soldiers slogging in Jackson's wake awoke to the success of their general and his campaign sooner than did the majority of their officers. The startling, thrilling onfall against the small Yankee garrison at Front Royal opened the eyes of Confederate musketeers to the purpose of the endless marching and lurking. Innocent of the considerations that still furrowed of-ficers' brows, the enlisted men decided that the Valley operations bid fair to be a rousing success. On the morning after Front Royal, Jackson's troops en-acted a scene that would soon become entirely routine but remained remark-able on May 24: "He [Jackson] took off his cap & galloped in the hot sun near 4 miles to pass us. What hollowering you never heard." When the triumphant Confederates captured a wagon load of lemons from enemy sutlers' stores, southerners gloated at drinking Yankee lemonade—and soon began talking of Jackson's fondness for the acerbic fruit.[18]

Col. Sam Fulkerson had undergone something of a metamorphosis in his own view of Stonewall Jackson, but perhaps he was not yet fully converted. Having been firmly in the anti-Jackson camp at the time of the Romney mutiny (signing the manifesto to Richmond near its head), Fulkerson could admit five days after Port Republic that "the privates of the whole army have the most unbounded confidence in him."[19] Was Fulkerson's careful con-struction of that phrase an indication that he and others were not yet ready to share the unbounded confidence of the private soldiers? If so, he had no opportunity to repent of his judgment; Fulkerson was killed thirteen days later at Gaines's Mill.

Not long after Jackson's meteoric rise to prominence, R. E. Lee, too, became a Confederate hero. The two men offered such markedly different public visages to the world that, not surprisingly, their respective legends varied considerably. "The difference in the manner in which" the two gen-erals were regarded "is one of the curious features of the war," a thoughtful veteran wrote years later. For Lee the soldiery exhibited "an explicit trust and reverent affection." Jackson inspired, by contrast, "diabolical yells and cheers," prompted by "admiration and enthusiasm." The disparate reactions made sense to some degree, but even so, concluded the reflective Confederate, "action and events are largely beyond the ken of pure reasoning facilities."[20] That rubric might well be posted in the academic halls where historiography is unveiled to innocents.

The Jackson legend crafted during a few weeks in the spring of 1862 was far too strong to be unhorsed by the general's costly failures during the Seven Days battles around Richmond that followed immediately after the Valley. In the aftermath of that bad performance—the only one of Jackson's career—popular opinion was inclined to blame Lee rather than the new Valley hero, entirely unfair though such a judgment was in relation to the facts of the case. When Stonewall's troops found triumph after triumph in succeeding months, men on both sides came to savor or fear the appearance of Jackson, depending on their allegiances.

The utterly unknown military school professor had, by the time of his death, become "the great dread of the Yankees," in the admiring phrase of one of his men. The legend continued to expand after the general's demise. An august Federalist court-martial convened in Atchison, Kansas, in the summer of 1864 sentenced a citizen named A. R. Earl to prison. The crime that had brought poor Earl before the Jacobins was of the most brazen and seditious sort: he had been offering for sale a biography of Stonewall Jackson. The book had been published in New York and copyrighted under laws promulgated by the U.S. Congress, but none of that mattered to the earnest protectors of Kansan readers' virtue.[21]

Northerners of less frenzied temperament openly admired their dead enemy. Herman Melville, who was anything but a southern sympathizer, wrote two contemporary poems lauding Jackson. In one the great northern writer declared that though "Relentlessly he routed us . . . We drop a tear on the bold Virginian's bier." The other Melville poem hymned Jackson's "great soul" and marveled how "his sword with thunder was clothed." Some vindictive northern journals attacked Melville as a traitor, but other newspapers, even in such stridently Federalist venues as Vermont, printed complimentary notices of Jackson's death. The same New Yorker who had grumbled in June 1862 that "very few in our army are fit to compete with him" admitted on Jackson's death, "I do not feel like exulting over the grave of such a brave, wise, and energetic antagonist—'peace be to his ashes.'" Northerners of that mien saw to the posting of sentinels, assigned from the Federal occupation force, to stand guard at Jackson's grave in Lexington in the weeks soon after Appomattox.[22]

Northern readers of *Harper's Weekly*, many of whom undoubtedly had followed Jackson's exploits in the Valley during the spring of 1862, saw this sketch of the general by British artist Frank Vizetelly in the pictorial newspaper's March 14, 1863, issue.

Countless thousands of southerners mourned bitterly the loss in May 1863 of a man who a few months earlier had been unknown or ignored. An entirely typical reaction was to blame the country's loss on a dour and vengeful god. A leading southern cleric suggested within days after Jackson's death that the news actually was good: obviously God now had "charged Himself [rather than Jackson] with the care and protection of this struggling Republic." "The army loved him almost to idolatry," a North Carolina captain wrote the morning after the fatal day; "I believe he was taken away to learn us not to depend upon the arm of flesh." A similarly pious Virginian, of the old Stonewall Brigade, reached the blissful conclusion that "it is all for the best" but could not help admitting in a less relentlessly pietistic moment, "I almost feel like we were without a general now."[23]

Those few Confederates not enamored of Jackson, even after his Valley triumphs, primarily were motivated by jealousy. Gen. Joe Johnston, who had more than ample room for jealousy but no credentials for pontification, insisted that Jackson was not a military genius but, rather, simply "possessed with a sublime enthusiasm." A Front Royal woman made the mistake of hymning Stonewall's excellence in front of one of Gen. James Longstreet's staff. Capt. Osmun Latrobe "was greatly picqued" by such good words about Jackson because he thought it "detracted from Longstreet's fame." The woman diarist was "much surprised that such a quiet self-possessed individual should have been startled out of his usual equanimity thus."[24] Longstreet, of course, spent many decades after both Jackson and Lee were dead awkwardly attempting to assail their reputations in service of his own. The embittered general accomplished infinitely more for his enemies than for himself in the process.

Interest in the Jackson of legend burned brightly in England. Not long after the general's death, there appeared for sale in London a popular song, "Stonewall Jackson Recitative and Air" by Charles Blamphin. The nine-page sheet music included these perfervid, if awkward, lines: "He was his soldiers' pride, and for his country died, on a bright May day in sixty three . . . on a battlefield for liberty."[25]

The emergence of Fool Tom Jackson, from chrysalis form as the crazy man of Virginia's Valley into the Mighty Stonewall for whom high schools are named, occurred as a direct result of his operations in the spring of 1862. Southern newspapers wryly admitted their conversion experiences. The *Richmond Daily Whig* had, in the immemorial journalistic tradition, known quite

Sheet music for "Stonewall Jackson Recitative and Air." Collection of Robert K. Krick.

certainly best how to run the Valley war in its early days and had catered to the theorems of Jackson as eccentric. Now the paper spoofed itself in a lengthy faux wanted circular:

STRAYED

A liberal reward will be given for the apprehension of a confirmed lunatic, named Old Stonewall, who escaped from the Asylum, in this place, early in the Spring of the present year. He endeavors to avoid detection by calling himself T. J. Jackson, and fancies he is an officer in the Confederate army. When last heard from he was offering personal indignity to an aged and feeble Ex Senator of the United States. . . . He is reported to have misdirected an imbecile cobbler from Massachusetts, who was making his way . . . towards Staunton [an allusion to General, former congressman, Banks]. . . . [Stonewall] is marked by an excessive irrascibility, a propensity to steal wagons and munitions of war, and an indisposition to sit down quietly and behave himself. The entire efforts of the United and Confederate Governments hav[e] failed to arrest him. . . .

BY ORDER OF THE SUPERINTENDENT OF
THE LUNATIC ASYLUM AT STAUNTON[26]

A Georgia newspaper took the same tack. Stonewall's surprising Valley victory "gives us a vertigo of delight," the paper crowed: "We hope he will keep on and give us an apoplexy before he stops." Editorial policy had been much less enthusiastic not long before. "Sometime ago," the editors admitted manfully, "we accused Jackson of being of unsound mind." Of late, they continued,

he has exhibited not the least symptom of improvement. In fact he gets worse and worse every day. Within the last two weeks he seems to have gone clean daft—crazy quite, crazy as a bedbug—crazy as two bedbugs. . . . He has been raving, ramping, roaring, rearing, snorting and cavorting up and down the Valley, chawing up Yankees by the thousands as if they were so many grains of parched pop-corn. The Lord send he may never recover his senses till his foot cavalry are stabled in the big barns of the Susquehanna Valley. Crazy or not, we but echo the voice of the whole Confederacy when we say "God bless Old Stonewall and Old Ewell, and Old Ned Johnson. God bless 'em a thousand times over and all the gallant fellows they so skilfully command. God bless them all!"[27]

The "quite lunatic" general, Tom Fool Jackson, had become Mighty Stonewall overnight, or at least over a few dozen nights. His newly won stature suddenly made him an apt pseudo-purveyor of Yankee soap to phrenologists. T. J. Jackson was well on the way to becoming an American legend.

NOTES

1. Advertisement in *American Phrenological Journal and Life Illustrated* 36 (November 1862): 118. The soap ad reproduced a fanciful note signed "Stonewall" vouching for the product's efficacy against all kinds of grime.

2. "From Western Virginia," *Columbus (Ga.) Daily Sun*, November 12, 1861; Clayton G. Coleman to Francis H. Smith, January 27, 1861 [1862], Virginia Military Institute Archives, Lexington (repository hereafter cited as VMIA); Emma Cassandra Riely Macon and Reuben Conway Macon, *Reminiscences of the Civil War* (Cedar Rapids, Iowa: Torch Press, 1911), 72–73; Lucy Walton Fletch diary, July 2, 1862, private collection of Lewis F. Fisher, San Antonio, Tex.

3. Wm. B. Taliaferro and others to Brig. Gen'l Loring, January 25, 1862, forwarded to the secretary of war, document 11158-1862, "Letters Received by the Confederate Secretary of War," M437, roll 27, National Archives, Washington, D.C. (repository hereafter cited as NA); Henry Kyd Douglas, *I Rode with Stonewall* (Chapel Hill: University of North Carolina Press, 1940), 57; T. J. Jackson to Mr. Fulkerson, September 2, 1862, Fulkerson Family Papers, VMIA. The three regimental-commander signatories not named in the text were, respectively, Vannoy H. Manning, James W. Anderson, and Andrew Van Buren Scott. Manning and Scott went on to make respectable records. Taliaferro's attempt to elbow into the spotlight shed on his once-loathed superior appears in Mary Anna Jackson, *Memoirs of "Stonewall" Jackson* (Louisville, Ky.: Prentice Press, Courier-Journal Job Printing Co., 1895), 508–26. An example of an officer willing to go forward with the Romney campaign was Thomas H. Malone of the 1st Tennessee Infantry, whose January 1862 letters are in Thomas H. Malone, *Memoir of Thomas H. Malone: An Autobiography Written for His Children* (Nashville: Baird-Ward, 1928), 116–17.

4. J. T. L. Preston account recorded by Jedediah Hotchkiss in manuscript notes on bare pages of a printed 1857 catalog for Mossy Creek Academy, Alderman Library, University of Virginia, Charlottesville (cited hereafter as Hotchkiss ms. notes). I have Stephen L. Ritchie of Muncie, Indiana, to thank for his diligence in uncovering this extremely important source. The best source on Jackson during this ill-fated campaign is virtually unknown: "Scraps from my Haversack," *Valley Virginian* (Staunton), January 16, 1866–May 2, 1867 (plus other numbers, apparently, not seen, as the above dates cover no. 4 to no. 11).

5. Turner Ashby to A. R. Boteler, April 25, 1862, Simon Gratz Collection, Pennsylvania

Historical Society, Philadelphia; Judah P. Benjamin to Turner Ashby, care of A. R. Boteler, February 22, 1862, Letters Received by the Confederate Adjutant and Inspector General, M474, roll 3, NA.

6. Jackson to A. R. Boteler, February 25, 1862, Frederick M. Dearborn Collection, Houghton Library, Harvard University, Cambridge, Mass.

7. *Winchester Virginian*, January 29, 1862; Algernon Sidney Wade to "Lou," February 10, 1862, private collection of Lewis Leigh Jr., Fairfax, Va.; "Gave Jackson Bread on His Famous March," *Winchester Evening Star*, June 20, 1923; "Twice-told tale," *Winchester Star*, May 7, 1997.

8. Elizabeth Maxwell Alsop Wynne diary, Virginia Historical Society, Richmond; *Columbus (Ga.) Daily Enquirer*, May 28, June 9, 1862.

9. J. T. S. letter dated June 15, 1862, in "From the 20th Georgia Regiment," *Columbus (Ga.) Daily Enquirer*, June 23, 1862; John W. Anthony to "Dear Callie," June 16, 1862, in possession of Claude Foster, Charlottesville, Va.

10. Robert Gaines Haile to wife, June 14, 1862, transcript in possession of Robert E. L. Krick, Richmond, Va.; Edmund Cody Burnett, ed., "Letters of Barnett Hardeman Cody and Others," *Georgia Historical Quarterly* 23 (December 1939): 365; William S. White, *Sketches of the Life of Captain Hugh A. White* (Columbia: South Carolinian Steam Press, 1864), 93; John Apperson letter, June 10, 1862, Dr. Harvey Black Papers, Virginia Polytechnic Institute and State University, Blacksburg; George P. Ring to wife, June 14, 1862, Ring Papers, Tulane University, New Orleans, La.; James L. Dinwiddie to wife, June 12, 1862, Virginia State Archives, Richmond; William H. Murray to "My dear friend," undated [May 1862], Maryland Historical Society, Baltimore (repository hereafter cited as MHS).

11. James Cooper Nisbet, *Four Years on the Firing Line* (Chattanooga: Imperial Press, [1911?]), 61, 78, 85, 351; James Cooper Nisbet, "From Stonewall Jackson," *Macon (Ga.) Daily Telegraph*, June 27, 1862.

12. William Wheeler, *Letters of William Wheeler* (Cambridge, Mass.: H. O. Houghton, 1875), 336; James L. Strain and Adolphus E. Fant, *Found among the Privates: Recollections of Holcomb[e]'s Legion* (Sharon, S.C.: privately printed, 1997), 97; U. R. Brooks, *Butler and His Cavalry in the War of Secession* (Columbia, S.C.: State Company, 1909), 78–79; J. A. Crose, "Letter from the Shenandoah Valley," *Indianapolis Daily Journal*, July 2, 1862; Lt. George Breck letter, August 13, 1862, published in the *Rochester Union and Advertiser*, August 19, 1862; Court Martial file #kk835, Records of the Judge Advocate General's Office (Army), entry 15, Court Martial Case Files, RG 153, NA, courtesy of Dr. L. Thomas and Bev Lowry's admirable Index Project, Inc. (for some reason, poor Simms's given name is not in the court file); Mary Warner Thomas and Richard A. Sauers, eds., *The Civil War Letters of First Lieutenant James B. Thomas, Adjutant, 107th Pennsylvania Volunteers* (Baltimore: Butternut and Blue, 1995), 167; Daniel B. Carroll, *Henri Mercier and the American Civil War* (Princeton: Princeton University Press, 1971), 174–75. For General

Banks's amusing insistence that "we ought not to have lost," see Banks to Josiah Dunham, June 10, 1862, Dearborn Collection, Harvard University. Banks wryly observed of the hubbub in Washington, "I do not believe men will be saved or destroyed by any system of salvation in vogue there."

13. Richard Taylor, *Destruction and Reconstruction: Personal Experiences of the Late War* (Edinburgh: William Blackwood and Sons, 1879), 99; David French Boyd, *Reminiscences of the War in Virginia*, ed. T. Michael Parrish (Austin: Jenkins, 1989), 7–10. Alison Moore, in *He Died Furious* (Baton Rouge: Ortlieb Press, 1983), 120–40, launches the interesting premise that Taylor never did come to admire Jackson but merely bowed to the popular image by pretending to have been an intimate of the Confederate hero. Less convincingly, Moore suggests that if Jackson did choose to sit by Taylor's campfires, it was to keep a careful eye on the Louisianan.

14. Richard S. Ewell, *The Making of a Soldier: Letters of General R. S. Ewell*, ed. Percy G. Hamlin (Richmond: Whittet and Shepperson, 1935), 108; J. William Jones, "From Port Republic to the Chickahominy," in *Southern Historical Society Papers*, ed. J. William Jones and others, 52 vols. (Richmond: Southern Historical Society, 1876–1959), 9:364–65; George E. Sipe, "Civil War Recollections," Harrisonburg-Rockingham County Historical Society, Dayton, Va.; Munford account, Munford-Ellis Papers, William R. Perkins Library, Duke University, Durham, N.C.

15. Charles S. Winder diary, MHS.

16. D. S. Freeman to Mrs. Delia Page Marshall, July 12, 1943, VMIA. The proceedings of the interrupted court-martial and the pro-Garnett correspondence by his subordinates are at the Museum of the Confederacy, Richmond, Va. Alexander Swift "Sandie" Pendleton, Jackson's aide and supporter before the court, wrote on the eve of the trial that "the case will most probably go by default in favor of Gen. Garnett" (Pendleton to mother, August 5, 1862, William N. Pendleton Papers, Southern Historical Collection, University of North Carolina, Chapel Hill). For the charges in the case, and excerpts from the testimony, see Robert K. Krick, "The Army of Northern Virginia's Most Notorious Court Martial," *Blue and Gray Magazine* 3 (June–July 1986): 27–32.

17. McHenry Howard, *Recollections of a Maryland Confederate Soldier and Staff Officer under Johnston, Jackson, and Lee* (Baltimore: Williams and Wilkins, 1914), 130–31. The uncertainty about the final two pessimists is Howard's. This anecdote throws interesting light on Taylor's subsequent depiction of himself as a Jackson intimate and an unswerving supporter. Hindsight is an incomparable tool, which is the central message of this historical essay. The staffer quoted is Henry Kyd Douglas, "Stonewall Jackson's Only Speech," *Shepherdstown Register*, February 5, 1876. In this article, which is far more thoughtful than Douglas's boastful published memoir, the quondam aide forwarded the premise of the next paragraph in the text of this essay—that the army's enlisted men enthused over Jackson sooner than did their officers.

18. Joseph M. Ellison (15th Alabama) to "My Dear Wife," May 26, 1862, in *Georgia*

Historical Quarterly 48 (June 1964): 231; *Augusta Daily Constitutionalist*, June 14, 1862. Despite revisionist attempts to debunk the Jackson-and-lemons legend, there are several solid sources supporting his fondness for that fruit—and in fact most other varieties, too.

19. Samuel V. Fulkerson to his sister-in-law, June 14, 1862, Fulkerson Family Papers, VMIA.

20. "Idols of the Army," *Shepherdstown (W.Va.) Register*, November 2, 1884.

21. Court-martial of A. R. Earl, file #nn2161, Records of the Judge Advocate General's Office (Army), entry 15, Court Martial Case Files, RG 153, NA, courtesy of Tom and Bev Lowry of the Index Project, Inc. The intended victim of a similar court-martial lynching, S. M. Kennedy of St. Louis, somehow won a verdict of not guilty, though he had been so bold as to sell eight copies of a Jackson biography (file #nn2732, ibid.).

22. Herman Melville, *Battle-Pieces and Aspects of the War* (New York: Harper and Brothers, 1866), 79–83. For one of a host of examples of friendly mortuary columns about Jackson, see the *Rutland (Vt.) Daily Herald*, May 16, 1863. The unvengeful New Yorker was William Wheeler, writing on May 14, 1863; see *Letters of William Wheeler*, 397. See also Hotchkiss ms. notes.

23. Benjamin M. Palmer in *Minutes of the General Assembly of the Presbyterian Church in the Confederate States of America* (Columbia, S.C.: Southern Guardian Steam-Power Press, 1863), 152–53; letter of Captain Eli Freeman, Company B, 14th North Carolina, May 11, 1863, copy in the author's possession. Freeman himself died in battle almost precisely two years later, whether or not as the penalty for someone else's fondness. The Stonewall Brigade veteran was Alexander Straith Baird [Beard in the Compiled Service Records] of the 2nd Virginia; see Baird to "Dear Ma," May 15, 1863, typescript in the author's possession.

24. Johnston quoted by Jeremiah Morton in Hotchkiss ms. notes; Lucy Rebecca Buck, *Diary of Lucy R. Buck*, ed. L. Neville Buck (Front Royal, Va.: privately printed, 1940), 116.

25. The 5th edition of the song sheet bears the London imprimatur of Brewer and Co., but without a date.

26. *Richmond Daily Whig*, June 13, 1862.

27. *Macon (Ga.) Daily Telegraph*, June 16, 1862.

WILLIAM J. MILLER

Such Men as Shields, Banks, and Frémont

FEDERAL COMMAND IN WESTERN VIRGINIA,

MARCH–JUNE 1862

Generations of students of Civil War history have taken as an article of faith that General T. J. "Stonewall" Jackson's operations in the Shenandoah Valley in the spring of 1862 were brilliant, miraculous, and ingenious. Writers and readers alike have come to see Jackson as a master strategist—a determined and wily warrior who almost literally marched his army in rings around a series of laughably inept Federal commanders. Few generals of the Civil War so dominated a campaign that historians have deigned to consider it "his," yet almost universally writers have given the lanky former professor deed and title to those springtime operations, referring to them more often than not simply as "Jackson's Valley campaign."

Jackson did dominate his enemies and achieve a signal victory for the South, but the very degree of that dominance raises important questions about his performance. Is not an interpretation of the campaign that extols the brilliance of Jackson's actions while ridiculing the bumbling incompetence of his foes illogical? If Nathaniel P. Banks, John C. Frémont, and James Shields were utterly without military capacity, does that not denigrate Jackson's military achievements against them? Gen. James Longstreet touched on this question long after the war when he wrote that "Jackson was a very skillful man against such men as Shields, Banks, and Frémont, but when pitted against the best of the Federal commanders he did not appear so well."[1] General Longstreet's point is no less interesting for its unseemly expression. The quality of Jackson's opposition is part and parcel of the quality of Jackson's generalship. To evaluate the latter, one must assess the former.

Furthermore, Jackson's admirers, including this writer, have long looked at operations in the Valley in 1862 almost entirely from a southern standpoint. This limited perspective has naturally left enormous gaps in our knowledge of what happened at Federal headquarters and in Washington between March and June 1862 and therefore with an imperfect understanding of why the principals acted as they did. Thus we must conclude that for a series of operations of major significance in the war, we possess a body of interpretative work that is, on the whole, incomplete and illogical. Further inquiry into and a reassessment of those operations seem imperative, beginning with an examination of Federal plans and operations.

Federal intentions in western Virginia were clear enough in the late winter of 1862. On February 3, 1862, Maj. Gen. George B. McClellan, general in chief of all Federal armies, presented a letter to Secretary of War Edwin M. Stanton and President Abraham Lincoln laying out his plan of operations for the coming spring. His strategy called for a general advance of all armies in all theaters. The principal effort was to be aimed at Richmond, the Confederate capital, but the other thrusts, McClellan argued, would both gain strategic points and keep the Confederates from concentrating all their strength at Richmond. A part of his plan was to "gain possession of the Eastern Tennessee Railroads" and to capture Nashville and the rest of eastern Tennessee. This was to occur with simultaneous advances in the Carolinas and Alabama and along the Mississippi River. Lincoln approved this grand strategy, and McClellan set army and department commanders from Washington to beyond the Mississippi to creating operational plans for the offensive.[2]

The Great Valley of Virginia, of which the Shenandoah Valley was a part, played a very small role in McClellan's grand scheme. The Young Napoleon was intent on Richmond, and he wished to take it from the east. His plan was to advance with an enormous army of 120,000 or more men up the Virginia Peninsula from the Chesapeake Bay and with this irresistible force capture the Confederate capital and crush the rebellion. He wished to protect Harpers Ferry and its railroads and bridges at the northern tip of the Shenandoah Valley because he understood that the Valley offered a shielded avenue by which a Confederate force might strike into western Maryland and possibly threaten Washington—a circumstance he heartily wished to prevent. He was interested in the Valley only to the degree that it would help or hinder his effort at Richmond.

In late February Maj. Gen. Nathaniel P. Banks led two divisions—his own and that of Brig. Gen. James Shields—across the Potomac into Virginia. Banks was, according to McClellan's orders, to occupy Winchester, about twenty-five miles south of Harpers Ferry, and secure the surrounding country. Within a week Banks and his 20,000 men had taken the city without a fight, having driven off Stonewall Jackson and his command of fewer than 4,000 Confederates. On March 16 McClellan sent new orders to Banks that clarified the commanding general's defensive policy. Banks was to rebuild the Manassas Gap Railroad to Strasburg, entrench a brigade (with cavalry) at Front Royal or Strasburg, and "occupy Winchester & thoroughly scout the country south of the R.R. & up the Shenandoah valley." McClellan thought Banks's men might protect these vital points by building blockhouses at railroad crossings and stressed the importance of cavalry scouting "well to the front." He also urged Banks to take "Great care to obtain full & early information as to enemy." In sum, McClellan stated, the "General object [was] to cover the line of Potomac and Washington."[3] That done, Banks could then move with most of his troops to Manassas Junction, near Washington, and thence, perhaps, to Richmond.[4]

McClellan's designs in the Shenandoah in mid-March were wholly defensive, but two events that month threw the Federal program into chaos. First, on March 11 Lincoln created the Mountain Department, a vast tract of land between the Shenandoah Valley on the east and Ohio on the west, and appointed Maj. Gen. John C. Frémont to command it. As an inexperienced, first-term president just a year in office, Lincoln struggled not only to restore the broken union of states but also to unify the fragmented northern war effort. Unionists, Democrats, and abolitionists all hoped to win the war on their own terms, and they often pursued different ends. Powerful factions within these camps sought to bend Lincoln to their will. Even within his own Republican Party the president faced formidable opponents, not the least of whom were supporters of John Charles Frémont.

Frémont ranked among the more famous men in America. He had run as the first Republican candidate for president of the United States in 1856. Before that, he had made a fortune in gold in California and earlier still had been the first U.S. senator from California. As a junior officer in the Army

Nathaniel P. Banks, at center with his arms folded, flanked by members of his staff. This engraving was first published in *Frank Leslie's Illustrated Newspaper* shortly before the beginning of the Valley campaign. Paul F. Mottelay and T. Campbell-Copeland, eds., *The Soldier in Our Civil War*, 2 vols. (New York: Stanley Bradley, 1893), 1:193.

Corps of Engineers between 1842 and 1853, Frémont led five expeditions through the American West. These were scientific journeys as well as mapping forays. The crews of 50 to 100 men under his command gathered samples of plants and animals and assisted their leader in making maps, charting trails, finding mountain passes, and fighting hostile Indians. It was a hard life, battling blizzards, frostbite, starvation, and mutineers, but Frémont survived it all. With the help of his wife Jesse, daughter of powerful Missouri senator Thomas Hart Benton, Frémont wrote and published exceptionally readable reports of his expeditions, and they brought him wide fame as "The Pathfinder."

Once the war came, a combination of Frémont's service in the engineers and his ideology earned him rank in the Union army beyond his abilities. A committed abolitionist, he became the darling of the radical wing of the Republican Party, and Lincoln appeased his bedfellows by appointing Frémont one of the North's first major generals—third on the seniority list behind only Winfield Scott and McClellan.[5] It was an appointment Lincoln would regret.

Frémont's first assignment was as commander of the Department of the West with headquarters in St. Louis. Assailed by Confederates, guerrillas, the Washington bureaucracy, thieves and black marketeers, patronage seekers, and an impatient administration, he was overwhelmed. High-level investigators from Washington traveled west to look into charges of corruption in the awarding of contracts. Frémont made a bitter enemy in Missouri congressman Francis Preston Blair, who denounced the general in a widely published speech in the House of Representatives. The Pathfinder's troubled tenure in the West came to an end soon after he tried to emancipate Missouri's slaves. Though intended as a military measure to weaken the wealthy Missouri planters bankrolling bands of Confederate guerrillas that plagued Frémont's troops, many in the North considered the proclamation an extreme act by a radical. Abolitionists praised Frémont, but Democrats and many moderate Republicans reviled him. Lincoln ordered him to rescind the proclamation. Frémont, proud and stubborn, refused, whereupon the president rescinded it himself and relieved his headstrong general in November 1861.[6]

But Frémont, a forty-eight-year-old sometime soldier, did not just fade away. His advocates took umbrage at the insult dealt him. They besieged Lincoln, chastened him for his indiscretion in relieving their man, and insisted that Frémont be given another suitable command. "Where?" Lincoln asked. "In the early Spring," the president later wrote to a friend, "Gen. Frémont sought active service again; and, as it seemed to me, sought it in a very good and reasonable spirit. But he holds the highest rank in the Army, except McClellan, so that I could not well offer him a subordinate command. Was I to displace Hooker, or Hunter, or Rosecrans, or Grant, or Banks? If not, what was I to do?"[7]

Lincoln knew that the Army of the Potomac had a full complement of corps commanders and that, in any case, McClellan, who loathed Frémont and his politics, would not accept him. Frémont had already failed in the West, and no appropriate place seemed in the offing there. Finally succumbing to what he called the "everlasting popular clamor!" to reinstate Frémont, Lincoln looked

John Charles Frémont in 1861, an engraving first published in *Frank Leslie's Illustrated Newspaper* during Frémont's command in Missouri before he transferred to western Virginia. Paul F. Mottelay and T. Campbell-Copeland, eds., *The Soldier in Our Civil War*, 2 vols. (New York: Stanley Bradley, 1893), 1:157.

at mountainous western Virginia.[8] There, at his headquarters at Wheeling, William S. Rosecrans, a mere brigadier, labored in obscurity. Another place could easily be found for him. But the mountains, the seam between the Eastern and Western Theaters, might well prove a suitable place to squirrel away the Pathfinder. A victory there might open the door to eastern Tennessee and the transportation hub of Knoxville. The strong Unionist sympathy in the Tennessee Appalachians might catch fire if Union troops occupied the region, and the railroads in southwestern Virginia, important to the Confederate defense of Richmond and the Old Dominion, might be vulnerable to Federal assaults from the mountains. On the other hand, the failure of a campaign through the mountains would mean little, especially if McClellan succeeded in his drive on Richmond. As he sat at his desk in the White House in March 1862, Lincoln had little to lose in proposing to Frémont that he take hold of matters in western Virginia. The president created the Mountain Department and installed Frémont as commander. The Pathfinder accepted the proposal at once, but rather than take to the field, he chose to begin his preparations in, of all places, New York City.[9]

As is often the case, an idea that made political sense was practical nonsense. Gen. Jacob Cox, an experienced Ohio politician and soon to be one of Frémont's subordinates, had been on duty in the wilds of western Virginia for months. He knew the region, yet no one consulted him about the feasibility of a campaign through the high country to Tennessee. "There was a little too much sentiment," Cox later wrote, "and too little practical war in the construction of a department out of five hundred miles of mountain ranges, and the appointment of the 'path-finder' to command it was consistent with the romantic character of the whole."[10]

The second event that deranged McClellan's plans west of the Blue Ridge was Stonewall Jackson's impetuous attack on Banks's force at Kernstown on March 23. Banks, convinced that Jackson and his 4,000 men were no threat, had begun to execute McClellan's orders to move most of his force toward Washington. Shields's 9,000-man division, by direction of McClellan, would remain in the Valley to protect the railroads while the rest of Banks's soldiers, some 10,000 strong, moved to Manassas. On March 22 Brig. Gen. Alpheus S. Williams's division broke camp in Winchester and headed eastward toward the Blue Ridge. The next day, Jackson struck at Kernstown. The Federals suffered 574 casualties, but Jackson lost 737 and the field as well. Forced to withdraw again, Stonewall slunk southward to Narrow Passage and on to Rude's Hill, just north of New Market.[11]

The small battle at Kernstown, though a Union victory, caused an extreme overreaction in the mind of George McClellan. Viewed rationally, Jackson's sally at Kernstown need not have altered McClellan's plans or his defensive posture in the Valley. Shields's 10,000 men could remain at Winchester to

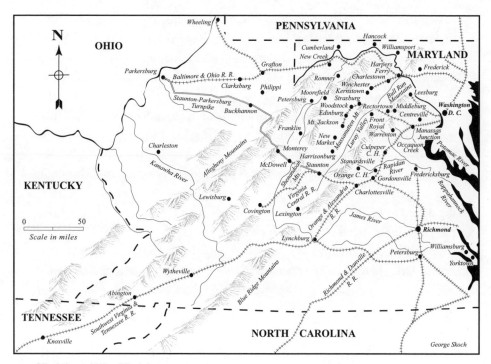

Virginia and West Virginia

cover the Baltimore & Ohio Railroad (B&O) and likely would have been
more than able to deal with Jackson's brigade-sized army. But for perhaps the
only time in his career, McClellan rejected deliberate thought and discreet
action. He boldly changed Banks's orders. "As soon as you are strong enough
push Jackson hard and drive him well beyond Strasburg, pursuing at least as
far as Woodstock, and, if possible, with cavalry to Mount Jackson." The army
commander reiterated his desire that Banks resume the movement on Manassas "the very moment the thorough defeat of Jackson will permit it," leaving a division behind "to cover the line of Potomac and Washington." Unfortunately, McClellan was unnecessarily vague about precisely how and where
the remaining troops should be posted. He told Banks to leave Shields's
command "at or near Strasburg and Winchester," but as the two towns were
twenty miles apart, Banks might have been forgiven any uncertainty. Mc-
Clellan closed with an exhortation: "Communicate fully and frequently and
act vigorously." Banks did just that, after a fashion. He recalled Williams and
set out up the Valley, intent that his 19,000 men should thoroughly defeat
Jackson's 3,500.[12]

After Kernstown and continuing through to the final week in May, Federal plans in the Valley region became ill defined or ill considered or both. Confusion marked the operations of Banks and Frémont. Two Federal forces operated in western Virginia, sometimes less than fifty miles apart, yet neither was instructed or encouraged to cooperate with the other. Banks reported to the commander of the Army of the Potomac and sought to execute his designs. Frémont reported directly to the War Department. One of these forces had begun on the defensive before its mission had been switched to an offensive pursuit of Jackson's little force. It was to finish its work as quickly as possible and then move elsewhere. The other force operated on the offensive as well but with a different and entirely unrelated goal, and that, too, was someplace other than the Shenandoah. As March closed, then, the Federals in the Valley region were on divergent courses.

On April 1, as McClellan sailed from Washington to join most of his army on the Virginia Peninsula southeast of Richmond, he sent revised orders to Banks. The latter's earlier goals had been to secure the Front Royal area, protect the railroad, and move eastward to defend Washington. Now, McClellan wrote, "the most important thing . . . is to throw Jackson well back & then to assume such a position as to enable you to prevent his return." McClellan did not state what that position should be and, with his mind occupied by the great task before him on the Peninsula, seemed unable to give Banks clear instructions. As soon as the Manassas Gap Railroad was repaired, wrote McClellan, Banks should move to Staunton (changing again from the defensive to the offensive). The army commander immediately negated that plan, however, by stating that because such a move would require 25,000 to 30,000 men, he thought Banks too weak to succeed. McClellan then further muddied the waters by declaring that an advance on Staunton should be made "nearly coincident with my own move on Richmond." He once again reversed himself, however, by writing that he did not think Banks could be ready in time for such a concerted movement.[13]

Confusion worsened as the days of April passed away. In the same order that had installed Frémont in command of the Mountain Department, Lincoln had relieved McClellan of command of all the armies and directed him to focus his attention on the Army of the Potomac and its effort to take Richmond. This did not immediately affect McClellan's command relationship with Banks, whose troops were included in the Army of the Potomac, but in the first week of April that changed. Having relieved McClellan, Lincoln and Secretary Stanton decided to assume the role of general in chief and attempt to direct grand strategy from Washington. After McClellan left for the Peninsula on April 1, they learned that he had not assigned as many troops for the defense of Washington as promised to receive approval for his operations on the Peninsula. Feeling duped and fearing for the capital's safety, Lincoln immediately reduced McClellan's force and took steps to provide for Washington's security by creating two new independent commands: the Department of the Rappahannock under Maj. Gen. Irvin McDowell and the Department of the Shenandoah under Banks.[14] Henceforth, Banks would not be answerable to McClellan. He would take orders from the two lawyers in Washington.

Because the War Department did not alter his instructions from McClellan, Banks resolved to move forward and keep contact with Jackson. He encountered two obstacles. The Confederates burned bridges and destroyed culverts behind them as they moved southward. What cavalry Banks had was inferior in quality to Turner Ashby's Confederate horsemen, and the Confederates set ambushes and shrewdly posted artillery on knolls and in blind bends in the road to slow the Federal advance. Banks found progress difficult, halting frequently to rebuild bridges.[15]

Repeatedly blocked in front, Banks also felt himself tugged on from behind. Supplies and rations did not follow the army promptly. The aborted move to Manassas a week or more earlier had interrupted the supply line. On March 22 Banks had sent most of his trains eastward, apparently ahead of the infantry. When he had to return to the Valley, his quartermasters had failed to get the wagons back and reestablish the old supply line. More than three weeks after the disruption, things still had not been set aright. Banks's command remained at Edinburg for more than a week awaiting rations and shoes. The Federals did not occupy Mount Jackson until April 17, forcing Jackson from his camps at Rude's Hill. Another five days passed before Banks covered the eighteen miles to Harrisonburg, and there he stopped. "The failure of our supplies," he wrote to the War Department, "made it impossible to continue the pursuit farther. . . . When we halted our troops had not a ration left."[16]

While at Harrisonburg, Banks sent a series of extraordinary messages to the War Department. "I believe Jackson left this Valley yesterday," he wrote to Stanton on April 19. "He is reported to have left Harrisonburg yesterday for Gordonsville." The next day he told the secretary that the "flight of

Jackson from this valley, by way of the mountains, from Harrisonburg toward Stanardsville and Orange Court-House, on Gordonsville is confirmed this morning by our scouts and prisoners." And on April 22 he reported, "Jackson has abandoned the valley of Virginia permanently." Anxious to explain how the clever Confederate had eluded him, Banks hastened to assure Stanton that the "crippled condition of our supplies alone enabled him to escape."[17]

Alpheus S. Williams was convinced otherwise. A week after the April 22 dispatch, Williams, who commanded a division under Banks, described the situation with perfect accuracy in a letter to his daughter: "Jackson's army is east of this from fifteen to twenty miles on the slopes of the Blue Ridge. He has a very large bridge between us and him. It is said he has it ready for burning. We fear he has been largely reinforced and intends to turn upon us here or wait for us in his strong position." At the time Williams wrote, the Confederates lay camped below Swift Run Gap in the Blue Ridge, and Jackson maintained headquarters in the village of Conrad's Store. The Federal War Department, however, accepted Banks's report as accurate, or at least completely discounted Jackson as a threat. On May 3 Stanton ordered Banks to detach Shields's 9,000-man division and send it to Fredericksburg, where it would join the drive on Richmond. Banks himself was to withdraw his remaining troops—two brigades of Alpheus Williams's division—to Strasburg and await further orders.[18]

It was at Strasburg and Front Royal that Banks would reap the fruit of his erroneous report of Jackson's abandonment of the Shenandoah. In March, Banks had led two divisions, more than 20,000 men, into the Valley to occupy Winchester. Not eight weeks later, now in command of the entire Department of the Shenandoah, he controlled fewer than 6,500 and lacked the strength to resist Jackson with any degree of certainty should the Virginian return. As a result, the Federal War Department had created a situation that jeopardized attainment of its chief and only significant goal in the Shenandoah: defense of the B&O.

Banks reached Strasburg by May 14 and put his men to work on building fortifications. He could call upon 4,476 infantrymen in two brigades, 1,600 cavalrymen, and 16 pieces of artillery—10 rifled Parrotts and 6 smoothbores. This seems a small enough force to hold the line in the lower Valley, but Banks's job almost immediately grew even more difficult. On May 16 the War Department, anxious to shift all available troops to eastern Virginia for the advance on Richmond, ordered Banks to extend his command farther and

In this sketch by Edwin Forbes, U.S. units occupy Front Royal, Virginia, in May 1862. *Frank Leslie's Illustrated Newspaper*, July 5, 1862.

protect the railroad from Strasburg to Front Royal. This would free Brig. Gen. John White Geary to deploy his troops elsewhere. Strasburg lay just west of Massanutten Mountain, and Front Royal stood at the head of the Page Valley, a subdivision of the Shenandoah Valley just east of Massanutten. Banks protested that he lacked sufficient men to cover both places but complied with the order by sending Col. John R. Kenly and 775 men of his 1st Maryland, two companies of the 29th Pennsylvania, some pioneers, and a section of Knap's Pennsylvania battery to Front Royal. This force of perhaps 1,000 was, Banks pointed out, "intended as a guard for the protection of the town and railway against local guerrilla parties that infested that locality." Kenly's detachment could do little good against a significant Confederate infantry force, but Banks informed the War Department that he detected "no indications of infantry in the valley." Except for some cavalry at Woodstock and Chester Gap, there were "no signs of enemy in this vicinity."[19]

Nevertheless, Banks was general enough to know he occupied vulnerable positions at Strasburg and Front Royal. Both numbers and terrain conspired against him. Alpheus Williams later complained that Washington's orders put Banks in a false position, obliging him "to hold the debauches of two valleys (at both points large public stores were in deposit) twelve miles apart," and that "good stone pikes led directly to our valuable deposits." Banks grasped that an aggressive foe could not ask for better circumstances than a weak enemy broken into detachments and spread too thin over too many miles with good roads leading to their isolated positions. He knew as well that Jackson was nothing if not aggressive. On May 22, less than a week after his arrival at Strasburg, Banks told Stanton that Jackson had resumed activity in the Valley and that he, Banks, could do nothing about it:

> The return of the rebel forces of General Jackson . . . increases my anxiety for the safety of the position I occupy and that of the troops under my command. . . . I am compelled to believe that he meditates attack here. . . . We are compelled to defend at two points, both equally accessible to the enemy—We are preparing defenses as rapidly as possible, but with the best aid of this character my force is insufficient to meet the enemy in such strength as he will certainly come, if he attacks us at all, and our situation certainly invites attack in the strongest manner. . . . To these important considerations ought to be added the persistent adherence of Jackson to the defense of the valley and his well-known purpose to expel the Government troops from this country if in his power. This may be assumed as certain. There is probably no one more fixed and determined purpose in the whole circle of the enemy's plans.[20]

Banks knew his man and had made a remarkably accurate reading of the situation. He correctly estimated Jackson's strength at 16,000, and as the New Englander wrote his dispatch, Jackson was just one long march away and closing the distance rapidly. The next day, May 23, Jackson attacked Kenly's bridge watchers and captured most of the Marylander's command. On May 24 he attacked Banks's retreating column at Middletown and along the Valley Turnpike and on May 25 routed Banks's infantry at Winchester, launching the beaten Federals on a pell-mell flight northward toward the safety of the Potomac River. Historians have been uniformly unkind to Banks for this small disaster. Blamed for the defeats at Front Royal and Winchester and the chaotic flight that so disorganized his force that it would be of no use for some weeks, the general is still mocked as "Commissary Banks," a reference to the rations and supplies he abandoned at Strasburg and Winchester. Viewed dispassionately, Banks's conduct seems reasonable. Unfortunately, most of those who have written about the campaign have based their criticism on a single source: Col. George H. Gordon.

Gordon wrote prolifically after the war about his 2nd Massachusetts Infantry Regiment and its campaigns. In the Valley in 1862, he commanded one of the two brigades in Alpheus Williams's division that remained with Banks in late May. We have no reason to disbelieve Gordon's accounts of what transpired at Banks's headquarters during the crisis, but neither should they be accepted uncritically. Did the relationship between the two men (Gordon seems not to have liked his commander) color Gordon's perspective? Rivalry between West Pointers and political appointees tainted many command relationships in both armies during the Civil War. A mere colonel despite having been graduated in the vaunted West Point class of 1846 and having earned a brevet for gallantry and hero status with two wounds in Mexico, Gordon might have resented Banks, the career politician who had never served in uniform until he became an instant major general only a year earlier.

On the afternoon of May 23, according to Gordon, while news filtered into Banks's headquarters of Jackson's attack at Front Royal, the colonel urged Banks to remove from Strasburg the sick and large quantities of supplies. Banks refused, declaring, "I must develop the force of the enemy." Gordon thought Banks seemed "spiritless and dejected." Later in the evening, in reaction to Gordon's continued urgings, Banks allegedly blurted out, "By God, sir, I will not retreat! We have more to fear, sir, from the opinions of our friends than the bayonets of our enemies." Gordon left Banks at 11:00 P.M., having concluded that his commander "was afraid of being thought afraid." That night, again according to Gordon, Banks began moving the wagons northward, called upon the War Department for help, then changed his mind and decided to stay in Strasburg. Sometime in the early morning of May 24, he changed his mind again and began sending his wagons toward Winchester.[21]

Gordon portrays Banks as an indecisive man afraid to act in a crisis. Other evidence, however, casts doubt on this portrait. As late as 7:15 on the morning of May 24, when he telegraphed the War Department, Banks was determined to "stand firm" at Strasburg. He had sent at least four dispatches to the War Department during the night and had in return been promised reinforcements and urged to not "give up the ship" until help arrived. Nothing in Banks's correspondence suggests the panic and fear reported by Gordon. More consistent with the facts is the account of David Hunter Strother, a member of Banks's staff. Strother noted that at the first reports of a crushing defeat at Front Royal, Banks acted quickly to pack up stores in Strasburg and withdraw. In his diary Strother frankly admitted that he thought the news exaggerated and that he dissuaded Banks from a hasty withdrawal—an admirable confession considering that events proved him utterly wrong. Only later, after more reports arrived, did Banks order his retreat for the morning of May 24. The most credible evidence Banks possessed that night suggested Front Royal had suffered a raid by a few thousand Confederates. There was no sense of crisis at Banks's headquarters on May 23, and the general went to bed expecting to see to the safety of the stores at Strasburg in the morning. Scouts brought word of many Confederates, but both Banks and Strother apparently considered the reports more the products of excitement than of cool observation. Banks nevertheless ordered a retreat. Only then, after the command was on the road north of Strasburg, did Banks come to learn the extent of Jackson's movement. He remarked pointedly to Strother, "It seems we were mistaken in our calculation." A sense of urgency, even dread, gripped the column, and it moved on to Winchester in haste.[22]

Gordon's account misleads in another sense. In sketching Banks as an inept bumbler, Gordon leaves the impression that Banks bore responsibility for the crisis. Yet the War Department had placed Banks in an exceptionally weak position and diminished and dispersed his force. Banks had not created the strategic situation that made him vulnerable and resulted in his defeat. Regardless of his response on May 23, he was not to any significant degree responsible for the creation of the emergency—a distinction made by neither Gordon nor the historians who have relied on him.

There is a still larger point to be considered regarding Gordon's testimony. Even if Banks had been as weak and indecisive as the colonel claimed, did it make a difference? Did it make the rout worse than it might have been? In the wake of the defeat at Winchester, Banks and his supporters cast the rout as something of a victory. The retreat to the Potomac, in the words of one writer, would "take its place as a masterly movement; and General Banks, with his gallant little corps, will take high rank in the esteem and affection of the people." From a Confederate perspective and from Gordon's, this line of argument seems almost laughable. Yet considering that Banks had been set upon by 16,000 men—more than twice the number of his dispersed force—and that of the 500 wagons he pushed northward toward the Potomac he lost only about 50 in the retreat, the idea that he managed his escape from Strasburg creditably does not seem so absurd. Banks lost two small battles and many supplies, but vastly outnumbered and in a weak position not of his choosing, he saved the bulk of his command.[23]

To the west, oblivious of Banks's movements and troubles, John C. Frémont prepared to mount a campaign. As he had in Missouri the year before,
Frémont proceeded slowly. After his appointment in mid-March, he had
remained in New York City, settling affairs, making preparations, and even
trying to purchase, at his own expense, matériel for his troops. Not until two
weeks later did he, accompanied by Jesse Benton Frémont, report in Wheeling, Virginia, to assume his command. For thirty-six days Frémont would
remain in Wheeling, assembling a staff (a rather large one composed, oddly,
mostly of Europeans), communicating with his subordinates and Washington, and creating the administrative machinery that would permit him to
begin his campaign into East Tennessee.

Frémont faced a difficult task. The enormous Mountain Department extended from Pennsylvania to Tennessee and from Kentucky to the Shenandoah Valley, an area of more than 35,000 square miles. It had been divided
into six districts, each commanded by a colonel or a brigadier general. Before
he could embark on an offensive, Frémont had to take stock of his command
and learn about the particular strategic, geographical, political, and logistical
problems of each district. What he discovered was daunting.

Frémont counted 34,271 men in the department, about 9,100 of whom—
those in eastern Kentucky and points in southwestern Virginia—were soon
assigned elsewhere. Between 20 and 25 percent of those remaining in the
department were sick or absent, due perhaps to the exceptionally severe
winter just past, leaving about 19,000 men present for duty. "With these
troops," reported Frémont, "it was necessary to guard a frontier of 350 miles,
approached by roads more or less at rectangles with lines in occupation, and
having few interior cross-communications." His men were assigned to guard
depots, bridges, and tunnels on 300 miles of railroad and more than 200 miles
of navigable rivers. They were dispersed by regiment, battalion, company,
and squad to defend dozens of important points throughout the department
from Confederate troops and from southern sympathizers, including numerous bands of bushwhackers who preyed on Federal supply trains, picket
posts, and Unionist citizens. Frémont assigned about half of his force to cover
the supremely important B&O, which functioned not only as the key segment
of his supply line but also as Washington's most important link to the West.
The War Department, understandably, was obsessed with protecting the
B&O, which had been broken by Jackson in 1861 and reopened only in
March 1862. Frémont had no choice but to defend about 90 percent of his

department with about 50 percent of his men—and plan an offensive in which his striking force would consist of approximately 8,000 soldiers.[24]

After studying his department, Frémont declared that the best line of advance on eastern Tennessee was through Kentucky rather than Virginia. Without enough men to execute such a plan, however, he stated that with 10,000 to 12,000 more soldiers he could mount an advance through the valley of the South Branch of the Potomac to hit the Southwestern Virginia & Tennessee Railroad at Salem and Newburg. Having severed that critical link between Richmond and the western Confederacy, he would move along the railroad to Knoxville with a force of 22,000 men. This proposal offered several advantages. It contributed to the effort in Virginia by exerting pressure away from Richmond, thereby preventing Confederate concentration against McClellan. Cutting the railroad west of Richmond also would hinder or at least complicate Confederate efforts to supply the army defending the capital. These factors would have made an offensive in western Virginia attractive to Lincoln and worthwhile to the Union effort, but Frémont explained that he could accomplish nothing without more men. The day after he read Frémont's proposal, Lincoln proved the sincerity of his interest and ordered to the Pathfinder a division of infantry—Gen. Louis Blenker's—originally earmarked for McClellan on the Peninsula.[25]

Not everyone shared the president's enthusiasm for Frémont's plan. Gen. Jacob Cox, the veteran campaigner in the region, believed "extensive military operations across and beyond the Alleghenies from west or east were impracticable, because a wilderness a hundred miles wide, crossed by few and difficult roads, rendered it impossible to supply troops from depots on either side. The country was so wild that not even forage for mules could be found in it, and the teams could hardly haul their own provender for the double trip." Cox considered it an "impossibility" to supply an army through the mountainous country in which he had worked.[26] Nevertheless, Frémont, with the president's support, moved ahead with the plan.

On May 3 Frémont at last took the field and moved his headquarters to the Mountain Department's chief supply base at New Creek on the B&O. Throughout the month in Wheeling, Frémont had struggled to get his force in condition to campaign. Horses had posed the chief problem. He had artillery batteries manned and equipped but idle for want of animals. The 6th Ohio Cavalry remained dismounted for the same reason. Requisitions to the War Department for horses had, in Frémont's words, "lingered in unknown channels." At the same time, Stanton would not permit Frémont to buy, let alone impress, animals. The most important use of horses, as well as mules, was to pull supply wagons. Frémont understood that unless he resolved his transportation problems, his campaign to Tennessee would be impossible.[27]

The Pathfinder moved his new headquarters to Petersburg at the end of the first week in May. There, in the heart of his department on the supply line, he could see with his own eyes the difficulties before him. Many days of rain ruined the roads. All the army's food had to come some fifty miles over one unsurfaced road from the supply base at New Creek. Furthermore, Blenker's division, sent from the Army of the Potomac five weeks earlier, still had not arrived.

Frémont had expected Blenker's 10,000 men to join him in the mountains in mid-April. He had based his expectation of a successful campaign to Tennessee on those reinforcements. None of Blenker's units arrived until early May, and Frémont would never see more than 60 percent of the men he expected. Those of Blenker's soldiers who showed up were so badly worn down and demoralized as to be arguably worth not more than half their number.[28] On May 11 the last of Blenker's command reached Petersburg and stood for inspection by Frémont's chief of staff, Col. Albert Tracy. Tracy was appalled. "This division," he wrote, "has been delayed by every imaginable difficulty, and from every imaginable cause. . . . Shoeless, are also many of the soldiers, and . . . with but a meager supply of blankets or overcoats." The division's arms were "old Austrian or Belgian refuse," ammunition was scarce, and horses and mules were "worn down to the ribs, and scarcely able to get over the ground either guns or wagons." A veteran of eight years in the regular army, Tracy declared, "This command should rest and recuperate on full supplies, for not less than ten or twenty days, and yet it is to move with us tomorrow!"[29]

Stonewall Jackson's unexpected aggressiveness had prompted the morning march. In the first week of May, Jackson had left the Shenandoah Valley and marched westward into the mountains in response to the activity of a lone brigade of Federals along the Staunton-Parkersburg Turnpike. Pushed vigorously by their energetic commander, Brig. Gen. Robert H. Milroy, the Federals, about 3,000 Ohioans and western Virginians, had advanced picket posts to within fifteen miles of Staunton, a railroad town served by excellent turnpikes. Staunton held immense importance as a Confederate transportation hub and supply base, yet it was sparsely defended and unfortified.

Throughout the winter and early spring, its sole defense from Federals in the mountains was the brigade of Brig. Gen. Edward Johnson, who had held his men deep in the mountains watching the northerners. Milroy's aggressive movements in April, along with Jackson's reverse at Kernstown and Banks's advance in the Valley, forced Johnson to withdraw from the mountains to Westview, just eight miles from Staunton.

On May 6 Jackson joined Johnson at Westview, absorbed the latter's command into his column, and marched into the mountains with 9,000 men, intent on defeating Milroy. Milroy knew the region well, and he was unwilling to surrender his hard-earned territorial gains (and his dream of capturing Staunton). He made a stand at the town of McDowell on the Bull Pasture River and was promptly reinforced by a brigade under Brig. Gen. Robert C. Schenck. A career politician from Ohio and a sometime soldier, Schenck had marched his men thirty-four miles in twenty-four hours to relieve Milroy at McDowell. When they met before noon on May 8, Milroy and Schenck agreed that the position at McDowell was indefensible and that they would have to withdraw. Milroy accepted that discretion formed the better part of valor in this case, but he resisted a retreat without at least determining the enemy's strength. With Schenck's concurrence, Milroy prepared to probe the Confederate position. Though the Federals attacked uphill, scaling steep, heavily wooded slopes, they inflicted 450 casualties on Jackson's regiments while suffering about 250 themselves. Milroy and Schenck gave their troops some rest in the evening and withdrew in the early hours of May 9. After pursuing the Federals to within a few miles of Franklin, whence Frémont had moved his headquarters in response to the Confederate advance, Jackson broke off contact and returned to the Valley.[30]

The fight at McDowell had national repercussions, at least for southerners, in providing a much-needed boost to flagging Confederate morale. Though Jackson's men had again been worsted tactically, despite immense advantages in terrain, they could claim a strategic victory. To the Federals, however, McDowell meant little. The withdrawal of two brigades that served primarily as an advanced outpost or a "corps of observation" on the road to Staunton had almost no influence on Frémont's operational plans. From his headquarters at Franklin, the Pathfinder let Jackson withdraw unmolested. In fact, Frémont treated the Virginian's foray into the mountains as merely an annoyance, after which he returned to his primary business: solving his supply

Robert H. Milroy, a sketch based on a wartime photograph. Benson J. Lossing, *Pictorial Field Book of the Civil War*, 3 vols. (Hartford, Conn.: T. Belknap, 1870–76), 2:103.

problems and making a lodgment on the Southwest Virginia & Tennessee Railroad. In the words of Gen. Jacob Cox, "Frémont resumed preparations for his original campaign."[31]

Washington, too, evinced little concern about Stonewall Jackson. On May 11, three days after the fight at McDowell and with Jackson opposite Frémont at Franklin, the War Department detached Shields's 9,000 men from Banks's command and ordered them to Fredericksburg. Banks, weakened by more than half, was to withdraw to Strasburg to protect the railroad. On May 16, a week after McDowell, Lincoln prodded Frémont to move—not after Jackson, but *on to southwestern Virginia*. In a surprising shift of focus,

Lincoln inquired if Frémont might not better abandon the Knoxville plan and march instead on Richmond.[32]

Frémont spent fifteen days at Franklin following the fight at McDowell. In the same period the Lincoln administration drastically reduced its forces in the region and ordered Banks to assume a purely defensive posture. This cycle of Federal passivity greatly assisted Jackson, who filled the time with extraordinary activity. In the twenty-five days between April 30 and May 24, Jackson increased his force from 6,000 to 17,000, marched his command about 270 miles, and fought two significant engagements 90 air miles apart.

Why did northerners appear to be so indifferent to Jackson through the first three weeks of May? The answer is as much historiographical as historical. Because virtually every history of the campaign has focused on Confederate intentions and performance and drawn on hindsight, students have not had a fair opportunity to consider Federal intentions and performance. From the Confederate viewpoint, Jackson's hyperactivity in May makes the Federals seem inert and foolish. The slothlike Yankees seem to play right into the hands of Stonewall, who marched another 150 miles and won three significant victories against three different Federal forces in eighteen days in late May and early June. From a northern perspective, however, neither Jackson nor the region in which he was operating gained importance until the final week of May. Richmond was the goal. Washington's primary military concern was supporting McClellan's move on the Confederate capital. No other military movement—whether in western Virginia, Tennessee, or Mississippi—mattered as much. The North cared about controlling the Shenandoah that spring only as the strategic flank of the Army of the Potomac's operations against Richmond. By mid-May the War Department deemed that McClellan's grand army had drawn in close enough for a killing blow against the heart of the rebellion. Furthermore, in Washington's understanding of Virginia's strategic landscape in mid-May 1862, Jackson posed no threat. Hindsight leads us to decry the Federals' cavalier disregard of the soldier we know as a formidable foe, but in May 1862 Jackson and his men were mere mortals rather than the legends they would become.

Much changed on May 24 after Jackson's attack at Front Royal. The Virginian's sudden appearance and victory in the lower Valley shocked Washington. For the first time since the Federals had begun active operations in the Valley more than two months earlier, Jackson represented a significant threat rather than a nuisance.

Lincoln and Stanton, distant from the field of events, had little idea of what was happening. "We are left in extraordinary state of uncertainty as to the real state of affairs," Stanton wrote on May 24. From Lincoln's perspective, things must have looked serious indeed when General Geary, commander of 2,200 railroad guards in an independent brigade on the Manassas Gap Railroad east of Front Royal, telegraphed (erroneously) on May 24 that Jackson was already east of the Blue Ridge and moving through Aldie Gap in the Bull Run Mountains toward Centreville with 20,000 men. As one of Washington's chief informants during the next few days, Geary badly misled his superiors and contributed immeasurably to the chaos.[33]

From his headquarters at Rectortown, Geary sent a series of dispatches that heavily influenced Lincoln's perception of the crisis in the Valley. Geary informed Washington on May 24 that heavy masses of Confederates were threatening to cross the Blue Ridge and move against Manassas and Warrenton. He feared for the safety of his outnumbered men and withdrew to White Plains to consolidate his command. Relying on testimony from deserters, contrabands, and a captured Confederate drummer, Geary reported that "bodies of the enemy are moving north of me and others to the south, to cut me off." On May 25 he estimated that 10,000 Confederates under Jackson were crossing Manassas Gap while another 10,000 moved eastward through Chester Gap. The next day he declared that "reliable" intelligence placed 20,000 Confederates passing through Middleburg.[34]

A thoroughly dispirited Geary withdrew again, this time to Broad Run at Thoroughfare Gap, where on May 26 he informed the War Department that "upon consultation with all my officers, they have, in consideration of the hopeless circumstances surrounding us, concluded to attempt to march to Manassas." Such messages of alarm and doom persuaded the War Department that there was, in addition to the enemy in the Valley pursuing Banks, a Confederate force of unknown strength in Geary's front proceeding toward Washington. Stanton fretted on May 25 that the capital's defenses were woefully undermanned: "Our condition is one of considerable danger, as we are stripped to supply the Army of the Potomac, and now we have the enemy here." The secretary acquiesced to Geary's decision to fall back yet again and worked to mass troops at Manassas to resist the advancing Confederate horde. "I think it not improbable that Ewell[,] Jackson and [Alleghany] Johnson," Lincoln wrote to a member of the cabinet that same day, "are pouring through the gap they made . . . at Front Royal, making a dash Northward."[35]

Always solicitous for the safety of the nation's capital, and crippled by the lack of accurate information about the Confederate advance, Lincoln put aside recent plans to support McClellan in driving on Richmond and worked to defuse what looked like a crisis. He had to be certain of Washington's safety, so the first step was defensive. The president ordered McDowell, who had begun his advance on Richmond from Fredericksburg, to Manassas, thirty miles from the capital. Next Lincoln sent Brig. Gen. Rufus Saxton to Harpers Ferry with orders to organize the troops there, protect the railroad bridge, discourage Jackson from taking the town or crossing the Potomac, and perhaps most important, keep Washington informed of what was happening in the Valley.

Lincoln's second step was offensive. He was determined to respond in kind to Jackson's aggressiveness. Shields's division, which had been detached from Banks's force a week or so earlier, had just arrived at Fredericksburg but was immediately ordered back to the Valley in the hope of catching Jackson somewhere near Front Royal.

More indicative of Lincoln's determination to catch Jackson, however, were his orders to John C. Frémont. The president saw in Jackson's deep penetration of northern Virginia not just a threat but a strategic opportunity, and Frémont was the key. On May 24 he ordered Frémont to aid Banks by moving "against Jackson at Harrisonburg . . . immediately." Harrisonburg, deep in Jackson's rear, lay on the Valley army's supply route. A lodgment there would cut Jackson off from Staunton, his supply base, and the most important transportation center in the Valley. To be certain that he had made himself perfectly clear, Lincoln sent another dispatch urging Frémont to "put the utmost speed into it. Do not lose a minute."[36]

Frémont received Lincoln's orders with dismay. He already knew of Banks's dilemma but remained focused on the railroad in southwestern Virginia and on Tennessee beyond. He was reluctant to give up the plans he had been maturing for so long. In addition, as department commander he had other responsibilities that could not be lightly dismissed, chief among them Jacob Cox's 9,000 men in the Kanawha, Guyandotte, and Big Sandy Valleys in southwestern Virginia. The Confederates had flexed their muscles in the region and attacked Cox the day before—just as Jackson was attacking at

Front Royal. Wishing to support Cox as soon as possible, Frémont also took seriously the charge of defending his enormous department. "Enemy seems everywhere re-enforced and active," he told Stanton. "Under the circumstances my force cannot be divided, and if I abandon this line and move eastward to the support of General Banks this whole country to the Ohio would be thrown open, and General Cox also immediately exposed to disaster."[37]

To his credit, Frémont accepted the realities of Banks's emergency and immediately planned to go to his relief; yet vexing obstacles lay ahead. Lincoln's isolation from the realities of campaigning in the mountains had prompted him to direct Frémont to do the impossible.

Just before Lincoln's orders arrived, Frémont had explained to Washington why he had made so little progress during his three weeks in the field. "Want of supplies," he stated, "has kept this force at Franklin." The refrain was familiar to those in the War Department offices on Seventeenth Street. Banks and George McClellan had endured similar difficulties, but Frémont was in the midst of a genuine crisis. At Franklin, Frémont lay sixty miles from his supply base at New Creek. Every cracker, every piece of salt pork, and every oat had to come to him by wagon. Rain had swollen rivers, washed away bridges, and soaked the single road on which his long supply line depended. Wagons simply could not get through the water and mud. His men suffered from hunger and grew disorderly. For almost two of the three weeks he had been in the field, Frémont's supply line had been all but nonexistent. For nearly two weeks the regiments had been on less than half-rations (by law, each soldier was to receive three pounds of food each day). "Money is of no use here," wrote one Ohioan, "as there is nothing to eat that money will buy." He added, "I should like to be in Ohio just to get something to eat!"[38]

Many men had nothing but beef to eat for days, and "salt, and sugar and coffee were unknown." Some companies received only flour (twenty pounds for eighty men), and others had only hardtack ("eleven crackers in seven days," according to one Pennsylvanian). Lt. T. Albert Steiger of the 75th Pennsylvania, one of Blenker's regiments, recalled that many of the men were so hungry that "out of sheer desperation . . . [they collected] such corn as they could gather from the ground of the cavalry and wagon camps where . . . the kernels . . . had been trodden into the ground as a waste by the horses and mule teams." Frémont's chief of staff moaned that "our people were next to starving," and Lieutenant Steiger agreed: "The great suffering from hunger . . . was almost beyond the possibility of human endurance" and would "never be effaced from the memory of those who participated in these memorable privations."[39]

Ignorant of these hardships, Lincoln ordered Frémont to march the forty miles from Franklin to Harrisonburg. The president looked at his map and saw that a direct road connected the two towns. He did not know that the road, steep and unsurfaced, crossed two mountain ranges. One of the more tortuous routes in that part of Virginia, it represented a nightmare for Frémont's supply wagons. Apart from failing to appreciate the poor quality of the road, Lincoln apparently did not consider how Frémont would feed his men once they reached Harrisonburg.[40]

Given his circumstances, Frémont scarcely could extend his line of supply an additional forty miles over wretched mountain roads. His chief of staff, Colonel Tracy, wrote that a movement to Harrisonburg was easy to order and, on its face, both plausible and feasible. But bad roads, too few horses and mules, and insufficient food for man and beast made a move away from the already malfunctioning supply line an impossibility. Frémont rightly decided that he could not obey Lincoln's orders. He first informed superiors in Washington that he could not go anywhere without more horses and asked permission to purchase any he found (the War Department had refused his earlier requests to do so). Lincoln immediately authorized Frémont "to purchase the 400 horses or take them wherever and however you can get them" and reminded him that "this movement must be made immediately." Choosing the only feasible course in the emergency, Frémont abandoned his plans to move southward and instead turned in the opposite direction. He fell back on his supply line, thereby relieving his crippling food and forage problem, increasing the battleworthiness of his troops, and moving them closer to Jackson's Confederates.[41]

Frémont's disobedience of orders—described by him as the exercise of a field commander's discretion—became the subject of heated debate among Lincoln's and Frémont's partisans that extended into the twentieth century. Yet Jackson had rendered the question moot as early as May 11. That morning his work parties had tumbled rocks and felled trees onto the road to Harrisonburg, which Colonel Tracy termed a wreck, with "culverts torn away, and trees felled across-the whole to an extent tending to involve great embarrassment and delay."[42]

The Pathfinder and his men left Franklin on the morning of May 25 and covered about fifteen miles. The troops got a good look at what one of

Blenker's men called the "most horrible roads." These were the routes that could not keep them supplied while at Franklin. The wagons had carved deep furrows into the rain-soaked road, and though the men could slog through the mire, the wagons and animals found the going much tougher. The wreckage of abandoned wagons, some full of supplies, littered the road, and broken-down horses, their skin stretched tight across ribs, stood helpless and weary or wallowed in the mud. The troops marched on only coffee, sugar, and crackers.[43]

On May 26 the Federals reached Petersburg and rested, having made twenty-eight miles, over miserable roads but mostly downhill, in two days. The worst lay before them, yet Frémont understood the need for haste. When his men left Petersburg at sunrise on May 27, they were stripped down to essentials for a rapid march. They left all baggage, knapsacks, and tents behind and carried only ammunition and five days' rations. The South Branch of the Potomac stopped the column at Moorefield, thirteen miles north of Petersburg. The river was high and swift and the bridge was gone. Frémont's officers rigged a crossing at a ford by slinging a rope across the river to help the men negotiate the strong current. Hand over hand they waded waist deep across the rushing river until the entire column had crossed by the morning of May 28. Blenker's men, in the advance, were on the road by 5:00 A.M.[44]

Frémont reported his position on May 27, and Lincoln wired back angrily: "I see that you are at Moorefield. You were expressly ordered to march to Harrisonburg. What does this mean?" Frémont explained about his supplies and transportation, but Lincoln seems to have been in no mood to listen to explanations. Frémont's unexpected movement apparently so deranged the president's plans as to leave Lincoln uncertain about what to do next. Ten miles east of Moorefield at Fabius on the morning of May 28, Frémont received new instructions from the War Department directing him "to halt at Moorefield and wait orders." This startling reversal of the president's earlier expressions ("Move against Jackson at Harrisonburg . . . immediately"; "Put the utmost speed into it. Do not lose a minute"; "This movement must be made immediately") caused Frémont to halt at Fabius, high in the mountains, and wait for his column to close up.[45]

The road from Moorefield had been exceptionally difficult, rising 1,500 feet in $8^{1}/_{2}$ miles. "This march is a real hardship for us," wrote Lt. Louis Biskey of the 45th New York in his diary, "since it starts to rain toward eight o'clock and

This wartime engraving, based on a sketch by Edwin Forbes, captured the exhausted, ragged condition of Frémont's soldiers as they marched up the Valley in pursuit of Jackson. *Frank Leslie's Illustrated Newspaper, War Supplement,* July 5, 1862.

the air has become so oppressive that when climbing mountains we cannot catch our breath. It is very hard, almost impossible, to carry our rubber blankets." The wet, taxing march demoralized much of Frémont's command. Upon arrival at Fabius, Chief of Staff Tracy noted that "upon the roads behind us, are left such scores of disabled and broken-down men, particularly from the division of Blenker, that our Medical Director, Doctor Sukely, protests against their further marching, except upon at least one day's rest." The surgeon's request coincided with the president's order to halt and await orders. Innocent of events in the Shenandoah but painfully aware of the condition of his own command, Frémont perhaps believed he had little to lose and possibly much to gain by granting Suckley's request. He ordered a day of rest on May 29, except for those portions of the column not yet closed up.[46]

Frémont made good use of the day of rest. He mustered his troops and counted heads, a process that yielded more unhappy news. Blenker's division, far from mustering the expected 10,000 men present for duty, totaled fewer than 6,000. Frémont's entire command numbered only about 11,000.[47]

On May 29 Lincoln directed Frémont to be at Strasburg the next day. A rapid march would put the Pathfinder on Jackson's retreat route, and the president saw the issue in starkly simple terms. It was, he told Frémont, "A question of Legs." As Lincoln soon learned, that was not a game in which Jackson could be easily beaten. The Confederates left their camps at Winchester and Charlestown on May 30 and headed southward. Jackson sent troops under Maj. Gen. Richard S. Ewell westward from Strasburg to delay Frémont. The Federals, already detained by rain and storms, met Ewell and deployed for battle, but Frémont restricted the action to some artillery dueling. Ewell tried in vain to precipitate a fight but finally withdrew, having accomplished his mission of keeping open the army's escape route until Jackson's far-flung brigades could pass.[48]

On June 2 Frémont placed his column in motion "with the earliest dawn" and passed through Strasburg. After struggling for long days through the steep, muddy roads of the mountains, the troops much appreciated the flat, hard, surfaced Valley turnpike. They appreciated as well that Jackson's force showed some distress. "On every hand," wrote one officer, "were evidences of the haste in which the enemy had retreated, and odd ends of camp equipage, knapsacks, blankets, and the like, with here or there a broken ambulance, or cast off extra artillery wheel—lined the way." According to one of his staff officers, Frémont rode "well up towards the head of all . . . earnest and determined and impatient only of delay in any form." But the going was slow. Turner Ashby's Confederate cavalry engaged in effective delaying tactics, compelling Frémont to halt twice during the day to deploy portions of his force and contest ground.[49]

Frémont's advance battled rain and hail but kept contact with Jackson's rear guard. On June 3 aggressive Federal cavalry saved the bridge over Mill Creek in Mount Jackson from destruction, but it failed to gain the more important bridge over the Shenandoah River just to the south at Meem's Bottom. Frémont's infantry, a few miles to the rear, watched the latter bridge go up in smoke. The Federals then struggled with the river for two days. They built a pontoon bridge, but high water threatened to sweep it away. Not until the morning of June 5 did the river drop enough for the army to cross.[50] The delay at Meem's Bottom gave Jackson the breathing room he needed, and he marched eastward from Harrisonburg toward the Blue Ridge, as he had in April. On the hills around Cross Keys and Port Republic, Jackson found the ground he wanted and turned to meet his pursuers.

Frémont's active advance guard, commanded by Brig. Gen. George D. Bayard, clashed with Ashby's cavalry and their infantry supports near Harrisonburg on June 6; the chief result of the skirmish was the death of Ashby.

WILLIAM J. MILLER

Frémont spent June 7 closing up his column and planning the next move. A Federal council of war decided to move against Jackson at Cross Keys the next day.[51]

Frémont did not manage the battle of Cross Keys well. The Confederates, directed by Ewell, held a strong position with their artillery, and aggressive southern infantry commanders delivered a few well-timed blows that kept the Federals off balance. Frémont later explained that he fought the battle haltingly because he was expecting to cooperate with another Federal column, commanded by James Shields, which was supposed to be approaching Jackson's rear. Hoping to catch Jackson between the two Union forces on the morning of June 9, the Pathfinder broke off the battle at Cross Keys and decided to wait.[52]

Gustave Cluseret, a French adventurer serving under Frémont with the rank of colonel, subsequently condemned what he saw as his commander's inactivity. Cluseret admired Frémont during the war but later fell out with him, so his account is suspect. But in his memoirs the French officer wrote that he had ridden to Frémont's headquarters on the afternoon of June 8 to urge further attacks. He claimed to have found the Pathfinder at his headquarters sipping tea. Cluseret said Frémont met his urgings with the bland remark, "It is a victory, isn't it? Then have a cup of tea." However damning the image, and granting that Frémont's generalship often lacked aggressiveness, it is worth noting that the Pathfinder had little with which to fight at Cross Keys. Having marched 150 miles in thirteen days, much of the distance over mountains and with half-rations or less, his soldiers were broken down, barefoot, and surly. An officer who joined Frémont's command on June 10 expressed shock at the condition of the troops. "The army had suffered much," he wrote, "continued rapid marches; extremely inadequate provisions, at times absolutely nothing to eat; shoes worn out, a large proportion of the men barefooted; the horses through want of regular feeding worn down and decrepit: the cavalry for the most part beneath contempt."[53] Frémont's 10,500 men were in such poor condition that they were likely worth less than their number. Undoubtedly Frémont believed so.

As Frémont withheld his blows on June 8, the man in whom he placed his hopes for success against Jackson wrestled with demons of his own many miles away. Brig. Gen. James Shields, like Frémont a former U.S. senator, was a native of Ireland and a friend of Abraham Lincoln. He had been a principal player in the opening act of the drama in the Valley as a division commander under Banks and the nominal Federal commander at the battle of Kernstown in March 1862. Fate brought him back to the stage in June just as the curtain was about to fall in the Shenandoah.

Perhaps the most controversial order of the campaign had flown over the wires at 5:00 P.M. on May 24, when Lincoln ordered Irvin McDowell, who commanded a Federal army near Fredericksburg, to send 20,000 troops to the Valley to "capture the forces of Jackson and Ewell." The president demanded speed: "Everything depends upon the celerity and vigor of your movement." McDowell protested that such a long chase of Jackson would be fruitless, and he informed Lincoln, "I shall gain nothing for you there, and lose much for you here." He complied with the order but told Stanton, "This is a crushing blow to us."[54]

General Shields's division, it will be recalled, had been ordered from Banks in the Valley to McDowell at Fredericksburg only a fortnight earlier. After a wearying march they had entered McDowell's lines on May 23, the day Jackson attacked the Federal garrison at Front Royal. Shields received orders the next day to return to the Valley.

Moving west along the Manassas Gap Railroad, Shields's lead brigade reached General Geary's position by May 27. The brigade's commander, Brig. Gen. Nathan Kimball, had been the hero of the battle of Kernstown. He quickly saw for himself how things stood in Geary's sector and minced no words in his report. Despite Geary's alarmist claims to the contrary, no significant Confederate force had reached the eastern slopes of the Blue Ridge. Kimball further noted that Geary's men had burned 1,000 new Enfield rifles and 700 carbines as well as their tents, concluding that "this is the all-firedest scare I ever heard of." Shields had correctly judged Geary's warnings to be the products of hysteria. When he met with Geary at Manassas, he expressed disgust. "The whole thing here was a shameful panic," wrote Shields, adding that all was well "except the commanders, who ought to be replaced to save us from disgrace." Shields advised that no more men be sent to Manassas because "they will be of no use to me." Full of confidence and spoiling to get at Jackson, whose force he accurately estimated at 16,000, Shields wrote Stanton, "If you send me supplies and forage I will do the work myself." To McDowell he boasted, "I will soon clear out the Shenandoah Valley."[55]

Shields and McDowell both recognized that obtaining food and forage would be a problem. The haste with which McDowell's troops had been withdrawn from their southern advance and directed westward forced the

This portrait of James Shields appeared in *Harper's Weekly* at the time of the Valley campaign. *Harper's Weekly*, April 12, 1862.

quartermasters to redraw their supply routes. The Manassas Gap Railroad could have served as an excellent supply line for the march to the Valley had it been sound, but it had fallen into disrepair. Then a train derailed on May 29, causing Shields to halt and wait for supplies. Furthermore, the Confederates had burned small bridges, so Shields's work gangs had to rebuild the spans as the division moved. The real difficulty would come once they were in the Valley, where Shields likely would leave the line of the railroad. McDowell doubted whether he had sufficient wagons to support a long march away from the rails, and already Shields had complained about horses "weak for want of grain." From Front Royal on May 30 he stressed that "no effort or expense should be spared" to repair the railroad.[56]

Regrettably for Federal efforts against Jackson, Shields seemed to fall into a fog of confusion when he entered Front Royal on May 30. For the next two weeks he would display poor strategic judgment and be utterly mastered by circumstances. He also proved himself a failure as a leader by lying and casting unfair blame on a subordinate.

Shields's lead brigade, under Kimball, reached Front Royal on the morning of May 30, capturing two locomotives, some rolling stock, quartermaster stores, and small arms lost by Kenly a week earlier as well as about 150 Confederates. The next day one of his brigades reconnoitered toward Winchester but withdrew after driving off some of Ashby's pickets. Shields did not press westward to the Valley Pike at Strasburg, where he might have interdicted Jackson's retreat route. He certainly had time enough to do so but, mysteriously, remained at Front Royal. Shields explained his inactivity to the War Department as an act of sagacity. "We would have occupied Strasburg," he wrote on June 2, "but dare not interfere with what was designed for Frémont." This seems curious logic for the aggressive man who just days earlier had boasted that he would "soon clear out the Shenandoah Valley." Lincoln had been urging haste and daring for a week and wished for nothing more than that Shields would "interfere" with the Jackson-Frémont minuet at Strasburg and clean out the Confederates. But the Irishman apparently considered his hands tied. Sadly shaking his head and clucking his tongue over Jackson's escape, Shields blamed Frémont, writing, "His failure has saved Jackson."[57]

Shields's confusion worsened after McDowell ordered him to march southward up the Luray Valley to operate against Jackson. Though uncertain of Stonewall's whereabouts, Shields expected him to withdraw up the Valley. With this premise, he drew on his experiences in the region in April to decide what Jackson would do next. He guessed the Confederates would move around the southern terminus of Massanutten to Conrad's Store, as they had six weeks earlier. Jackson would be bound for Richmond, Shields reasoned, which meant he would pass through Swift Run Gap to Stanardsville. Thence the Valley army would ride the rails to Charlottesville and on to the Confederate capital. "Our route," Shields decisively told a subordinate, "is to Stanardsville, which if we reach before the enemy he is lost."[58]

The least of the flaws in this speculation was that no railroad served Stanardsville. The Orange & Alexandria Railroad lay about fifteen miles beyond at Orange and Gordonsville. The more serious flaw was that whatever Shields might have done to a railroad at Stanardsville, Jackson could have marched to Charlottesville via Brown's Gap, which breached the mountains ten miles south of Conrad's Store. Perhaps Shields realized the hollowness of his plan, for when the time came to write his report two weeks later, he never mentioned Stanardsville and claimed that his intentions had been quite different. His first object, he wrote, had been "to find some mode of crossing the Shenandoah, in order to fall upon [Jackson's] flank [at New Market] while Frémont assailed him in the rear."[59]

Shields might well have entertained both schemes at different times, but in the end he reached neither Stanardsville nor New Market for reasons well known to every Federal commander in the Valley: bad roads, burned bridges, and supply problems. Rain fell hard for the first three days of June. The Shenandoah overflowed its banks, and streams became small rivers. Federal wagons sank to their axles on the unsurfaced roadway (Jackson's men marched far more rapidly on the macadamized Valley Pike), and Shields found that his column could move neither forward nor backward. On June 4 floodwaters swept away the bridges at Front Royal, isolating part of McDowell's command and making it impossible to transfer supplies up the Luray Valley to Shields's force.[60] Beset by crisis, Shields forgot about Jackson. "In this condition," he wrote, "the first question was to live, to obtain supplies, as none could reach us over such roads."[61]

Despite the horrendous weather conditions, Shields initially tried to send a portion of his men after Jackson. Movement in the upper Luray Valley required gaining control of at least one of two bridges south and west of Luray before the Confederates could destroy them. Once across the river at either the White House bridge or the Columbia bridge, Shields's men would be in a central position. Less than a day's march across Massanutten Mountain through New Market Gap would take them to Jackson's column on the Valley Turnpike, and in two days they could reach Stanardsville. Despite what he would claim later, Shields focused on Stanardsville rather than on a strike across the mountain to catch Jackson's column in motion along the Valley

Pike. He sent a vanguard under Col. Samuel S. Carroll southward into the Luray Valley on June 1. He hoped Carroll would seize and hold the key bridges and then move on to Conrad's Store to burn the bridge over the South Fork of the Shenandoah River (which would isolate Jackson on the river's west bank). Shields wished Carroll to travel light and fast so as to cover the nearly fifty miles to Conrad's Store in less than forty-eight hours. Carroll was to abandon broken-down horses along the way and impress fresh animals as needed. "Everything depends on speed," wrote Shields; "Jackson must be overtaken." Carroll was also to hold the two key bridges so the rest of the division could pass rapidly up the Valley. Shields closed with what he hoped young Colonel Carroll would find a motivational flourish: "You will earn your star if you do all this."[62]

But Carroll would accomplish none of it. The heavens opened as he headed south. With the main body of Shields's force floundering, out of contact, behind them, Carroll's soldiers slogged along mud-choked roads through torrential rains. Samuel Coyner of Ashby's cavalry grasped a fine opportunity to stymie Carroll's beleaguered Federals. Coyner and some troopers, sent across Massanutten Mountain in a driving thunderstorm, battled the same bottomless thoroughfares in the Luray Valley. "Oh! the roughest road!" Coyner exclaimed in a letter to his sister: "For two miles at one place we had to almost crawl." The Confederates overcame the storms and the wretched roads, burning the White House and Columbia bridges before dawn on June 2 and thus ensuring that the Federals could not cross the rampaging Shenandoah to interfere with Jackson's retreat past New Market Gap. The next morning Coyner's company destroyed the bridge at Conrad's Store. Just one span remained across the Shenandoah: the covered bridge at Port Republic. Jackson wished to possess that bridge himself. Thanks to Coyner, the Confederate chieftain could rest assured that Shields and Frémont were divided and would remain so.[63]

Shields viewed Captain Coyner's handiwork at White House on June 5 and apparently could see little else through the fog of his befuddlement. In his report he stated that at this point he "pushed forward the advance as rapidly as possible, in hopes of finding the bridge at Conrad's Store still standing." Yet he himself had sent arsonists to that bridge and could not have been hoping that Carroll's men had failed. The chagrin he expressed in his report over the demise of the Conrad's Store bridge appears to have been an afterthought, the product of deliberation after events made plain to him the folly of his focus on Stanardsville. As it was, after finding the White House and Columbia bridges gone, Shields simply returned to Luray.[64]

The bridge at Port Republic beckoned to Jackson. Shields could not decide whether it was better to capture the span or destroy it. In his report, written after Jackson held and made good use of the bridge, Shields claimed he had wished to burn it and constructed a fantastic scenario in which Stonewall would be brought to his knees. Without access to the bridge, stated Shields, the enemy would have had an impassable river in his front and Frémont's cannon in his rear. "This river could not become fordable in less than three days," he wrote: "It was only necessary to place him between Frémont's artillery and mine, with an impassable river in his front, to insure his destruction." Shields sent his artillery forward in the hope of effecting this cross fire while another column was to head for Waynesboro, eighteen miles south of Port Republic, to cut the railroad there and, the Irishman thought, seal the Confederates' fate. This done, Jackson "would be compelled to lay down his arms."

According to this program, however, Shields would be too busy to attend the surrender ceremonies somewhere near Port Republic. About the same time, Shields said, scouts brought him word that Gen. James Longstreet was approaching Luray from the east with 10,000 men. "This," he explained, "compelled me to post two brigades at Luray and remain there in person to make head against Longstreet, so that he might not fall on my rear." So while two of his brigades commanded by subordinates were to cooperate with Frémont, Shields would remain at Luray with two brigades, not more than 4,000 men, to confront Longstreet's 10,000. What had begun as an offensive to clean out the Valley had turned into a defensive campaign to fend off an imaginary foe. Only in his report was Shields clearheaded and offensive minded.

But all of Shields's speculation about Jackson's fate had the bridge at Port Republic been burned appears to be post facto hokum. On June 4 he had given Carroll specific orders to "save the bridge at Port Republic." Carroll set off on June 7, with Erastus B. Tyler's brigade following. Carroll successfully entered the village of Port Republic on the morning of June 8, created some havoc among Jackson's headquarters, captured two of the general's staff and very nearly the general himself, and gained control of the bridge over the North River. Jackson roused his infantry, however, and Carroll retreated with the loss of two field guns.[65]

Carroll would have done well to burn the bridge. That would have placed Jackson in a dangerous position, separated from his trains and with his back to a river. Shields belatedly realized this and claimed to have ordered Carroll to destroy the covered bridge. He blamed Jackson's success and escape on Carroll, who by "some unaccountable misapprehension" neglected to burn the bridge, "although he held possession of it three-quarters of an hour." The "misapprehension" is accounted for by Shields's explicit order to hold the bridge, though how Shields expected Carroll to do so unsupported and deep in the Confederate rear is difficult to understand. Shields showed his worst in attempting to cover up his own blunder by faulting a colonel who "wanted the good sense" to torch the bridge.[66]

Shields had managed to string his command out over twenty-five miles, with one brigade at Luray, another at Columbia Bridge, and a third—Kimball's—near Conrad's Store, toward which Carroll and his advance brigade fell back from Port Republic. Tyler's brigade fought with Jackson on June 9 northeast of Port Republic, but the Confederates concentrated their more numerous infantry and threw the Federals back. Shields met and halted the retreating column south of Conrad's Store that afternoon and, with most of his division in hand, intended to attack Jackson. "On the evening of the 9th," he wrote later, "I was concerting a combined attack on Jackson next morning with General Frémont." Shields's plan seems to have been for Frémont—"whose conduct throughout cannot be too highly praised"—to throw a pontoon bridge across the Shenandoah on June 10 "to attack Jackson's flank, while I with my whole command should attack him in front. The result could not have been doubtful."[67]

But the game was over. Frémont was by then dragging his weary corps back to Harrisonburg, and Lincoln, having new ideas, sent word to Shields, through McDowell, to withdraw to Front Royal. Wrote Shields, "I never obeyed an order with such reluctance, but I had to return."[68]

So ended Shields's chaotic excursion up the Luray Valley. Bewildered by his notions about Jackson's intended escape to Stanardsville and Charlottesville, he had moved indecisively. Though wise enough to know that he had to control the bridges between Luray and Port Republic, he did not seem to know how to use them. Because Shields had no grasp of the region's geography and no understanding of Frémont's or Jackson's circumstances, he was handicapped from the outset. Poor intelligence gathering and inefficient supply operations further aggravated his circumstances, contributing to an utterly ineffectual performance.

Jackson rested his tired men at Mount Meridian for a week before marching eastward. As his men crossed the Blue Ridge en route to join Robert E. Lee at Richmond, the Valley campaign ended. The campaign's greatest irony is that by then the Federals had a carefully considered, clearly expressed plan for operations in the Valley. On June 8, after three months of rudderless drifting, Lincoln at last put his ship before the wind and set a course for Federal operations in Virginia. Having studied a map, he wrote to Stanton what in retrospect seems to have been obvious: "Richmond is the principal point for our active operation." This could not have been a revelation to the president, for McClellan had been saying as much for more than half a year. "Accordingly," Lincoln continued, "it is the object of the enemy to create alarms every where else and thereby to divert as much of our force from that point as possible. On the contrary, as a general rule, we should stand on the defensive everywhere else, and direct as much force as possible to Richmond." McDowell was ordered to leave Front Royal and return to Fredericksburg to operate against Richmond. Part of this new policy for conducting the war in Virginia was a "general plan for the valley of the Shenandoah," as Lincoln called it. Both the Mountain and Shenandoah departments were reduced, their boundaries redrawn to protect the railroads at Strasburg, Front Royal, Winchester, and Harpers Ferry. Jacob Cox was left on his own to protect western Virginia, and Banks was to stand at Front Royal and maintain a presence far up the Luray Valley and eastward along the Manassas Gap Railroad through northern Virginia.[69] Frémont was to be the linchpin. "Halt at Harrisonburg, pursuing Jackson no farther," Lincoln wrote to the Pathfinder on June 9. "Get your force well in hand and stand on the defensive, guarding against a movement of the enemy either back toward Strasburg or toward Franklin, and await further orders, which will soon be sent to you."[70]

And so the blueprint outlining Federal intentions in the Shenandoah Valley came at the end rather than the beginning. Lincoln's "general plan" showed insight, massing strength against the vital point at Richmond while also articulating the subordinate status of operations in all other regions of Virginia. Lincoln recognized the important points in the Valley and intelligently placed available troops where they were likely to do the most good. By June 9, however, Confederate leaders had decided the time had come to deliver

Richmond. The Valley receded in importance for them. Lincoln's new plan offered a classic example of slamming the barn door after the horse had fled. If the president had invested even a day in studying his map in late March or early April and deployed his troops as intelligently as he wished to in June, he would have controlled most of the Valley, protected the railroads and the approaches to Maryland on the upper Potomac (and therefore the northern and western approaches to Washington), and assisted the drive on Richmond by both reinforcing McClellan and threatening Staunton. Frémont's force at Harrisonburg would have stood only thirty miles from Staunton, and even small signs of aggressiveness from the Pathfinder would have compelled the Confederates to deploy units in the Valley that were badly needed to help repel McClellan. Had Lincoln or Stanton contemplated such ideas in the early spring, they might not have taken Richmond or even won a great victory anywhere in Virginia—but they almost certainly would have avoided the fiasco that deranged Federal plans in the Old Dominion during those critical months before Robert E. Lee attacked McClellan in late June and reversed the course of the war.

Federal command in the Valley was, in the most important sense, nonexistent. Banks, Frémont, and Shields all exercised a measure of control, but so did Lincoln, Stanton, and McClellan. Only Lincoln and Stanton saw each other regularly, and most of the military officers never saw any of their collaborators between March and June. Nor did the Federals develop an overall plan or even pursue a single goal. Frémont and Banks never worked toward the same end. Frémont looked toward Tennessee while Banks was pursing Jackson. When the Pathfinder chased Jackson, Banks was licking his wounds after Winchester. Superiors changed James Shields's goals five times between mid-March and late May. Only on May 24, just two weeks before the end of the campaign, did the Federals attain a unity of purpose with Frémont and Shields being sent in pursuit of Jackson. The Federals previously had been so divided in their agendas that Jackson often had meant little to them, and therein lay much of the reason for his success. For eight weeks between late March and late May, the Federals concerned themselves with their own problems—among them Tennessee, horses, reinforcements, bad roads, half-rations, no shoes, and Richmond—and left Jackson to do as he wished.

In 1861 John Charles Frémont labored ineffectually in Missouri, prompting Congressman Frank Blair to declare him a failure. While the Pathfinder called for more men and matériel, Blair countered that "a man to be great must be able to do great things with small means."[71] This seems a fair measure of greatness. Frémont's means were small in Missouri and smaller still in Virginia, and in neither place did he achieve great things. Nor did Banks or Shields. To say they failed of greatness, however, is not to condemn the three generals as bumbling fools. Shields's performance, particularly in the Luray Valley, seems the most inept, largely because he was overwhelmed by confusion. Banks and Frémont struggled against enormous obstacles. Although they also made mistakes, each deserves some credit for modest accomplishments in bad situations not of their making, particularly in late May and early June. But if all three generals failed the test of greatness, so also did Lincoln and Stanton. The men running the war had little at their disposal in the way of talented commanders, and with their small means they achieved nothing great.

Stonewall Jackson emerged as the one great commander in the Valley that spring. He accomplished so much with so little in the Shenandoah that his subsequent performances, most notably in the Seven Days battles, sometimes paled by comparison. Ever afterward held to the standard he set in the Valley, Jackson sometimes has been criticized when he failed to meet it. The same principle seems to have been at work in evaluating Federal commanders in the Valley. Banks, Frémont, and Shields repeatedly have been judged harshly—indeed ridiculed—for not being the equal of Jackson of the Valley. That they did not measure up to Jackson's level of performance is plain, but where is the officer who could in the spring of 1862?

NOTES

1. James Longstreet "'The Seven Days,' including Frayser's Farm," in *Battles and Leaders of the Civil War*, ed. Robert Underwood Johnson and Clarence Clough Buel, 4 vols. (New York: Century, 1887–88), 2:405.

2. McClellan to Stanton, June 25, 1862, in George B. McClellan, *The Civil War Papers of George B. McClellan: Selected Correspondence, 1860–1865*, ed. Stephen W. Sears (New York: Ticknor and Fields, 1989), 216–17. A problem inherent in this plan is that it disperses Federal forces as well. They must advance on many different points in order to keep those Confederates occupied.

3. McClellan to Banks, March 16, 1862, in ibid., 212; U.S. War Department, *The War of*

the Rebellion: A Compilation of the Official Records of the Union and Confederate Armies, 127 vols., index, and atlas (Washington, D.C.: GPO, 1880–1901), ser. 1, 5:56 (hereafter cited as *OR*; all references are to ser. 1).

4. McClellan to Banks, March 16, 1862, in McClellan, *Civil War Papers*, 212.

5. When Scott resigned in November 1861, McClellan, Frémont, and Banks moved up to occupy the top three places on the seniority list.

6. The best biography of Frémont remains Allan Nevins, *Frémont: Pathmarker of the West* (1955; reprint, Lincoln: University of Nebraska Press, 1992). Nevins provides a good general account of Frémont's troubles in the West on pp. 473–549.

7. Lincoln to Isaac N. Arnold, May 26, 1863, in Abraham Lincoln, *The Collected Works of Abraham Lincoln*, ed. Roy P. Basler, 9 vols. (New Brunswick, N.J.: Rutgers University Press, 1953–55), 6:230.

8. Andrew Rolle, *John Charles Frémont: Character as Destiny* (Norman: University of Oklahoma Press, 1991), 217.

9. *OR* 5:54; Lincoln, *Collected Works*, 5:155. Lincoln signed the order creating the Mountain Department on March 11, the same day he relieved McClellan of command of all the armies.

10. Cox further observed that quick raids were the only type of operation that ever proved feasible in the region. See Jacob Cox, "West Virginia Operations under Frémont," in Johnson and Buel, *Battles and Leaders*, 2:278.

11. George H. Gordon, *Brook Farm to Cedar Mountain* (Boston: J. R. Osgood, 1883), 120; Gary L. Ecelbarger, *"We Are in for It!": The First Battle of Kernstown* (Shippensburg, Pa.: White Mane, 1997), 275–77.

12. *OR* 12(3):16.

13. McClellan to Banks, April 1, 1862, in McClellan, *Civil War Papers*, 220–21.

14. *OR* 12(3):43.

15. *OR* 12(1):1, 418.

16. Alonzo Hall Quint, *The Potomac and the Rapidan: Army Notes from the Failure at Winchester to the Reenforcement of Rosecrans, 1861–3* (Boston: Crosby and Nichols; New York: O. S. Felt, 1864), 134; *OR* 12(1):2, 426, 446.

17. *OR* 12(1):446. "So far as the matter of supplies is concerned," wrote Alonzo Hall Quint, "there has been no difficulty which energy could not have easily remedied. The reason, therefore, of the exceeding slowness of movements, and the present retrograde, is to be found in other directions, and is, in all probability, attributable to directions from Washington" (Quint, *Potomac and the Rapidan*, 146).

18. Williams to daughter, April 29, 1862, in Alpheus S. Williams, *From the Cannon's Mouth: The Civil War Letters of General Alpheus S. Williams*, ed. Milo M. Quaife (1959; reprint, Lincoln: University of Nebraska Press, 1995), 72.

19. *OR* 12(1):522–23, 556, 536; Gordon, *Brook Farm to Cedar Mountain*, 172–73.

20. *OR* 12(1):524–25. "I have forborne until the last moment to make this representation," observed Banks in his letter to Stanton, "well knowing how injurious to the public

service unfounded alarms become, but in this case the probabilities of danger are so great, that it should be assumed as positive and preparation made to meet it."

21. Gordon, *Brook Farm to Cedar Mountain*, 191–93, 197.

22. David Hunter Strother [Porte Crayon, pseud.], *A Virginia Yankee in the Civil War: The Diaries of David Hunter Strother*, ed. Cecil D. Eby Jr. (Chapel Hill: University of North Carolina Press, 1961), 38–41.

23. Quint, *Potomac and the Rapidan*, 150–51; *OR* 12(1):551.

24. *OR* 5:54; 12(1):4; 12(3):9–12.

25. Specifically, Frémont's plan called for Blenker's division of about 9,000 men to be transferred to his department. Blenker would unite with Schenck at Franklin, and that combined column of 12,000 would join Milroy at Monterey. This column of 15,500 men, presumably led by Frémont, would then strike the railroad at Salem. A second column of 7,000 men under Gen. Jacob Cox would advance from a base at Gauley on the Kanawha River near Fayetteville to strike the railroad at Newburg. See *OR* 12(3):32; Lincoln, *Collected Works*, 5:175–76.

26. Cox, "West Virginia Operations under Frémont," 278.

27. *OR* 12(1):6.

28. See *OR* 12(3):81, 93, for reports about the condition of Blenker's men.

29. Francis F. Wayland, ed., "Frémont's Pursuit of Jackson in the Shenandoah Valley: The Journal of Colonel Albert Tracy, March–July 1862," *Virginia Magazine of History and Biography* 70 (April 1962): 177, 171.

30. *OR* 12(1):462–67.

31. Cox, "West Virginia Operations under Frémont," 280.

32. *OR* 12(1):10; 12(3):197.

33. *OR* 12(3):226; 12(1):626; Lincoln, *Collected Works*, 5:234.

34. *OR* 12(3):223–24, 234, 240, 242, 246–47.

35. *OR* 12(3):241, 247; Lincoln, *Collected Works*, 5:235.

36. *OR* 12(1):642; Lincoln, *Collected Works*, 5:230; *OR* 5:231.

37. *OR* 12(3):9–12; 12(1):642.

38. Oscar D. Ladley, *Hearth and Knapsack: The Ladley Letters, 1857–1880*, ed. Carl M. Becker and Ritchie Thomas (Athens: Ohio University Press, 1988), 32–33.

39. Wayland, "Frémont's Pursuit of Jackson," 174–75; Ladley, *Hearth and Knapsack*, 32–33; T. Albert Steiger, "Address [History of the 75th Pennsylvania Volunteer Infantry]," in *Pennsylvania at Chickamauga and Chattanooga* (Harrisburg, Pa.: State Printer, 1897), 169–70.

40. In 2001 this road was known as U.S. Route 33 and, though surfaced, remained steep in places. Signs warned trucks of 9 percent grades. In the Civil War, strong, healthy horse or mule teams could, on a good, dry road, draw a fully loaded wagon weighing 3,000 pounds up a grade of no more than 10 percent. Frémont had neither a good, dry road nor rested teams.

41. *OR* 12(1):642; Wayland, "Frémont's Pursuit of Jackson," 174–75.

42. Wayland, "Frémont's Pursuit of Jackson," 174–75.

43. Louis Biskey diary (45th New York), May 25, 1862, Fredericksburg and Spotsylvania National Military Park, Fredericksburg, Va.

44. Wayland, "Frémont's Pursuit of Jackson," 176; Biskey diary, May 25, 27, 1862.

45. *OR* 12(1):644, 628–29, 642; Lincoln, *Collected Works*, 5:243, 230–31.

46. Biskey diary, May 28, 1862; *OR* 12(1):31; Wayland, "Frémont's Pursuit of Jackson," 177. Tracy misspelled Surgeon George Suckley's name.

47. Wayland, "Frémont's Pursuit of Jackson," 177, 332.

48. *OR* 12(3):267; 12(1):14.

49. Wayland, "Frémont's Pursuit of Jackson," 183–86.

50. Biskey diary; *OR* 12(1):15–16; Wayland, "Frémont's Pursuit of Jackson," 187–91.

51. Biskey diary; Wayland, "Frémont's Pursuit of Jackson," 193.

52. *OR* 12(1):21–22.

53. Gustave P. Cluseret, *Mémoires du Général Cluseret* (Paris, 1887–88), 3, 22, translated and quoted in Lowell L. Blaisdell, "A French Civil War Adventurer: Fact and Fancy," *Civil War History* 12 (September 1966): 253; Carl Schurz to his parents, June 12, 1862, in Carl Schurz, *Intimate Letters of Carl Schurz, 1841–1869*, ed. Joseph Schafer (Madison: State Historical Society of Wisconsin, 1928), 272–74.

54. *OR* 12(3):219–20.

55. *OR* 12(3):255, 248, 256–59, 243.

56. *OR* 12(3):272–73, 276–78, 281–82, 260, 270.

57. *OR* 12(1):682; 12(3):322.

58. *OR* 12(1):686; 12(3):316.

59. *OR* 12(1):686.

60. The waters remained high throughout the week. By June 9 no bridges had been built at Front Royal, and communications between shores was still by ferry. See *First Maine Bugle* 2 (July 1891): 5, 61.

61. *OR* 12(1):686.

62. *OR* 12(3):317.

63. Samuel Brown Coyner to sister, June 5, 1862, in "Memoir of Captain Samuel Brown Coyner," Augusta County Historical Society, Staunton, Va.

64. *OR* 12(1):686; Franklin Sawyer, *A Military History of the 8th Ohio Vol. Inf'y: Its Battles, Marches, and Army Movements* (1881; reprint, Huntington, W.Va.: Blue Acorn Press, 1994), 53.

65. *OR* 12(1):686–87; 12(3):335; 12(1):683.

66. *OR* 12(1):684.

67. *OR* 12(1):685, 688.

68. *OR* 12(1):685.

69. Lincoln to Stanton, June 8, 1862, in Abraham Lincoln, *The Collected Works of Abraham Lincoln: Supplement, 1832–1865*, ed. Roy P. Basler (Westport, Conn.: Greenwood, 1974), 138; Lincoln, *Collected Works*, 5:264; *OR* 12(1):542. On June 8 Stanton directed Banks to "take position in force at or near Front Royal, on the right or left bank of the

Shenandoah, with an advance at Luray or other points in supporting distance of General Frémont [who had been ordered to remain near Harrisonburg]; also that you occupy with sufficient detachments the former positions of Brigadier General Geary on the line of the Manassas Gap Railroad as far as the Manassas Junction" (*OR* 12[1]:541).

70. *OR* 12(1):655. See also Lincoln, *Collected Works*, 5:270–71.

71. F. P. Blair, "Frémont's Hundred Days in Missouri," delivered March 2, 1862, *Congressional Globe* (Washington, D.C., 1862).

JONATHAN M. BERKEY

In the Very Midst of the War Track

THE VALLEY'S CIVILIANS AND THE

SHENANDOAH CAMPAIGN

On March 19, 1862, as the Shenandoah Valley campaign began in earnest, Augusta County farmer Jacob R. Hildebrand pondered a dream his wife had the preceding evening. She dreamt that a barn had caught on fire, causing a neighborhood panic. Many of the barn's shingles burned before the fire was out, but some escaped the conflagration along with the barn's rafters, which remained upright. "Now I do not pretend to be a Daniel to interpret dreams," Hildebrand confessed in his journal, "but [I] will call the barn the Southern confederacy, the Rafters the States composing the confederacy, [and] the shingles the People of the States."[1]

Mrs. Hildebrand's image of the burning barn seems apt for the impact of the Valley campaign on the region's civilians. As her dream suggests, the hopes of the state of Virginia and the Confederacy survived the Valley campaign and, indeed, thrived because of it. However, like the shingles in Mrs. Hildebrand's barn, Valley civilians faced grave dangers during the campaign. The preceding year of war had transformed antebellum Valley households as men went off to the armies and women attempted to manage farms and homes. The military action in the spring of 1862 hastened this transformation by seriously disrupting Valley households. As the Valley's civilians reacted to military authority during the campaign, they saw their antebellum power relationships altered significantly. White men who had not joined the army fled at the prospect of being drafted. African Americans utilized the Federal presence in their midst to escape bondage or to gain leverage in the master-slave relationship. Women stepped out of their antebellum role of deference to challenge military authority. Because the military events of the Valley campaign had such a great effect on local households, civilians attempted to influence the operations in any way they could. The impact of the contending armies went beyond the military results of the campaign, encouraging a process of social change that continued throughout the war.

The Shenandoah Valley's geography and agricultural productivity virtually ensured that it would be contested by Union and Confederate armies. The Valley forms a corridor between the Blue Ridge Mountains in the east and Little North Mountain and the Shenandoah Mountains in the west. It runs southwest for more than 150 miles, from the Potomac to the James River. Its width varies from 12 to 24 miles. The Shenandoah River begins in the mountains and travels toward the Potomac; thus anyone traveling "down" the Valley is actually heading north. The lower Shenandoah Valley flanked Washington, D.C.; any point above Strasburg was north of Washington, and any point above Martinsburg was north of Baltimore. The Baltimore & Ohio Railroad (B&O), which linked Washington to the Midwest, traveled through Harpers Ferry and Martinsburg. Thus a Confederate army in the lower Valley would flank any attempt to advance on Richmond from the North. A Union army occupying Winchester would relieve Washington's right flank, have use of the B&O and the Chesapeake & Ohio Canal, and being within 100 miles of Staunton, threaten the western supply lines of the Confederacy. "Stonewall" Jackson deemed the Valley so critical that he exclaimed, "If this Valley is lost, Virginia is lost."[2]

The Valley's agricultural importance rivaled its strategic significance. Unparalleled throughout Virginia for its wheat production, the Valley yielded almost 2.5 million bushels in 1860, accounting for roughly 19 percent of that crop in the entire state. Livestock raising was also common in the region. Thus whoever held the Valley controlled a vital food source.[3]

In March 1862 it seemed that the Confederacy could not protect the Valley. The 4,000 soldiers of Stonewall Jackson's command camped in the area around Winchester, facing a Union force more than twice as numerous under Maj. Gen. Nathaniel P. Banks. To the southwest another Union army under Maj. Gen. John C. Frémont threatened a small Confederate force under Brig.

Gen. Edward "Alleghany" Johnson. After abandoning Winchester on March 11, Jackson retreated before the Federal advance. On March 23 he turned to attack the Federals at Kernstown, a few miles south of Winchester. Although a defeat for Jackson, this action kept in the Valley a Union division slated to reinforce George B. McClellan on the Peninsula below Richmond. After Kernstown, Jackson retreated up the Valley to Swift Run Gap. On May 8 he united with Alleghany Johnson and defeated part of Frémont's army at the battle of McDowell. After this action, Jackson bided his time and by the third week of May received reinforcements. A force under Maj. Gen. Richard S. Ewell joined him on May 21, nearly doubling his strength to about 17,500.

Jackson then took the initiative, advancing down the Valley and routing a Federal detachment at Front Royal. He next attacked Banks at Winchester on May 25 and pursued the retreating Federals to the Potomac. After spending only a few days in the lower Valley, Jackson raced back up the Valley to avoid being trapped by the forces of James Shields and Frémont. This stage of the campaign culminated in the battles of Cross Keys and Port Republic on June 8–9, where Jackson successfully kept the armies of Shields and Frémont from crushing his force. Shortly after the battle of Port Republic, Jackson left the Valley to reinforce the Army of Northern Virginia outside Richmond.[4]

As the contending armies squared off in the Valley, civilians learned one of the first lessons of the Shenandoah campaign: proximity to either army inevitably led to property loss. Anna Maria Henkel, living near New Market, noted that Yankees who passed by her dwelling stole "every thing they could lay their hands on." Union soldiers' penchant for thievery distressed Lt. Col. Thomas Clark of the 29th Ohio. Upset that many members of the 110th Pennsylvania had stolen chickens from an old widow's coop, Clark seethed, "I've seen lots of men this Eve that only lack bristles to make them hogs. Some of them would steal a bit of sausage from a blind Puppy." Clark posted a guard with orders to shoot the next soldier who attempted to bother the widow or her property. One Valley newspaper asserted that from Smith's Creek Valley to New Market, Federal soldiers helped themselves to all of the cattle, horses, hay, corn, and other goods that they could carry.[5]

Confederates also did their share of property damage. John Casler, who served in the Stonewall Brigade, recalled with some humor that the soldiers would not allow anyone's chickens to come out into the road and bite them. "We would not steal them!" he recalled, "No! Who ever heard of a soldier stealing? But simply take them." David W. Barton of Frederick County noted

JONATHAN M. BERKEY

· 88 ·

that Confederate stragglers caused many problems for local noncombatants. "They are more troublesome than the Yankees," he said, "because they go anywhere without fear." Civilians especially felt the pinch of military necessity as Jackson hurried back up the Valley in late May and early June. From Front Royal, Maj. John A. Harman, Jackson's profane quartermaster, impressed horses and wagons throughout the upper Valley in order to move captured Federal stores to a safe place. Confederate officers were directed to collect "everything that can be made available to haul stores" and send them to Front Royal. In a brief time Harman had trains of civilian wagons carrying captured supplies to Winchester and Front Royal.[6]

Of all of the contending military forces, Union German-speaking units, or "Blenker's Dutch," as Valley civilians knew them, inspired the most bitterness. Laura Lee lamented that the Germans forged a path of destruction through Clarke County. "They went to Carter Hall, Page-Brook and other places," she recalled, "drank all the liquors, and broke up the furniture, stealing and destroying wherever they went." When word reached Winchester that the German soldiers would soon enter the town, many residents were in "a state of terror about them." As some of the German troops began a search of Clara Strayer's room during the battle of Port Republic, she admonished them that gentlemen would respect the privacy of a lady's chamber. The leader of the squad replied, "Yah, yah! if dere be any Dutch gentlemen! Come boys, let's go to town!" Union brigadier general Robert H. Milroy formed a comparably unfavorable opinion of the German-speaking units, whom he claimed were "composed of the most infernal robbers, plunderers and thieves, I have ever seen, our army is disgraced by them."[7]

Even when soldiers did not actively plunder Valley homesteads, civilians suffered from property loss. Cornelia McDonald grudgingly allowed Union soldiers into her home but despaired at the scene she encountered in her parlor. "Mud, mud, mud," she recalled, "was everywhere, over, and on, and in everything. No colours were visible on the carpets, wet great coats hung dripping on every chair, great pools of water under them where they hung." Looking out on her lawn, she saw "a sea of deep mud." Lucy Rebecca Buck's family had a disturbing experience when 4,000 soldiers of Brig. Gen. Nathan Kimball's brigade quartered around "Bel Air," the family home. Lucy observed the columns of men arriving, "like a great black serpent." Next came the artillery, the wheels of which cut up the green fields. The stone fence was pulled down to allow all of the troops entry. Next came some cavalry, which

Cornelia Peake McDonald, a photograph made more than twenty-five years after she recorded valuable impressions of the 1862 Valley campaign in her diary. Cornelia McDonald, *A Diary with Reminiscences of the War and Refugee Life in the Shenandoah Valley 1860–1865*, ed. Hunter McDonald (Nashville, Tenn.: Cullom and Ghertner, 1934), opp. p. 1.

pastured their horses in a clover field. When the troops received permission to break ranks, even more destruction occurred. All of Mr. Buck's fencing disappeared, or as Lucy termed it, "melted." "If I live a century," she confided to her diary, "I do not think I can ever forget this day." Similar scenes occurred throughout the Valley. Lucy's Uncle Marcus noted in June that the "whole

Valley [is] almost white with the tents and wagons of the armies of McDow-ell, Shields, and Banks."[8]

The proximity of Federal armies resulted in a more disturbing form of property loss for Valley slaveholders. The disruption caused by the Shenan-doah campaign weakened the foundations of the master-slave relationship. African American residents of the Valley often played an active role in weak-ening the bonds of slavery, but their actions usually depended on military movements. The proximity of U.S. forces provided the key, affording slaves a reasonable chance to escape their bondage. Valley civilians, white and black alike, quickly acknowledged through actions and words that one of most cru-cial effects of Jackson's campaign was the erosion of the "peculiar institution."

Although slaves were never numerically significant in the Valley, the institu-tion nevertheless functioned as an important part of local social relations. In 1860 the Valley held about 5 percent of the state's slaves. Most slaveholders owned a very small number of slaves, and only one planter had more than 100. Valley inhabitants commonly hired out slaves for housekeeping and agricultural work. Because of this practice, many nonslaveowning Valley resi-dents believed that they had a stake in perpetuating slavery.[9]

As Federal troops moved up the Valley in March and April, many African Americans ventured into their lines. Harpers Ferry, one of the first areas secured by Union troops, faced a flood of "contrabands" pouring into town. Resident Annie Marmion claimed that the influx of escaped slaves increased the population of Harpers Ferry to unprecedented heights. The Federals faced a similar "invasion" in Charlestown. Federal staff officer and Valley native David Hunter Strother noted that the first slaves who entered the lines at Charlestown were arrested. When the jail filled, the slaves were organized into work squads and marched off to Harpers Ferry. "Hundreds of contra-bands are hourly seeking refuge within our lines," noted a reporter in Charles-town. One Front Royal resident termed the flight of African Americans from the vicinity a "stampede." The black exodus would continue as the Federals moved south.[10]

The Federals struggled with the question of how to manage so many contrabands. Col. Charles Candy, commanding the provost guard at Stras-burg, expressed this uncertainty when he asked a superior, "What instructions are there in regard to Contrabands? . . . Do not know what to do with them or whether to receive them." A reporter for the *Baltimore Sun* captured the laissez-faire essence of Federal policy toward the Valley contrabands. "They

The Valley's Civilians

are allowed to roam at large without espionage or care," he stated. "In fact, but little notice is taken of them, except to prevent their return beyond our posts."[11]

The experience of Charles Yates Aglionby of Charlestown demonstrates the speed of the black exodus and the crippling effect it had on individual farms. In 1860 Aglionby's 375-acre farm, Mount Pleasant, was home to twenty slaves. By March 3, 1862, the Federals occupied Charlestown, and soon thereafter Aglionby's slaves began leaving. On March 10 Aglionby awoke to find that five slaves had fled during the preceding evening. One, Laura, would be especially missed because she was "handy at all works." Laura's husband, Henry Robinson, owned by Elizabeth Striden, was included in the group of escapees. Three days later, Ralf Madison Hall, who made boots and shoes, fled with Silas Hall, who was working at a neighboring farm. The two apparently were father and son. On March 24 George W. Cockerell informed Aglionby that his slave Rebecca left with her husband the night before. Aglionby described Rebecca as "active[,] intelligent, [a] good seamstress and handy at all woman's work." Zachary Blair left the Aglionby plantation on April 24, and three more slaves attempted to escape ten days later. The slaves did not go empty-handed, taking a wagon, two horses, and two mules with gear. In less than a month Aglionby lost at least seven slaves, more than a third of his 1860 workforce. In the year before the Valley campaign, he had lost only three slaves.[12]

Why did some slaves flee so quickly? The arrival of Federal troops made younger male slaves less tolerant of abusive masters. George Williams, seventeen-year-old slave of M. L. Greggs, escaped to Federal lines because his master "was mean and knocked us about." Ned, a ten-year-old owned by Abe Isler, had seen his mother and father sold south. When his master whipped him, Ned had little reason to remain on the farm. The ironically named slave John Brown fled when an overseer tried to whip him.

A few slaves needed no specific personal threat to escape bondage. George Washington, a slave of Bushrod Herbert, had served as a farm laborer and hotel waiter. He claimed that his master never harmed him; he simply "prefers freedom to slavery." Miles Sanders, perhaps a friend of Washington's, proclaimed to Union officials, "I don't wish to continue in slavery." Another official noted that Clarke County slave John Ford "came to be free." Laura Lee, a Winchester resident, captured the complexity of African American reactions to the prospects of freedom. "The servants still keep pouring in from the country," she observed in April, "some looking very much elated by their new-fledged freedom, and others wandering about forlorn and depressed."[13]

Even when slaves remained with their owners, the occupation of much of the Valley by Federal troops loosened the bonds of the masters' authority. Though she remained with the Lees, the slave Betty became more assertive. One day Laura Lee's behavior offended Betty, who promptly put on her bonnet and walked off to her mother's, "saying she supposed she was not wanted here any more." After some persuading, Betty returned to the household. In May, Marcus B. Buck of Front Royal remarked that the slaves were "doing but little, and that only in their own way." Mary Greenhow Lee noted what many Confederates would have considered more disturbing behavior by African Americans in Winchester. The Union troops persuaded many to watch for and report anyone who refused to pass under the American flags set up in town. Anna Andrews deplored that slaves in Shepherdstown acted in an "*up-ish*" way, "but we can expect nothing else when Jno. Brown's party is at the very thresh holds." A letter from Winchester published in the *Richmond Enquirer* commented on the restlessness of the African American population during the Federal occupation, claiming, "the weighty question of freedom was too much for them to digest, and it caused a moral dyspepsia, which made them irritable and uncomfortable."[14]

Many incidents among white civilians, contrabands, and occupying Federal soldiers shocked the racial sensibilities of the Confederates and helped to demonize Yankee soldiers in their eyes. Some slaves took advantage of Federal military might to assert power over their former superiors. Shipley, a Maryland slave who had been hired out in Frederick County, Virginia, utilized an escort of twenty-five Federal troops to go to Newtown and reclaim his wife, Mary. Lucy Rebecca Buck of Front Royal grew infuriated when she saw a black man at the head of a Federal cavalry patrol. "This boy a short time since had fled from the best of masters and joined these miserable hypocrites," she noted: "Yes, there he rode at the head of the detachment as grandly as the first officer among them, and he looked as if he felt a savage satisfaction in thus coming back to his old home and lord where he had once served." Another black man from Front Royal teamed up with a Federal soldier and planned to burn the depot, but the two were captured before doing any damage. Winchester resident John Peyton Clark reported with amazement that one of his neighbors, a Mr. McDowell, had been arrested for striking his slave woman. Although released from jail, the neighbor had to listen to a stern lecture from a Union colonel named Clark while in the presence of an African American. Colonel Clark chastised the man, who had the appearance of a gentleman, for striking a "defenceless female." McDowell explained that the slave woman had hit his wife and that his attempt to discipline her complied with the laws of Virginia. The colonel responded that McDowell should not use force in managing a servant. When McDowell asked how a servant should be managed, Clark replied, "by love."[15]

Physical relations between black women and Federal soldiers scandalized many Valley civilians. This reaction must be considered disingenuous, at least to a significant degree, because white citizens of the Valley must have known that such liaisons also occurred frequently between masters and slaves. John Peyton Clark set down in his journal examples of what he deemed improper incidents. Someone had overheard a black woman asserting that Union general Banks was "sweet" and kissed her when she left. It was rumored that Susan Robinson, a member of a well-known free black family, planned to marry a Yankee soldier with whom she frequently walked on the street. Clark lamented that "such scenes should ever have been enacted within the limits of Virginia! And yet the half is not told." Kate Sperry expressed shock at hearing of two Federal officers who walked arm in arm with free black women in Winchester. "To think that white men could place themselves upon an equality with niggers!" she exclaimed in her journal. A Confederate officer claimed that three Yankees married black women during the Federal occupation of Winchester. When Union soldiers reached New Market, Anna Maria Henkel probably had already heard some of the rumors. "One of the Yankey's thought he must press my house for a couple of their concubines," she wrote. "I gave him as good as he sent."[16]

However vexing the thought of interracial romance involving Yankee soldiers and local African American women, most white residents of the Valley would have agreed that the loss of black labor represented a far more serious consequence of Union invasion. The departure of slaves disrupted the social and productive functions of many white households. Even if slaves remained faithful in the presence of the Yankees, many slaveowners dreaded the prospect of losing their favorite servants and prepared themselves for the worst. Laura Lee struggled with the disintegration of her relationship with the black members of her sister-in-law's household during the Federal occupation of Winchester. When a contingent of Federals began to withdraw from the town just before the battle of Kernstown, a slave named Evans left with them. "It was a great shock," wrote Laura, "for I thought if there was one who would be faithful, it would be Evans, but there are few who can stand the temptation to be free." Evans's departure so traumatized Laura that she had to lay down to recover from the shock. Anna Andrews reacted to the uncertain status of her family's slaves with scorn. "They are nothing but an ungrateful, discontented lot," she wrote, "& I don't care how soon I get rid of mine except that I don't like Lincoln's gang to do it."[17]

Many Valley women dreaded the prospect of laboring without their servants. Laura Lee confessed, "We are doing a little spring sewing, and *talking* of housecleaning." Kate Sperry felt the pinch of a reduced labor force in her household as well. She confessed to her diary, "Such a time as I've had on yesterday and today—never was as tired and worn out in all my life—that Levi being off with the Yanks and no woman to do the work I've been compelled to 'fall in ranks.' " Writing on May 25, Susan Nourse Riddle of Berkeley County succinctly recorded the effect of the campaign on Valley households: "Banks *Grand Retreat* from Winchester. Confederates here in evening. Darkies gone. Go to kitchen ourselves."[18]

As if the loss of slave labor was not disruptive enough, many Valley men faced the prospect of arrest for disloyalty. During the spring of 1861, secession had not enjoyed widespread popular support in most of the Valley counties. Even after secession became a foregone conclusion in April 1861, many Unionist families remained in the Valley. The Confederates had been known to arrest civilians suspected of disloyalty, and many Valley residents expected Union troops to respond in kind. In April 1862 the Confederacy enacted the first national draft in American history, placing all males between the ages of eighteen and thirty-five in line for Confederate service. Thus a Valley male not only might face imprisonment for being disloyal to the Confederacy, but the conscription act meant that he might also be forced to fight for a cause he abhorred. To further complicate the issue, a small portion of the Valley's population belonged to the Quaker, Mennonite, or Dunker religions, all of which embraced pacifism. Not surprisingly, civilian men became scarce that spring. A northerner at Edinburg observed the fine wheat fields in the region but concluded "that when the grain becomes ripe there will be few reapers to gather it. There are few men through the country, unless they hide themselves, as some are known to have done." A reporter at Harrisonburg noted that, like "all the towns in this valley, but few males remain here."[19]

Traveling civilians proved especially vulnerable to arrest. Union troops captured the father of Valley historian John W. Wayland when he was traveling in the vicinity of New Market; they released him about three weeks later. In June, "Justice" wrote to the *Richmond Daily Enquirer* from Staunton that Federal soldiers were arresting male civilians age fourteen years and older; Justice believed that the Union army adopted this policy because Stonewall Jackson had arrested so many Unionists. The writer feared that women soon would become the targets of military arrests. When some of the Unionist prisoners returned to Winchester in late March, Minister Benjamin Brooke admitted, "It was wrong to take them in the first place."[20]

Jackson's men displayed brutal efficiency in rounding up Unionists. During three days in February, Sarah McKown reported that the Confederates had arrested five of her neighbors. One Federal soldier in Winchester wrote that "their is a good many Union people here and they have suffered much Jackson took with him all he could catch Irrespective of age or constitution." Indeed, Jackson had some problems with the large number of civilian prisoners he collected. "With regard to putting the female Tories in the Winchester jail," he wrote, "I think it would be impolitic, as the Lawyers have even annoyed me about my disloyal male prisoners."[21]

In the upper Valley many civilians fled from the prospect of impressment into military service. Augusta County resident Harvey Bear remembered that "some men from our neighborhood disgraced themselves and [their] families by running to the mountain, to avoid being drafted." Isaac N. Smith declined traveling to Richmond from the Valley because any man who appeared along the roads risked immediate arrest and transfer to the army. In early March a group of about seventy Dunkers and Mennonites attempting to escape through Confederate lines over the Shenandoah Mountains were seized and held in Richmond for about a month. Another group of eighteen religious objectors was captured in Pendleton County. In May a northern reporter noted a "continuous stream" of Unionists passing through Strasburg. These individuals feared the area would be abandoned to the Confederates and that Unionist men would be pressed into rebel service.[22]

Upper Valley residents dissatisfied with the prospect of being placed in military service threatened to become violent in Rockingham County. Members of the militia went into the mountains and determined not to leave their stronghold as long as impressment loomed. Jackson ordered Lt. Col. John R. Jones of the 33rd Virginia to subdue the "Rockingham Rebellion." Jones shelled the area near Swift Run Gap where many of the militiamen were hiding; twenty-four men surrendered, and one was killed. Jones remained in the region for some time, capturing at least fifty deserters.[23]

The arrest of loved ones had a great impact on Valley families. Following his detention of Charles Moore near Mount Jackson, Reuben Scott wrote, "I feel very sorry for his family they are so very much distressed for their father they wept bitterly when I sent for him as if he had been dead." When Union troops arrested Mr. Kendrick of Front Royal, Letitia Blakemore commented about the effect of the arrest on his family. Mrs. Kendrick was "inconsolable and the children grieve very much." The following day Mrs. Kendrick remained in bed all day, suffering "in both body & mind." The arrest of Unionist Charles S. Chase just before the Confederates evacuated Winchester angered his daughter Julia. She confided to her diary, "Oh, how indignant I felt towards the whole town. To take an old man lying sick on the Sofa is outrageous, but we will hope for the best, thou' we look upon it as a high handed piece of business."[24]

The threat of arrest or imprisonment and the destruction of property caused a great deal of movement among Valley civilians, who fled from a hostile army or sought protection from a friendly one. By early March many lower Valley residents realized that Jackson's tiny army would be no match for Nathaniel Banks's much larger force. They fled, initiating a stampede of refugees. Mapmaker Jedediah Hotchkiss observed part of this exodus as he headed down the Valley to meet Jackson. He recalled seeing "wagons of citizens loaded with furniture and carriages filled with families, many of them accompanied by servants, moving up from the Lower Valley." Among the most prominent refugees was Mildred Lee, one of Robert E. Lee's daughters, who had been attending Mr. and Mrs. Charles L. Powell's Female Seminary in Winchester. Belle Boyd, another famous refugee, left Martinsburg in the spring of 1862 to live in Front Royal. In Shepherdstown, on the Potomac, many Confederate sympathizers crossed to Maryland, with Baltimore, Hagerstown, and Frederick being the most popular destinations.[25]

The pattern of military operations in the Shenandoah Valley directly affected the refugee experience. Some civilians became involuntary refugees when one of the armies sealed off the towns they were visiting or in which they resided. In early May, Jackson stopped all traffic out of Staunton, stranding civilians who had come into town to visit relatives and friends in the rebel army. When the Confederates drove the Union army back to the Potomac in

May 1862, many Valley refugees followed them. In Shepherdstown the vanguard of the Union retreat called out, "Union friends and colored friends pack up! pack up!" One reporter observed that Williamsport and Hagerstown were "thronged with soldiers and refugees" after the Federal retreat. Laura Lee noticed that as the rebels passed back through Winchester on their retreat up the Valley in late May, "the numbers of fugitive citizens who returned so joyfully to their homes but a few days ago, have had to fly again." John G. Cockrell, who lived near Harpers Ferry, typified civilians whipsawed by the ebb and flow of military events. In the course of the Valley campaign, Cockrell sold flour to both armies and was first arrested by the Confederates and later by John W. Geary's Union soldiers. The pattern of flight and return that refugees began during the Valley campaign continued throughout the war.[26]

As General Banks's army advanced up the Valley, residents who chose to remain assumed unfamiliar roles. Most of the men in occupied areas exercised caution when dealing with Union authorities. They realized that they could be arrested if they were uncooperative. Mary Lee complained that the older men of Winchester were "too courteous" in their dealings with the Federal soldiers. However, many Valley women, aware that nineteenth-century gender assumptions would protect them from physical harm, boldly challenged the authority of the Federals. When the Union army occupied Harrisonburg, Rufus Meade noticed that while most of the men were gone, "the women and children have got the grit in them." Brig. Gen. Alpheus S. Williams was "much disgusted" with the female secessionists he encountered in the Valley. "It has been my endeavor to treat them all courteously and kindly," he commented, "but their manners, even under the gentlest language . . . are anything but maidenly or ladylike." After a visit to Winchester in April, Secretary of State William H. Seward characterized the town's women as "she devils." Jedediah Hotchkiss took heart that, despite the "iron rule" in Winchester, "our women there are not afraid of them [Union soldiers] and tell them freely what they think of their conduct." Mary Greenhow Lee boasted, "This is surely the day of women's power; the men are afraid to do, or say any thing, & leave all to us."[27]

As Mary Lee suggested, Valley women often held their own in clashes with the Federals. Anna Andrews feared that Shepherdstown would suffer because of its female inhabitants. She recalled, "They make low lived speeches to the soldiers & they have threatened the town for it—our refuge is under the well known proverb concerning 'barking dogs.'" In Winchester many women

"Refugees Returning," sketch by David Hunter Strother. The Valley campaign produced both Union and Confederate refugees. Strother noted the volume of displaced civilians near Martinsburg as Banks's army prepared to march south on June 3: "The road was alive with the fugitive population, now *en route* for home." *Harper's New Monthly Magazine*, May 1867, 723–24.

refused to walk under the American flag, which prompted the Union army to stretch large flags across streets or fly many of them at close intervals. Mary Magill told General Shields that if the Yankees killed all the men of the South, the women would fight them, and that when they were destroyed, the dogs would bark at them. One Winchester provost marshal found his hands full with Mrs. John Campbell, whom he arrested for "speaking her mind too freely." He soon dismissed the charge in order to be rid of her, as she had become "outrageously abusive" after her arrest. Samuel Miller Quincy of the 2nd Massachusetts asserted that the women of Edinburg were "perfect devils & swear like troopers." One of Quincy's comrades assaulted a townswoman after she spit in his face.[28]

The experience of Cornelia McDonald reveals the give-and-take that often occurred between strong secessionist women and Federal soldiers. One of McDonald's "weapons" in her battle against Federal authority was her use of gender assumptions to insult the Union invaders. When accompanying a soldier on a search of McDonald's home, Col. John S. Clark commented that the man seemed unused to such duty. McDonald disagreed and "complimented" the soldier on his skills. "I should think he had been long accustomed to examining ladies' and children's wardrobes," she interjected, "but if he feels unequal to the task, I will assist him." As the situation became more heated, she boasted that southerners would never be conquered by Union soldiers of Clark's caliber. Clark became quite angry but accepted the gender conventions of the time. "Should the fortunes of war place your husband in my hands, Madam," he icily replied, "you will wish you had used less intemperate language." At another time McDonald offended a soldier who had come up to her back door. When she asked the soldier what he wanted, he claimed to be a gentleman who wished only to look around. McDonald replied that she had misinterpreted his status because gentlemen usually did not come to the back door. The soldier, though angered, did not retaliate.[29]

Unlike this man, other soldiers who took exception to McDonald's behavior did retaliate. Laura Lee reported that some Federals beat and kicked Cornelia's son Harry in front of his mother because he claimed to be a secessionist. Col. Charles Candy played on McDonald's sympathy when he brutally punished a soldier whom Cornelia caught milking the family's cow. Cornelia observed the soldier riding a barrel—a common military punishment—and regretted causing his pain. She went to Colonel Candy and requested the soldier's release. She remembered the colonel's reaction: "I saw his eyes twinkle as if he enjoyed the fun of seeing me take it [the soldier's punishment] to heart." McDonald did not bother Colonel Candy with any complaints following this incident. Another soldier hurt McDonald by reading aloud some private notes in a mocking tone while searching her house. Cornelia recorded that the incident so enraged her that she could have shot the man.[30]

Perhaps more typical was Letitia Blakemore's experience with Union soldiers. Throughout early June, countless Union soldiers occupied "Riverside," the family home. Rather than exchanging heated barbs with the Yankees, Letitia worked relentlessly to keep her household functioning. She complained that the soldiers put her home in disarray, noting that "the dining room and passage are like a Barroom, but we bear with it as they are polite in their deportment." A few days earlier she had remarked, "This house is full. It keeps us all busy to wait on them[.] I am so tired I can scarcely go about the house."[31]

The increased boldness of Valley women marked a departure from antebellum gendered experiences. Mary Greenhow Lee noted that Winchester women began to pride themselves on their clever retorts to the Yankees. She experienced discomfort with this development, as the women became "so utterly fearless & indulge in such strong language, that I fear Billingsgate style will become habitual." In April she grew alarmed when her sister-in-law Laura "was heard to indulge in a little profanity to-day." Mary feared that the women of Winchester would "never be fit for refined society again." After learning of an exchange between Cornelia McDonald and some soldiers, Mary wondered, "Will we ever be gentle, refined ladies again, using mild terms & walking the street with pleasant, friendly countenances. Scorn & contempt are such habitual expressions, that I fear they will not readily give place to more lady-like ones." Kate Sperry expressed surprise at her own behavior when interacting with the Yankees. She took out her aggressions in cursing, noting that she had become "reckless—stonehearted and everything, hard and pitiless—never knew I was so revengeful." Long after the close of Jackson's 1862 campaign, Valley women struggled with military authority whenever Federal soldiers appeared in their midst.[32]

Because military events led to critical decisions for different members of Valley households in the spring of 1862, residents did their best to follow them, despite the scarcity of reliable information. Most African Americans knew that their widened scope of opportunity came as a result of Federal military success. Also realizing that Union reverses in the Valley could lead to the return of Confederate troops and a resumption of bondage, black people paid close attention to the military developments in their midst. On April 21, 1862, a rumor spread through Winchester that when Stonewall Jackson came back, free black people would be sold to compensate owners who lost their slaves. This rumor caused a general panic among Winchester's free black population. Later in the month African Americans in Harrisonburg revealed their understanding of the relationship between Union success and their own power when they became the only civilians in town who joined Federals in commemorating the fall of New Orleans. Toward the end of May many black people in Winchester took heed of a new rumor, passed along by Federal soldiers, that Jackson was murdering all African Americans as he advanced. "Numbers of them believe it," noted Laura Lee, "and are terrified beyond belief." As a result of the rumor, a large group of African Americans, including some always free and some recently escaped, fled the town.[33]

David Hunter Strother commented about the degree to which local secessionists pinned their hopes to the latest rumors of military action. "There is nothing too absurd for them to accept on the one side," he noted, "or too plain for them to reject on the other." When Strother informed a Winchester

"Jordan Is a Hard Road to Travel," a rather cruel sketch of black refugees by David Hunter Strother. Strother described fear among these refugees during the Union retreat northward from Winchester after the battle on May 25. "While the troops regarded them with no especial favor," he added in reference to Union soldiers' behavior toward the African Americans, "they gave them no wanton abuse that I observed." *Harper's New Monthly Magazine*, March 1867, 446.

woman that Gen. George B. McClellan had possession of Manassas, she exclaimed, "Good God! . . . Then Jackson is cut off!" At a Front Royal church service, "everyone seemed stupefied" by the news that Manassas and Winchester would be evacuated by the Confederates, discussing it in hushed whispers throughout the service. When the rumors favored the Confederate cause, civilians reacted accordingly. On March 22, with predictions of Jackson's return swirling around Winchester, Union soldier Oscar Rudd encountered many smiling ladies in the street. Rudd thought this strange, as he had always observed expressions of scorn from them in the past. In the days before the battle of Winchester, many town residents suspected that a Federal reverse lay ahead. A number of them began stocking up on supplies to distribute to the Confederates when they returned.[34]

Secessionist hopes became reality in May 1862 when Jackson's Confederates raced back down the Valley. Many African Americans joined Federals who retreated toward the Potomac River following the battle of First Winchester. David Hunter Strother, who accompanied the retreating body, termed the scene "pitiable and ludicrous." One weeping woman proclaimed, "O Lord, they will kill us. They will kill us." Wagons full of African Americans were pushed out of the road to make way for army equipment and cannons. Federal troops forced Sarah Lovett, her husband, mother, and eight children out of a wagon needed to haul artillery supplies at Martinsburg. The old grandmother and the very young children had to walk the remaining fifteen miles to the Potomac. Many black refugees made it to the river and beyond. Two weeks after the retreat, the *Chambersburg (Pa.) Times* reported that the roads from Virginia remained crowded with black refugees making their way northward. Some continued farther, but many remained in Chambersburg, where a number of houses were "crowded almost to suffocation" with contrabands.[35]

Although many white civilians hypothesized that slaves ran away because Yankees told them tall tales about being killed by Stonewall Jackson, events in the wake of the Confederate sweep down the Valley proved that the contrabands had good reason to flee. As they struggled to keep up with the retreating Federals, some fell behind and were overtaken by the Confederates. One rebel soldier encountered several black refugees with bundles of personal items. "They had evidently started for the land of sweet freedom and glorious ease," wrote George Neese, "but had cut loose from home a 'leetle' too late to make a success of it." The Confederates started a "whole caravan" of contrabands back to Winchester, there to be reunited with their owners. Mary Lee noted a few days after the battle at Winchester that the town's slaves were coming back. Some did so voluntarily, and others were returned to their owners by the Confederate cavalry. Still others languished in the jails of Charlestown and Martinsburg. Jacob Lemley, a musician with the 48th Virginia, returned from a brief furlough on May 27. He observed that the Confederates were "still bringing in prisoners. White and black ones."[36]

For a few days in the spring of 1862, home front and battlefront merged in the Shenandoah Valley. Living on a battlefield intensified the disruption of Valley households begun earlier in the campaign. Families faced not only the prospect of property loss or separation, but also the possibility of violent physical danger. A skirmish near Edinburg in April led to little damage to either army, but a misdirected artillery shell fell into a house near the Federal lines and destroyed the cookstove of a woman whose husband served with Jackson. As the armies faced off at Port Republic, civilians who had yet to experience a military campaign in their region fled their homes to the safety of the nearby woods. Those who remained endured harrowing experiences. Clara Strayer, the nineteen-year-old daughter of a prosperous farmer, recalled that a rifle shell passed near the corner of her home and another landed within two feet of an aged slave named Uncle Daniel. Thomas Ashby was caught traveling through town during the Confederate attack at Front Royal on May 23. As he ran toward his home, he recalled hearing artillery fire, "and I felt that each gunner was looking for me." During the same engagement, another Front Royal resident took advantage of the confusion for personal gain. Dr. Charles Eckhardt passed the courthouse in Front Royal and saw people plundering Yankee tents. The doctor entered a tent and took coffee, sugar, and blankets—and returned twice to secure more plunder. During the battle of Winchester, Cornelia Wilson recalled that bullets rattled on her roof "like hail."[37]

Many Valley civilians braved the physical dangers of the battlefield to aid their respective causes. Civilians, including women, took an active role in the fighting at Winchester on May 25. Members of the 21st Georgia felt grateful for the aid of a Winchester woman who hailed them as they approached a stone wall on the outskirts of town. She leaned out her window, waved a handkerchief, and pointed to the wall. The Georgians perceived the message she was trying to convey and fell to the ground just as a sheet of Federal musket fire erupted from behind the wall. Another secessionist lady led Confederates to nine Union prisoners, including four officers, she had locked in her parlor. Federal colonel Othneil De Forest of the 5th New York Cavalry also had reason to be thankful for the aid of Valley residents. When his unit tried to join General Banks in Winchester, a "German Unionist" guided him safely through some woods into the town. Later, when it grew too hot for the Federals in Winchester, another Unionist refugee led the regiment to a mountain road to Martinsburg.[38]

Some of Winchester's civilians took a more active role during the battle on May 25. Federal soldiers insisted that civilians, including women, fired on them from the town's doorways and windows. One Union officer claimed that as his men retreated through Winchester, ladies were "firing from the

A U.S. battery shooting over a building toward a Confederate rear guard in the Valley, a sketch by Edwin Forbes that suggests the danger artillery fire posed to civilians and their property. *Frank Leslie's Illustrated Newspaper*, June 28, 1862.

houses, throwing hand-grenades, hot water, and missiles of every description." A correspondent of the *Philadelphia Press* reported that during the retreat a soldier who was wounded in the foot stopped to rest on the steps of a house. A woman came out of the house and asked if he could walk. He replied in the negative, whereupon the woman asked to see his revolver. The man innocently gave her the pistol, and she held it to his head, demanding that he leave her steps. After he had limped out into the street, the woman allegedly killed him. Unionist Julia Chase remarked that the civilians in Winchester "have become demons almost." Some civilians did not escape unscathed. One woman yelled to a retreating officer, "You can insult women, but you can't stand before our men." The officer struck her in the face with the flat of his sword as he went by. Cpl. George C. Peoples of the 46th Pennsylvania and Jim Kearyon of the 27th Indiana testified that they fired at armed civilians in the houses of Winchester.[39]

In the aftermath of battle, civilians struggled to cope with the dead and wounded. The prospect of a loved one's death in combat added to their burdens. Many of the soldiers campaigning in the Valley hailed from the region, which tinged news of Jackson's victories with sadness for Confederate civilians. Cornelia McDonald recalled that most residents reacted cheerfully to news of military success, "but no good news . . . served for a moment to drive from the faces of the older people whose sons were in the army, the look of anxious care; and constant anticipation of evil gave them a sad and weary expression that was painful to see." After the battle of Kernstown, a northern reporter observed, "Scarcely a family in the town [Winchester] but has one or more relatives in Jackson's army, and there is scarcely a family in the county but will have to bemoan the loss of some friend." After the battle of McDowell, Jedediah Hotchkiss encountered many civilians heading to the battlefield to look after friends and relatives who had fought there. The experience of Fannie L. Barton exemplifies the threat to Valley households. She had four sons, four brothers, one son-in-law, and two neighbors serving in the Stonewall Brigade at the battle of Kernstown.[40]

Many Valley households focused on caring for the campaign's casualties. After the Confederate victory at McDowell, for example, Jacob Hildebrand ventured to the battlefield to look after his son, who was serving in the 52nd Virginia. He was glad that he made the trip, "though I seen sorrowfull sights among the woundet." On the evening of the battle of Kernstown, Cornelia McDonald observed that wounded soldiers filled the courthouse, the vacant banks, and even the churches. Mary Greenhow Lee, who assisted in one of the Winchester hospitals after the battle, recalled that the "dead, the dying, the raving maniac, & agonising suffering, in its most revolting forms, were before us." General Banks still found houses full of the wounded twenty-six miles south of Kernstown. While they cared for the wounded, the women and the mayor of Winchester buried the Confederate soldiers killed at Kernstown. Jed Hotchkiss claimed that after the battle of Winchester, women kept busy putting out fires, caring for the wounded, and burying the dead. Civilians at the Lynnwood home in Port Republic returned after the battle to find dozens of wounded soldiers in the main house "lying on the floor amidst pools of blood."[41]

The fruits of Confederate victory comforted many who faced the horrors of the battlefield and its aftermath, but the secessionist joy at deliverance from the Federal army proved short lived. By May 31 Jackson had withdrawn from the lower Valley. J. William Thomas, a member of the Confederate rear guard, noted that as the troops passed through Charlestown, "many làdies were in tears and the men serious." John Peyton Clark observed that in the week before the Confederates retreated, "agitation between the joy of being with our friends and the fear of being again within the power of our enemies has prevailed with all our citizens." By June 4 the Yankees had returned to

"Bel Air" in Front Royal, home of William Mason Buck, whose nineteen-year-old daughter Lucy Rebecca commented in her diary about the Valley campaign's impact on civilians. Warren Heritage Society, Front Royal, Virginia.

Winchester. General Banks ordered a search of the town for the supplies that the Yankees had abandoned two weeks earlier. In Front Royal, General Kimball returned to camp on the grounds of Bel Air, where his troops again destroyed fences, some recently repaired from their first visit. As the Valley campaign wore down, Laura Lee tired of its erratic pace. She had heard a rumor that Confederates would be back soon to liberate Winchester, but she wished for their return only if they could stay. She feared that the Federal occupation would become more odious with each successive occupation. A northern friend wrote to Carrie Bedinger of Shepherdstown, "Seriously we feel uneasy about you in these troublous times—placed as you are in the very midst of the war track."[42]

How much destruction did civilians suffer in the course of the Valley campaign? It is impossible to offer a precise monetary figure, but white civilians obviously paid a terrific financial and emotional price during the four months. A few examples will suggest the level of loss. Andrew J. Baugher of Cross Keys suffered looting on his farm after the battle. He lost 18 hogs, 15 sheep, 4 cows, 25 bushels of corn, 1 wagon, 1 1/2 barrels of flour, 25 gallons of molasses, 200 pounds of bacon, and 75 pounds of dried beef. John Strayer of New Market lost between $20,000 and $25,000 in property during the campaign. In the vicinity of Port Republic a Virginia journalist visited forty-nine households. Of these, twenty had suffered damage in excess of $1,000. At the end of May, Marcus B. Buck of Front Royal wrote, "Terrible waste and destruction of property around town. Hope for the future is gone." The comment of a Federal provost at Winchester applied to many residents of the Valley after the campaign: "Everything profitable taken and everything expensive left." The *Rockingham Register* asserted that the activity in the Valley had made it literally the "dark and bloody ground" of the conflict. African Americans also paid an emotional cost. In the early part of the campaign, many took the initiative to flee to Union lines for their freedom. After a few months, most either had moved far north in front of Jackson's advancing soldiers or had been caught and returned to slavery. Many of the African American families separated by the military events of the Valley campaign remained so until the end of the war.[43]

The campaign also hampered the short-term productivity of Valley households. Farmers faced labor shortages (of both free and unfree labor) and suffered from military impressment of wagons and horses. In April, General Banks asserted that there were not more than 300 serviceable horses remaining between Harpers Ferry and Woodstock. Despite this lack of horseflesh, Banks admitted that his troops had "pressed many and foraged very heavily, giving receipts for property taken." Banks's discussion of the forage situation in Clarke County in April 1862 would apply to many areas of the Valley by the end of Jackson's campaign. He noted that Clarke had been "occupied by two armies, and is exhausted on the lines of the roads." One reporter stated that Union depredations were so extensive in the Valley that "the farmers have been unable to get in their usual crops of corn and oats, their horses being stolen and their slaves running at large." Another reported in April from Woodstock that the Valley "shows great neglect of agriculture."[44]

In July 1862, long after Stonewall Jackson's army had left the Valley, the *Rockingham Register* reported more optimistically about the summer crops. "It cheers our heart to see our farmers gathering the crop which the Yankees hoped and expected to reap," the editor remarked. The *Register* observed that farmers were especially busy due to the acute shortage of labor, but their harvest exceeded the usual yields, totaling enough to feed a Confederate army for another year.[45]

The Shenandoah campaign produced a Confederate strategic victory but a more ambiguous result for the Valley's civilians. The presence of armies commanded by Jackson and his Federal opponents contributed to the disintegration of innumerable Valley households, a process that continued throughout the war. Slaves would exploit opportunities to weaken the "peculiar institution," citizens would pin their hopes on one of the opposing armies while fearing the loss of property and the arrest of family members, and women would continue to adapt to untraditional roles. Over the next two summers, Valley farmers would harvest their crops in the wake of contending armies. Much of the destruction and uncertainty that plagued the area in 1862 would return with a vengeance in 1864, when Union general Philip H. Sheridan carried out a more purposeful and systematic assault on the Valley's economy. Only in the spring of 1865 would the Valley's civilians be liberated from the effects of war they had first experienced during Jackson's campaign three years earlier.

ACKNOWLEDGMENTS

The author would like to thank Thavolia Glymph, John L. Heatwole, Gary Ecelbarger, and Ben Ritter for their assistance with earlier drafts of this essay.

NOTES

1. Jacob R. Hildebrand, *A Mennonite Journal, 1862–1865: A Father's Account of the Civil War in the Shenandoah Valley*, ed. John R. Hildebrand (Shippensburg, Pa.: Burd Street Press, 1996), 5–6.

2. Robert G. Tanner, *Stonewall in the Valley: Thomas J. "Stonewall" Jackson's Shenandoah Valley Campaign, Spring 1862* (Garden City, N.Y.: Doubleday, 1976; rev. ed., Mechanicsburg, Pa.: Stackpole, 1996), 34–37; William Couper, *History of the Shenandoah Valley*, 3 vols. (New York: Lewis Historical Publishing, 1952), 2:872; Thomas J. Jackson to A. R. Boteler, March 3, 1862, in Henry Kyd Douglas, *I Rode with Stonewall* (1940; reprint, St. Simons Island, Ga.: Mockingbird Books, 1974), 38. All town names have been modernized.

3. Statistics compiled from Joseph C. G. Kennedy, *Agriculture of the United States in 1860 Compiled from the Original Returns of the Eighth Census* (Washington, D.C.: GPO, 1864).

4. For a brief but effective synopsis of the final stage of the 1862 Valley campaign, see Robert K. Krick, *Conquering the Valley: Stonewall Jackson at Port Republic* (New York: Morrow, 1996), 2–17. The best modern treatment of that entire operation is Tanner, *Stonewall in the Valley*.

5. Editors of Time-Life Books, *Voices of the Civil War: Shenandoah 1862* ([Alexandria, Va.]: Time-Life Books, [1997]), 30–31, 38; Anna Maria Henkel diary, June 7, 1862, Special Collections, James Madison University, Harrisonburg, Va. (repository hereafter cited as JMU).

6. James Power Smith, "With Stonewall Jackson in the Army of Northern Virginia," in *Southern Historical Society Papers*, ed. J. William Jones and others, 52 vols. (1876–1959; reprint, with 3-vol. index, Wilmington, N.C.: Broadfoot, 1990–92), 43:22; John O. Casler, *Four Years in the Stonewall Brigade* (1893; reprint, Dayton, Ohio: Morningside, 1971), 78–80; Margaretta Barton Colt, *Defend the Valley: A Shenandoah Family in the Civil War* (New York: Orion, 1994), 186; Tanner, *Stonewall in the Valley*, 326.

7. Editors of Time-Life Books, *Shenandoah 1862*, 30–31, 38, 143; Laura Lee diary, April 17–18, 1862, photocopy in Ben Ritter Collection, Handley Regional Library, Winchester, Va. (repository hereafter cited as HL) (original located at Swem Memorial Library, College of William and Mary, Williamsburg, Va.); Peter Svenson, *Battlefield: Farming a Civil War Battleground* (Boston: Faber and Faber, 1992), 164.

8. Cornelia Peake McDonald, *A Woman's Civil War: A Diary, with Reminiscences of the War, from March 1862*, ed. Minrose C. Gwin (Madison: University of Wisconsin Press, 1992), 44; Lucy Rebecca Buck, *Sad Earth, Sweet Heaven: The Diary of Lucy Rebecca Buck during the War between the States*, ed. Dr. William P. Buck (Birmingham, Ala.: Cornerstone, 1973), 65–66; Marcus Blakemore Buck diary, June 16, 1862, Warren Heritage Society, Front Royal, Va. (repository hereafter cited as WHS).

9. Statistics compiled from Kennedy, *Agriculture of the United States in 1860*. The planter with 100 slaves most likely was George H. Burwell of Clarke County, who is listed as owning 97 slaves in the 1860 manuscript slave census of Clarke County.

10. Annie P. Marmion, *Under Fire: An Experience in the Civil War*, ed. William Vincent Marmion Jr. (n.p., 1959), 9; David Hunter Strother [Porte Crayon, pseud.], *A Virginia Yankee in the Civil War: The Diaries of David Hunter Strother*, ed. Cecil D. Eby Jr. (Chapel Hill: University of North Carolina Press, 1961), 10; *Baltimore Sun*, March 4, 1862; Buck diary, April 5, 1862.

11. Charles Candy to Col. Lewis, n.d., Colonel W. D. Lewis Papers, HL; *Baltimore Sun*, March 4, 1862.

12. Charles Aglionby claim, Southern Claims Commission, M1407, fiche 1517, no. 14627, RG 233, National Archives, Washington, D.C. (repository hereafter cited as NA); Jefferson County slave census, 1860; Charles Aglionby daybook, March 10, 13, 24, April 14, 24, 1862, typescript, Harpers Ferry National Park, Harpers Ferry, W.Va. (repository hereafter cited as HFNP). Regarding the final incident mentioned in the text, Aglionby

notes, "retaken and brought back." It is unclear whether he is referring to the equipment, the slaves, or both.

13. Information in the preceding two paragraphs comes from the sources listed in n. 12. The Laura Lee quotation is from Laura Lee diary, April 23, 1862.

14. Laura Lee diary, April 14, 1862; Buck diary, May 22, 1862; Mary Greenhow Lee diary, May 18, 1862, HL; Anna (Robinson) Andrews to My dear Sister, April 27, 1862, Charles Wesley Andrews Papers, William R. Perkins Library, Duke University, Durham, N.C. (repository hereafter cited as DU); *Richmond Enquirer*, June 9, 1862.

15. William D. Wintz, ed., *Civil War Memoirs of Two Rebel Sisters* (St. Albans, W.Va.: William D. Wintz, 1989), 33; Buck, *Sad Earth, Sweet Heaven*, 59, 81; John Peyton Clark journal, March 15, 1862, HL.

16. Clark journal, April 10, 1862; Kate Sperry diary, April 6, 1862, HL; *Richmond (Daily) Whig*, June 2, 1862; Henkel diary, May 6, 1862.

17. Laura Lee diary, March 13, 22, 1862; Anna (Robinson) Andrews to My dear Sister, April 27, 1862.

18. Laura Lee diary, April 24, 1862; Sperry diary, March 20, 1862; Susan Nourse Riddle diary, May 25, 1862, quoted in Mabel Henshaw Gardiner and Ann Henshaw Gardiner, *Chronicles of Old Berkeley: A Narrative History of a Virginia County from Its Beginnings to 1926* (Durham, N.C.: Seeman Press, 1938), 159.

19. U.S. War Department, *The War of the Rebellion: A Compilation of the Official Records of the Union and Confederate Armies*, 127 vols., index, and atlas (Washington, D.C.: GPO, 1880–1901), ser. 4, 1:1094–97 (hereafter cited as *OR*; all references are to ser. 1 unless otherwise noted); *Baltimore American*, April 10, 1862; *Baltimore Sun*, April 28, 1862. For treatments of Unionism in the Valley, see Daniel W. Crofts, *Reluctant Confederates: Upper South Unionists in the Secession Crisis* (Chapel Hill: University of North Carolina Press, 1988), 140–42; Henry T. Shanks, *The Secession Movement in Virginia, 1847–1861* (1934; reprint, New York: AMS Press, 1971), 157–213. The classic work on Confederate conscription is Albert Burton Moore, *Conscription and Conflict in the Confederacy* (New York: Macmillan, 1924). For the arrest of religious pacifists during the Valley campaign, see Samuel Horst, *Mennonites in the Confederacy: A Study in Civil War Pacifism* (Scottsdale, Pa.: Herald Press, 1967), 50–52, 56, 58; *OR*, ser. 2, 3:835.

20. Treadwell Smith diary, April 7–9, 1862, HL; William C. McDowell to W. D. Lewis, April 9, 1862, Lewis Papers; John W. Wayland, *A History of Shenandoah County, Virginia* (1927; reprint, Baltimore: Regional Publishing, 1980), 299; letter of "Justice," June 7, 1862, in *Richmond Daily Enquirer*, June 12, 1862; Benjamin F. Brooke journal, March 28, 1862, HL.

21. Sarah Morgan McKown diary, February 16, 19, 20, 1862, Thorton Tayloe Perry Collection, no. 17, Mrs. Sarah Morgon (Groff) Papers, Mss1G658a, Virginia Historical Society, Richmond; Ralph Haas, *Dear Esther: The Civil War Letters of Private Aungier Dobbs*, ed. Philip Ensley (Apollo, Pa.: Closson Press, 1991), 71; Thomas J. Jackson to D. H. Hill,

February 16, 1862, quoted in James I. Robertson Jr., *Stonewall Jackson: The Man, the Soldier, the Legend* (New York: Macmillan, 1997), 327.

22. Buck diary, March 10, 1862; Harvey Bear diary, March 15, 1862, in "The Valley of the Shadow: Two Communities in the American Civil War," ⟨http://etext.lib.virginia.edu/etcbin/toccer-valley?id=AD1003&tag=parsed&images=images/modeng&data=/texts/english/civilwar/diaries&part=0⟩; Isaac N. Smith to Col. C. Q. Hopkins, May 5, 1862, in ibid., ⟨http://etext.lib.virginia.edu/etcbin/civwarlett-browse?id=A0111⟩.

23. Lowell Ridenbaugh, *Jackson's Valley Campaign: The Battle of Kernstown* (Lynchburg, Va.: H. E. Howard, 1996), 112–13.

24. R. A. Scott to Dear Mollie, February 1, 1862, Margaret B. Burruss Collection, JMU; Letitia Blakemore diary, March 25–26, 1862, WHS; Julia Chase diary, March 11, 1862, HL.

25. Jedediah Hotchkiss, *Make Me a Map of the Valley: The Civil War Journal of Stonewall Jackson's Topographer*, ed. Archie P. McDonald (1973; reprint, Dallas: Southern Methodist University Press, 1989), 4; Roger U. Delauter Jr., *Winchester in the Civil War* (Lynchburg, Va.: H. E. Howard, 1992), 19; Edward H. Phillips, *The Lower Shenandoah Valley in the Civil War: The Impact of War upon the Civilian Population and upon Civil Institutions* (Lynchburg, Va.: H. E. Howard, 1993), 63; Belle Boyd, *Belle Boyd in Camp and Prison* (1865; reprint, Baton Rouge: Louisiana State University Press, 1998), 92.

26. Champ Clark and the Editors of Time-Life Books, *Decoying the Yanks: Jackson's Valley Campaign* (Alexandria, Va.: Time-Life Books, 1984), 101; C. to My dearest Mother, June 12, 1862, Carrie Bedinger letterbook, Bedinger-Dandridge Family Papers, DU; Frank Moore, ed., *The Rebellion Record: A Diary of American Events*, 11 vols. (New York: G. P. Putnam, 1861–1868), 5:64; Laura Lee diary, May 31, 1862; John G. Cockrell claim, Southern Claims Commission, M1407, fiche 1019, RG 233, NA.

27. Mary Greenhow Lee diary, March 13, 1862; Rufus Meade to Dear Friends at Home, April 30, 1862, Rufus Meade Jr. Papers, Library of Congress, Washington, D.C. (repository hereafter cited as LC); Alpheus S. Williams, *From the Cannon's Mouth*, ed. Milo M. Quaife (1959; reprint, Lincoln: University of Nebraska Press, 1995), 91 n. 12; Laura Lee diary, April 7–8, 1862; Hotchkiss, *Make Me a Map*, 31; Mary Greenhow Lee diary, April 1, 1862.

28. Anna (Robinson) Andrews to My dear Sister, April 27, 1862, Andrews Papers; Mary Kate McVicar, "Echoes of the War," 1, Ritter Collection; Mary Greenhow Lee diary, March 16, 1862; Laura Lee diary, May 10–16, 1862; Samuel Quincy Miller to Dear mother, April 13, 1862, Quincy-Wendell-Upham-Holmes Families Papers, LC.

29. McDonald, *Woman's Civil War*, 31, 57. Federal soldiers searching a house in Shepherdstown made a gender-based threat similar to Colonel Clark's. They told Virginia Bedinger that they would like to cut her brother's throat; her brother served in the Confederate army. See [Virginia Bedinger] to My dearest Ma, April 4, 1862, Bedinger-Dandridge Family Papers.

30. Laura Lee diary, April 24, 1862; McDonald, *Woman's Civil War*, 29–30. One must attempt to put the rage of secessionist women in proper perspective. For the most part, Federal soldiers acted with great restraint toward civilians. See Mark Grimsley, *The Hard Hand of War: Union Military Policy toward Southern Civilians, 1861–1865* (New York: Cambridge University Press, 1995), esp. chaps. 1–2. Grimsley used Cornelia McDonald's fury toward the Yankees as an example of how hard it was to conciliate a Confederate civilian; see *Hard Hand of War*, 48.

31. Blakemore diary, May 31, June 2, 1862.

32. Mary Greenhow Lee diary, March 17, April 3, 23, 1862; Sperry diary, March 31, 1862. For a discussion of antebellum expectations of women, see George C. Rable, *Civil Wars: Women and the Crisis of Southern Nationalism* (Champaign-Urbana: University of Illinois Press, 1991), chap. 1.

33. Mary Greenhow Lee diary, April 21, 1862; Rufus Meade to Dear Friends at Home, April 30, 1862, Meade Papers; Laura Lee diary, May 24, 1862.

34. Strother, *Virginia Yankee*, 11, 13; Buck, *Sad Earth, Sweet Heaven*, 33; Oscar Rudd diary selections, March 22, 1862, HL; Delauter, *Winchester in the Civil War*, 28.

35. Strother, *Virginia Yankee*, 43; A. Mercer Daniel, "The Lovetts of Harpers Ferry, West Virginia," *Negro History Bulletin*, 1971, HFD 552, HFNP; *Chambersburg Times*, quoted in *Baltimore Sun*, June 5, 1862.

36. George M. Neese, *Three Years in the Confederate Horse Artillery* (1911; reprint, Dayton, Ohio: Morningside, 1983), 61; Jacob Lemley diary, May 27, 1862, HL; Mary Greenhow Lee diary, June 3, 1862. For examples of the stories told by Federal soldiers to slaves, see Blakemore diary, May 26, 1862; McDonald, *Woman's Civil War*, 64.

37. Editors of Time-Life Books, *Shenandoah 1862*, 67, 142; Tanner, *Stonewall in the Valley*, 376; Thomas A. Ashby, *The Valley Campaigns: Being the Reminiscences of a Non-Combatant While Between the Lines in the Shenandoah Valley During the War of the States* (New York: Neale, 1914), 117; Dr. Charles Eckhardt diary, May 24, 1862, WHS; Cornelia Wilson to Dear Bro., July 22, 1862, typescript in the Ritter Collection (original in possession of George Rinsland, New Milford, Pa.).

38. Delauter, *Winchester in the Civil War*, 30; Laura Virginia Hale, *Four Valiant Years in the Lower Shenandoah Valley, 1861–1865* (Strasburg, Va.: Shenandoah Publishing, 1968), 155; *OR* 12(1):583.

39. *OR* 12(1):617; Moore, *Rebellion Record*, 5:49; Delauter, *Winchester in the Civil War*, 30; Chase diary, May 25, 1862; testimony of George C. Peoples and Jim Kearyon, RG 94, NA. There is considerable Federal testimony on the question of civilians firing on soldiers during the battle of Winchester. See *OR* 12:602, 608, 624–625, and Metzer Dutton to My Dear Mother, May 27, 1862, HL. For the few sources that dispute the Federal testimony, see Cornelia L. Wilson to Dear Bro. Martin, July 22, 1862, HL; Sperry diary, June 5, 1862; account of George A. Roelke, *Baltimore Sun*, June 3, 1862; account of "Nemo" (Kate McVicar), *Winchester Evening Star*, October 20, 1917.

40. McDonald, *Woman's Civil War*, 48; *Baltimore American*, March 31, 1862; Jedediah Hotchkiss diary extract, May 10, 1862, Hotchkiss Papers, roll 2, LC; Laura Lee diary, March 25, 1862.

41. Hildebrand, *Mennonite Journal*, 11; McDonald, *Woman's Civil War*, 37; Mary Greenhow Lee diary, March 25, 1862; Moore, *Rebellion Record*, 4:336; Hotchkiss, *Make Me a Map*, 12; Jedediah Hotchkiss, *Confederate Military History: Virginia* (Atlanta: Confederate Publishing, 1899), 245; Krick, *Conquering the Valley*, 482, 488.

42. Laura Lee diary, [May 31], June 9, 1862; J. William Thomas diary, May 31, 1862, Allan Tischler Collection, HL; Clark journal, June 2, 1862; *OR* 12:541; Buck, *Sad Earth, Sweet Heaven*, 90; M. L. Bogert to My Dear Carrie, June 4, 1862, Bedinger-Dandridge Family Papers.

43. Krick, *Conquering the Valley*, 302, 489; Editors of Time-Life Books, *Shenandoah 1862*, 142; *Rockingham Register*, May 30, June 20, 1862; Buck diary, May 31, 1862; Clark journal, May 9, 1862.

44. *OR* 12(3):61–62, 76–77; *Richmond Dispatch*, May 21, 1862; *Baltimore Sun*, April 4, 1862.

45. *Rockingham Register*, quoted in the *Richmond Enquirer*, July 14, 1862.

KEITH S. BOHANNON

Placed on the Pages of History in Letters of Blood

REPORTING ON AND REMEMBERING THE 12TH

GEORGIA INFANTRY IN THE 1862 VALLEY CAMPAIGN

May 9, 1862, was a day of anxious waiting for many people in Macon, Georgia. Citizens read a notice that morning in the *Macon Telegraph* about a "skirmish in the mountains of Virginia" in which Confederate brigadier general Edward "Alleghany" Johnson had been wounded. Johnson's command included the 12th Georgia Volunteer Infantry Regiment, which had a company of men from Macon, but the newspaper said nothing about losses in that unit.

In a prayer meeting held that morning in Macon's Christ Episcopal Church, someone read a telegram stating that a battle had been fought the preceding day at McDowell, Virginia. The southern forces claimed it a victory, but the 12th Georgia Infantry had been "cut to pieces." Georgia Conner, the twenty-one-year-old daughter of Col. Zephaniah Turner Conner of the 12th, became distraught over his safety. After creating "quite a scene" in church, Georgia went home to tell her twin sister, Virginia, the news. Later that day the frightened Conner family learned that Colonel Conner's name was not on the list of the Macon men killed or wounded at McDowell. "I do not know how to be thankful enough for Pa's protection," wrote Virginia Conner in her journal; "God's mercy spared him to us." Everyone thought his regiment had "fought nobly," she continued, although no one knew any particulars of the fight.[1]

Southern civilians with relatives and loved ones serving in the Confederate army obviously placed enormous importance on the timely reporting of battlefield news. Private telegrams and brief newspaper reports were usually the first means by which civilians learned about battles, followed later by personal letters from soldiers. Although the Confederate government never officially censored the southern press, patriotic newspaper editors and soldier correspondents often practiced self-censorship when reporting events, being aware of the enormous impact they had on public morale.

The efforts of Georgia newspaper editors, soldier correspondents, and civilian contributors to recount and memorialize the role of the 12th Georgia Infantry in the 1862 Shenandoah Valley campaign provide an illustration of how the Confederate press helped sustain morale on the home front. Such reporting often involved the public suppression of news that reflected poorly on the reputation of a renowned organization such as the 12th Georgia. Aged veterans of the 12th, like most other former Confederate and Federal soldiers, engaged in a similarly selective process in the decades after the Civil War, ignoring embarrassing episodes when recording the service of their regiment for posterity.[2]

The 12th Georgia Infantry was organized in Richmond, Virginia, in early June 1861 from ten companies raised primarily in counties of the lower eastern Piedmont and central cotton-belt regions of Georgia. These counties produced some of largest cotton yields in the state in 1860, and in at least half of them slaves comprised the majority of the population. The planters' sons and small farmers who joined the 12th Georgia, noted contemporary observers, were the "flower of the young manhood" in their neighborhoods.[3]

Fortunately for the eager volunteers, the 12th Georgia had a fine cadre of field and company-grade officers with antebellum military experience or education. Col. Edward Johnson was a West Point graduate, a veteran of the Florida and Mexican Wars, and a career army officer. Zephaniah Turner Conner, the regiment's first lieutenant colonel, was a longtime member of an antebellum volunteer company known as the Macon Volunteers and had served in that unit as a first lieutenant during the Second Seminole War. Maj. Abner Smead was a West Point alumnus and career U.S. Army officer, and Adj. Edward Shackelford Willis had been at West Point before he resigned to join the Provisional Army of the Confederate States. Several of the company-

Pvt. George C. Smith, Company C, 12th Georgia Infantry. Courtesy George M. Smith.

grade officers had served in the Mexican War or in the 1850s attended the Georgia Military Institute, a school whose curriculum and academic rigor mirrored that of West Point.[4]

A month after it was organized, the 12th Georgia left Richmond for the mountains of western Virginia. There the regiment spent the next ten months and participated in two minor engagements, at Greenbrier River and Alleghany Mountain in October and December 1861. Both battles were Confederate victories and helped lay the foundation for the 12th's reputation as a fighting regiment. During the winter of 1861–62 the Georgians suffered in the frigid confines of Camp Bartow and Camp Alleghany on the crest of Alleghany Mountain, losing dozens of men to disease and exposure.[5]

The December 1861 promotion of Colonel Johnson to the rank of brigadier general for the victory at Alleghany Mountain prompted rumors in the 12th about the identity of his successor. On January 2, 1862, two days after the men heard of Johnson's promotion, Pvt. James W. Atkins wrote in his diary that Lieutenant Colonel Conner "was greatly exercised at the idea now prevolent in camp that he may be passed over" for the colonelcy. Five days later the *Lynchburg Republican* announced that Capt. James Deshler, an artillery officer acting on Edward Johnson's staff, had been appointed colonel of the 12th Georgia. Rumors continued circulating for several days, but on January 27 Capt. Shepherd Green Pryor wrote home that Conner had received confirmation of his promotion. Pryor further noted that most of the men, including himself, were pleased at the appointment.[6]

Pryor may have been pleased at Conner's promotion, but other company-grade officers in the 12th were not and might have tried to stop it. According to a 12th Georgia enlisted man who visited the Conner family in Macon on March 6, 1862, Capts. James Gustavus Rodgers, William Lowther Furlow, Mark Harden Blandford, and Willis Alston Hawkins were all "striving to raise themselves" and acted "in an unprincipled manner" toward Conner. When Captain Hawkins visited the Conner residence several days later, he claimed that the colonel "had been thrown overboard at Richmond" and someone else had been given the office. Virginia Conner wrote in her diary that her father, who was home on leave, did not believe the news, but it still troubled him. She further noted that despite unkind treatment her father had received "at the hands of President Davis, Genl Johnson, [and] Capts. Hawkins, Furlow and Blandford," he did "not seem to cherish enmity towards them."

By the time Z. T. Conner left Macon on April 6 to return to Virginia, he undoubtedly knew of the March 25, 1862, confirmation of his promotion to the colonelcy of the 12th Georgia, to take rank from December 13, 1861.[7]

The 12th Georgia's tenure at Camp Alleghany ended in the first week of April 1862, when the regiment marched eastward with the balance of Gen. Edward Johnson's small Army of the Northwest through Monterey and McDowell to a position on Shenandoah Mountain. On April 19–20 Johnson again moved eastward in an effort to protect his lines of retreat, halting seven miles west of Staunton at West View. There on May 6 Johnson's force united with the army of Maj. Gen. Thomas J. "Stonewall" Jackson. Jackson hoped that the combined force could turn westward to strike a blow at the advance elements of a Union command under Maj. Gen. John C. Frémont, then march back into the Shenandoah Valley to face another Federal army under Maj. Gen. Nathaniel P. Banks. Because of Edward Johnson's familiarity with the mountainous region, his two brigades led the Confederate advance against Frémont.[8]

On May 7 Johnson's men marched westward on the Staunton and Parkersburg Turnpike, seizing some hastily abandoned Federal camps on Shenandoah Mountain and ending the day camped on Shaw's Fork. Early the next morning Johnson's men resumed the march, eventually moving up Bull Pasture Mountain. When the head of the column reached the top of Bull Pasture, Johnson and a reconnoitering party moved southwestward off the turnpike and ascended a steep rocky ravine. They eventually reached the open crest of Sitlington's Hill, an isolated spur of Bull Pasture Mountain that offered a commanding view of the Union forces in and around the town of McDowell to the west. Jackson ordered Johnson to secure Sitlington's Hill, and several regiments, including the 12th Georgia, began toiling up the ravine. When the 500 Georgians halted, Jackson rode by rapidly with his cap in hand, receiving cheer after cheer as he passed along the lines.[9]

The 12th was the second Confederate regiment to reach the top of Sitlington's. There the Georgians received orders to lie down on their arms in an old field filled with small bushes to await the progress of events. For the next half-hour the regiment endured sporadic Union artillery fire, which strained the men's nerves and resulted in several close brushes with death. In Company A, Sgt. Charles S. Darley was "blown up by a bomb," being "considerably stunned but not injured." Pvt. Henry Thomas Davenport in the same company wrote home how he and Thomas J. Stewart "were laying side by side with our heads towards the enemy, when a bomb fell in six feet of our heads & bursted," harming no one.[10]

Soon the cry went up: "To arms, the enemy is advancing!" Instantly the Georgians sprang to their feet and marched in column toward a "large hilly old field" on a spur of Sitlington's Hill, described by one of the 12th as "a small knoll between two large hills, running to a point as it approached" McDowell. As the Georgians neared the position, they saw Federals clambering toward them up the wooded slopes. Each company of the 12th "wheeled into position," wrote Capt. James G. Rodgers, "and opened fire and received that of the enemy in return."

The curvature of the open ground resulted in the 12th Georgia deploying into a V-shaped formation in the center of the Confederate line. This position exposed the two wings of the 12th to enemy fire from several directions at once. One Georgian told his father that during most of the engagement the regiment endured a cross fire, "the fire from both columns of the enemy converging at the angle occupied by us." Pvt. Henry T. Davenport claimed that two enemy regiments "fired on the rear of our reg. obliquely, while the other division fired on our front. I can't see how we escaped."[11]

To make matters worse for the Georgians, many if not all of them carried antiquated .69-caliber smoothbore muskets with a maximum range of no more than 100 yards. Several accounts mention that while the 12th's left wing engaged the enemy, the regiment's right wing stood under fire from one to two and a half hours before being able to respond. The men in the 12th's right wing held their fire, noted a Virginian who fought nearby, because "the Yankee scoundrels would not advance near enough" for the Georgians to bring their guns to bear on them. Clearly many of the Federals fired at their opponents with rifle-muskets from several hundred yards downslope and out of the range of the 12th's guns. When the Georgians finally responded, they succumbed to the tendency of troops aiming downslope to fire too high.[12]

After fighting for roughly an hour, Company H of the 12th suffered its first casualty when a minié ball pierced the head of Orderly Sgt. Asa Ernest Sherwood. His comrades immediately began shouting to "avenge his death," and it was with difficulty that their captain could keep some of them from "rushing madly at the foe." Such scenes were commonplace during the regiment's four-hour fight.

KEITH S. BOHANNON

Pvt. Henry T. Davenport, Company A, 12th Georgia Infantry. Hargrett Rare Book and Manuscript Library, University of Georgia, Athens.

While men in the Virginia regiments adjacent to the 12th fell back several paces after firing and lay down to load their weapons, the Georgians refused to do so. "Having been advanced . . . in front of the crest of the hill where their lines showed to their enemies from beneath, in bold relief," wrote Jackson's staff officer the Reverend Robert L. Dabney, the Georgians "could not be persuaded to retire to the reverse of the ridge." When the 12th's commanding officer passed along the ranks amid the roar of musketry fire and persuaded one wing of the regiment to withdraw, "they rushed again to the front while he was gone to expostulate the other."[13]

Alleghany Johnson inspired the men of his original regiment throughout much of the engagement. Known as "Old Blucher," after the Prussian field marshal of that name, Johnson's entry onto the field elicited joyful shouts from the Georgians. Johnson told the men that he considered the 12th "the crack Regiment of the Confederate Army" and pointed out the heroism of its field officers, including Colonel Conner, the acting brigade commander; Maj. Willis A. Hawkins; and Capt. John McMillan, acting major commanding the regiment's left wing. After having a horse shot from under him, Johnson received a wound in the ankle around dusk. While being carried from the field, the general proclaimed that "if he had four such regiments as the 12th Georgia, he would go on that night and take the last one of them."[14]

The Confederate line became silhouetted against the evening sky as the sun settled, affording "an excellent mark" for the Federals. Shortly after proclaiming that "the boys fight nobly!" and giving a loud cheer for Jefferson Davis, the 12th's Lt. William A. Massey fell shot through the side. Turning to his captain, the mortally wounded Massey proclaimed, "I am willing to die, for it is in a righteous cause." Lt. James Allen Etheridge of Company G, becoming "enraged at the slaughter of his men," seized a musket and began firing at the enemy. Soon Etheridge noticed "a yankee with murderous intent, seeking to form his particular acquaintance." Simultaneous discharges from the muskets of the lieutenant and the Yankee sent both men hurtling to the ground. Etheridge lay on the battlefield for several hours with a severe wound through the waist before he was taken away, but not before he checked on his Federal antagonist and found him dead.[15]

Firing continued on Sitlington's Hill after sundown, when several Virginia regiments moved up to reinforce the 12th Georgia. Soon the exhausted Georgians began running out of ammunition. Their company officers ordered them to lie down and if necessary hold the position with the bayonet. In Company H, Lt. Oliver F. Evans volunteered to find cartridges, a task his captain thought impossible to perform since "the enemy were cross firing from three points." Evans disappeared and returned an hour later, his hat filled with rounds. Each man eagerly took his allotment, noted Captain Rodgers, "as though they were so many diamonds." Numerous members of the 12th rejoined the fray, their firing guided by the flashes of the enemy's guns.

Around 9:00 P.M. the order passed along the Confederate lines to "cease firing," the Federals having withdrawn from the field.[16]

The 12th Georgia suffered a total of 182 casualties in four hours of fighting at McDowell, roughly 40 percent of the total Confederate losses in the engagement. The battle devastated the ranks of the 12th's company-grade officers; five captains and four lieutenants were killed or died within a few days after the battle. The 12th's earlier engagements paled in comparison with McDowell. Capt. Shep Pryor wrote his wife that "the 'Green Briar' I know, was a mere skirmish, compared with this bloody fight, and the boys say, that 'Alleghany' was a perfect child's play in comparison." The battleground, wrote a badly shaken Colonel Conner to his family, looked like a slaughter pen.[17]

Conner's men took pride in their bravery and sacrifice at McDowell and expressed their sentiments in letters that often appeared in hometown newspapers. "Our regiment bore the brunt of the action," wrote one, "and Gen. Johnson says none could have done better." Another noted that despite the Federal cross fire, the Georgians "stood like veterans, without flinching or quailing." Henry T. Davenport boasted to his father that "no reg. ever fought with more invincibility, or manifested more plainly a determination to conquer or die, than did the 12th Ga. on the evening of the 8th of May."[18]

Colonel Conner and Major Hawkins performed well at McDowell, receiving praise from their superior officers. General Johnson acknowledged the gallantry of the two officers in his official report of the engagement and introduced Conner to Stonewall Jackson after the battle as a regimental commander whose "skill & bravery could be implicitly relied upon." Jackson apparently agreed with Johnson. Ten days after McDowell, Colonel Conner had dinner with Stonewall and several of his staff members at a private home just outside the town of Bridgewater.[19]

Members of the 12th Georgia also lavished accolades on their regiment's field officers. Captain Pryor wrote his wife in a letter that appeared in their hometown newspaper that Conner "stood up bravely all the time" and Hawkins "conducted himself gallantly . . . leading and cheering the men to victory." Capt. James G. Rodgers, who only weeks earlier had apparently opposed Conner's promotion, said that the colonel "handled his troops with the skill of a veteran General" and had "proven himself to be among the best officers in the Confederate service." Henry T. Davenport told his father that Conner and Hawkins "proved themselves to be heroes," noting that the major "had two holes shot through the breast of his coat & one through the crown of his hat." A wounded member of the 12th in a Staunton hospital wrote home that the colonel and major "immortalized themselves. . . . Conner is certainly one of the bravest of men."[20]

The 12th's deeds also elicited tributes from editors of Georgia newspapers. "Through her chivalric sons," wrote the editor of the *Augusta Constitutionalist*, Georgia had "been placed on the page of history in letters of blood, most honorably shed." The *Macon Telegraph* published a long casualty list of "the fighting 12th," noting that "all hearts at home bleed in sympathy with this gallant and suffering corps, and the afflicted families and friends of the honored dead; but all feel that the regiment immortalized itself . . . and has set a glorious example to Georgia volunteers."[21]

The 12th's slain company-grade officers, all well-educated lawyers, planters, and leading citizens, drew the most attention in Georgia newspapers. Editors and friends filled columns with lengthy tributes and obituaries that included praise for the hometown "patriot martyrs" and vilification of the Yankee vandals. Such pieces not only honored the dead but also steeled soldiers and civilians for further sacrifice to the southern cause. Editor Joseph A. Turner of Eatonton, Georgia, mourned the death of fellow townsman Capt. Richard Tarpley Davis. A prominent lawyer who left a wife and three children, Davis had "possessed refined and cultivated belles-lettres tastes, and acquirements." Turner blamed the death of Davis on "the monster murderer in Washington, who is assassinating so many of our citizens in cold blood!" Resolutions passed by the Marshallville, Georgia, Masonic Lodge noted that the mother, relatives, and friends of Capt. John McMillan, a popular antebellum school principal, could draw consolation "in the reflection that he fell nobly battling for them and his beloved county."[22]

Some eulogists memorialized the dead in mawkish and awkward verse, expressing sentiments similar to those found in prose tributes. In a poem titled "Capt. Samuel Dawson" that appeared in the *Sumter Republican*, the writer extolled the martial prowess of Dawson and his company:

> Loud were the shouts, in Yankee land,
> When dauntless Dawson fell
> Keen was their fear of his command,
> How dreaded, none can tell.

The poet, who identified himself only by the name "Senex" ("old man" in Latin), also compared the fallen officer to the Revolutionary War partisan hero Francis Marion, claiming that Dawson "punish'd Yankee crimes, / And broke up half their plans."[23]

Another of the 12th's slain company commanders was Capt. William L. Furlow, a wealthy twenty-six-year-old planter. Furlow's last words, "Never mind me boys, fight on," became the title of another poem in the *Sumter Republican*. "Though born to wealth and ease," wrote "Amicus" ("a friend" in Latin), Furlow and his "company of Calhoun braves" responded to the Old Dominion's cry for aid.

> With rail-road speed did Furlow's clan,
> Rush forth to her relief;
> The fires that burned in every man,
> Burned brightest in their chief.

The poetic tribute to Captain Furlow in the *Sumter Republican* accompanied a lengthy obituary that praised the dead officer for fulfilling his Christian responsibilities as a slaveowner. Furlow had "devoted his attention entirely to the interests of his farm," claimed the eulogist, "not forgetting . . . to make provision for all the wants of his negroes." He had also built for the slaves "a house of worship, principally at his own expense, in order that they might have the Gospel preached to them."

Several Georgia newspapers reported "with much pleasure" the faithfulness of Captain Furlow's black servant Peter, who went to great lengths after McDowell to procure coffins for the bodies of his master and two other officers and then assisted in transporting them back to Georgia. "We commend this instance of genuine and unyielding affection, of the slave for the master," wrote the editor of the *Sumter Republican*, "to the false friends of the race who are warring upon us." The highly publicized actions of servants such as Peter bolstered the long-standing southern defense of slavery as a benevolent institution.[24]

While Peter might have shown loyalty to his master, Furlow's other slaves had not, something that, not surprisingly, went unmentioned in the newspaper tributes. Four months prior to McDowell, on January 10, 1862, Furlow wrote the Confederate secretary of war asking for a sixty-day leave because his slaves were in "a high state of insubordination," made worse after their overseer had shot one of them, supposedly in self-defense. Prior to his enlistment, Furlow had "always personally superintended" his plantations and never left them "under the full control of an overseer." The slaves "have been

Capt. William L. Furlow, Company D, 12th Georgia Infantry, killed at the battle of McDowell. Henry L. Thomas, *History of the Doles-Cook Brigade* (Atlanta: Franklin Printing and Publishing, 1903), unpaginated pictorial section following p. 310.

gradually growing more open in their disobedience," he continued, "until it has created considerable excitement throughout the whole country." If allowed to go home, Furlow promised to "quiet all excitement and quell all insubordination" by administering "the proper corrections." In an ominous postscript, the young officer warned, "If one of my negroes were to kill my overseer, the community incensed would hang half my negroes and probably hang many innocent negroes—without law or jury." Confederate authorities granted Furlow a leave.[25]

While southern newspaper editors refused to acknowledge the omnipresent threat of violence that attended slavery, they also often failed to report accurately on Confederate military defeats, especially if they reflected poorly on hometown soldiers. This was the case following an engagement at Front Royal, Virginia, on May 30, 1862, involving the 12th Georgia. Stonewall Jackson had detached the 12th from the Army of the Valley three days earlier, ordering it to march from Winchester to Front Royal. At Front Royal the regiment would guard and cover the removal of a sizable quantity of quartermaster and commissary stores captured when the Confederates had seized the village and its Federal garrison on May 23.[26]

Shep Pryor of the 12th thought that Stonewall also sent the bloodied regiment to Front Royal to recover. "Gen. Jackson has favoured us . . . all he could," wrote Pryor to his wife, noting that although the regiment had "been kept up ready for any imergency," it had not been engaged since the fight on Sitlington's Hill. Pryor's belief that Jackson favored the 12th is doubtful; Stonewall likely sent the 12th to Front Royal believing that he could count on Colonel Conner to fulfill an important assignment.[27]

The 12th Georgia arrived in Front Royal on the morning of May 28. At 6 A.M. the next day, Conner wrote his immediate superior, Brig. Gen. Arnold Elzey, that a prisoner brought in the night before claimed that a Union division of 14,000 men under Brig. Gen. James Shields was en route to Front Royal from Fredericksburg. The prisoner, who had been captured with a detachment of troops at Rectortown only eighteen miles east of Front Royal, did not know the location of Shields's main body.

With only the 12th Georgia (numbering fewer than 400 men), a section of William H. Rice's Virginia Battery, and a small detachment of southern cavalry to guard Front Royal, Conner asked Elzey for orders. "Shall I burn stores on approach of the enemy and come up to the division?" queried Conner. "Please answer." Conner might have received additional intelligence that day concerning the location of Shields's force; the May 29 diary entry of one 12th Georgia soldier noted the arrival of "a Dispatch [that] the Enemy was camped in 18 miles of this place advancing on us with 15000."

Shep Pryor wrote his wife on May 29, "Our reg. is in a good position here— 19 miles from our main army—to all be captured: I fear the consiquences." Pryor nonetheless reassured his wife that he had "no reason to doubt Gen. Jackson's ability to get out of here successfully, for he is an able man." Lucy Buck, a nineteen-year-old woman living in a home overlooking Front Royal, wrote in her diary on May 29 that "there is some excitement in town in consequence of the reported advance of Shields."[28]

Despite the small size of the Front Royal garrison, Jackson clearly expected Colonel Conner to defend the town. At 8:15 A.M. on May 30 Stonewall wrote Conner to "let me hear from you at least once every day & more frequently if necessary." While Jackson probably knew by this time of the Federals' advance toward Front Royal, he may not have realized how close they were to the village.[29]

Conner and his Georgians apparently had little idea of exactly how close Shields's division was to Front Royal in the early morning hours of May 30. A diarist in the 12th's Company D, which guarded prisoners in town, noted that "the Day open fine." Shep Pryor wrote his wife early that morning that Jackson had whipped the enemy the day before at Charlestown and that the Federals were crossing the Potomac. In a dramatic change of opinion from his sentiments of the preceding day, Pryor declared, "This part of Virginia is as clear of yanks as its been in 9 months." The Federals, wrote another Georgian about the events of May 30, "were on us almost before we knew it."[30]

Capt. Beckwith West of the 48th Virginia, one of many ill soldiers in Front Royal at that time, wrote in his diary that on the morning of May 30 Conner informed them of the town's evacuation only one hour before the Federals marched in. By the time the advance infantry brigade of Shields's division began deploying on the hills around Front Royal at 11:30 A.M., Confederate quartermasters had gotten all the wagon trains out of town and heading northwest toward Winchester. Conner's regiment followed, along with scattered squadrons of Confederate cavalrymen and panicked citizens. Lucy Buck and her family despairingly watched the Confederate retreat. She claimed that the southerners "did not go 'hurry-scurry' like the Yankees but marched out with becoming dignity."[31]

Conner managed with difficulty to get most of his regiment and a large wagon train moving toward Winchester, but a Confederate quartermaster who volunteered to remain in Front Royal burned the depot and the adjacent warehouse containing captured stores valued at $300,000. Soon several sections of Federal artillery opened fire on the retreating southerners while Shields's small cavalry contingent, consisting of 100 weary troopers from the New Hampshire Battalion of the 1st Rhode Island Cavalry, charged in column of fours into the village.

Although one Federal noted that balls and buckshot fired "from secret places" were "uncomfortably abundant" in the streets of Front Royal, the troopers and accompanying infantrymen quickly seized "a large amount of transportation, including 2 engines, 11 railroad cars, 5 wagons with teams, much quartermaster stores, and a quantity of small-arms recently captured from us." The Union cavalrymen also apprehended a number of sick and injured Confederates, freed some Federal prisoners, and disarmed squads of Georgians cut off from their regiment. The late Captain Furlow's Company D of the 12th was particularly unlucky; having been detached in town to guard prisoners, most of the command surrendered to the Federals.[32]

The main body of the 12th Georgia made it over a bridge spanning the South Fork of the Shenandoah River. Although the Georgians attempted to set the span on fire, pursuing Federal horsemen stopped and extinguished the blaze. As Conner's men began crossing a second bridge, over the North Fork of the river, a small squad of Confederate cavalry galloped onto the span and into the ranks of the retreating infantrymen. The stampeded southern horsemen raised the ire of the Georgians. The cavalrymen had retreated "through ignorance or cowardice," wrote the 12th's Sgt. William L. Robinson.[33]

While the Confederates crowded together on the bridge, Union cavalrymen charged onto and across the span, brandishing sabers and firing pistols and carbines. Sergeant Robinson related that the Georgians "had no orders to fire, the Colonel's horse having run away with him; but when we found the Yankee cavalry in our line, cutting and slashing with their swords, we waited no longer for orders and fired into them." The volley killed eight Federals, including their commanding officer, and wounded seven more. Despite these losses, the Federal charge succeeded in scattering the Georgians, killing at least one of them and wounding several others.[34]

With Colonel Conner on his way to Winchester, Maj. Willis A. Hawkins ordered his men of the 12th Georgia to put down their guns and surrender. Most of them would not obey, being prompted and supported by the remaining company-grade officers. Instead the 12th continued retreating under the command of Capt. William Frederick Brown, a grizzled officer commended on later battlefields for his "cool daring." Although the Georgians refused to surrender, those companies in the rear of the retiring column found it impossible to maintain their formations. Pvt. Irby Goodwin Scott wrote that they "had to run some distance to save ourselves. . . . A good many of the boys tired down and scattered through the woods, where they were picked up by the enemys cavalry some few escaping." The section of Rice's battery assisted in stalling the Federal pursuers. At one point the two unsupported guns repulsed enemy horsemen "by a close fire at 80 yards."[35]

General Shields reported capturing 6 officers and 150 enlisted men on May 30, as well as releasing 18 Federal prisoners who had been captured in the town the previous week. While some of the southern prisoners were patients in Front Royal's hospital, at least 128 belonged to the 12th Georgia. Most of the Georgians spent only a few months in Federal prisons before they were exchanged. Some of those who avoided capture had great difficulty getting back to their regiment. Irby G. "Chap" Hudson "traveled 13 days through the mountains being a prisoner twice" before returning to his company. Shep Pryor told his wife in mid-July 1862 that two men separated from his company at Front Royal were still "playing off as citazens working in the farms untill they can get a chance to get away."[36]

Those members of the 12th Georgia who avoided being captured in Front Royal or in the subsequent retreat trudged into Winchester on the evening of May 30. Colonel Conner had preceded them into town, arriving around 6:30 P.M. and sending a panicked message to Gen. Richard Ewell stating that the enemy was in close pursuit and that "unless you can throw re-enforcements here by morning all will be gone." Later that evening Conner went to Jackson's headquarters at Taylor's Hotel. Jackson had learned of the Front Royal debacle earlier in the afternoon while on a railroad car en route from Charlestown to Winchester.[37]

Upon entering Stonewall's office, Conner asked, "Gen. I suppose you have heard of my misfortune at Front Royal?"

"Yes," Jackson replied.

"Well Gen. I did the best fighting I could," stated Conner, "but we were overpowered."

"Col Conner how many men did you have killed?" asked Stonewall.

"I had no men killed Gen."

KEITH S. BOHANNON

"Col Conner do you call that fighting?" was Jackson's response.

Conner then left the room along with Jackson's chief commissary officer, Maj. Wells J. Hawks. Turning to Hawks, Conner said, "Major I believe Gen Jackson is crazy."

Stonewall's assistant adjutant general, Alexander S. Pendleton, then told Conner, "Col. consider yourself under arrest."

Conner said to Hawks, "Now I know he is crazy."[38]

That evening and the next day, several members of Jackson's staff vented their disgust over the Front Royal debacle. Jedediah Hotchkiss noted in his diary that Conner showed "great want of judgement and was surprised, completely." Ordnance officer William Allan wrote that Conner and the 12th Georgia were "not worth a d——n & from all accounts behaved badly." Quartermaster John A. Harman told his brother that the "affair at Front Royal was a disgraceful one on the part of both Conner and Hawkins" and that Jackson had "arrested both of them for cowardice."[39]

Jackson agreed with his staff officers about the deportment of Conner and Hawkins. In Stonewall's official report of the Valley campaign, he blamed Conner for "hastily and improvidently" abandoning Front Royal and losing Federal prisoners, numbers of his own men, and considerable commissary and quartermaster stores. Jackson promptly issued a general order calling for a court-martial of Colonel Conner on two charges: neglect of duty and violation of the 52nd Article of War. The 52nd Article, leveled against an officer or soldier "who shall misbehave himself before the enemy, run away, or shamefully abandon any fort, post, or guard which he . . . may be commanded to defend," prescribed the death penalty for the guilty party or any punishment that the court-martial found fit. Although the exact charges brought against Maj. Willis Hawkins are not known, Capt. G. Campbell Brown of General Ewell's staff wrote that the major was charged with cowardice "for ordering his men to lay down their arms and surrender to a very inferior force of Yankee cavalry."[40]

The disaster at Front Royal and subsequent arrests of Conner and Hawkins received scant coverage in Georgia newspapers, in dramatic contrast to the extensive number of articles on the 12th at McDowell. One of the only accurate accounts of Front Royal appeared in the *Macon Telegraph* in a letter written by Sgt. William Robinson, who blamed much of the disaster on the retreating southern horsemen for creating confusion in the ranks of the 12th just prior to the Union cavalry charge. Robinson admitted, without going into

Maj. Willis A. Hawkins, 12th Georgia Infantry. Hawkins undoubtedly escaped being court-martialed for his conduct at Front Royal by resigning his commission on January 15, 1863, citing poor health. Henry L. Thomas, *History of the Doles-Cook Brigade* (Atlanta: Franklin Printing and Publishing, 1903), unpaginated pictorial section following p. 310.

detail, that Conner and Hawkins were "under arrest for disobeying orders." "We made good our retreat," Robinson wrote, and "saved all our wagons." A bizarre article claimed that the Union seizure of Front Royal was due to one Ed Randolph, an insane man who had killed his wife the preceding fall and surreptitiously guided the Federals into the town.[41]

Not surprisingly, soldiers were less reticent in their private correspondence about the Front Royal affair and the arrests of Conner and Hawkins. The only surviving testimony from Colonel Conner concerning his arrest comes indirectly through the diary of his daughter Virginia. "He says Stonewall Jackson acted more like a madman than anything else (he was once in an insane asylum)," wrote Virginia, "and has about half of his officers under arrest." Virginia also noted the capture of members of the 12th Georgia at Front Royal and the subsequent arrest of Major Hawkins for cowardice, but she made no direct mention of her father's predicament.[42]

Opinions varied within the ranks of the 12th regarding the culpability of Conner and Hawkins for the Front Royal disaster. Shep Pryor of the 12th told his wife on June 13 that "Conner and Hawkins are under arrest. . . . They ought [to] both be cashiered, no doubt in my mind." Eleven days later Pryor had at least partially changed his mind, stating that "Hawkins is under arrest yet; very injustly, I think, Conner is, too." Another member of Pryor's company complained of the "slanderous reports" concerning Hawkins, claiming that the major had "fully sustained his reputation as a brave and gallant soldier on the bloody field at McDowell." When Hawkins obtained a hearing, the soldier claimed, he would "clear his skirts of the foul accusation of cowardice and misconduct."

The Front Royal disaster had little long-term effect on the reputation of the 12th Georgia. During the remainder of 1862 the regiment performed well and lost heavily in the Seven Days, Second Manassas, Maryland, and Fredericksburg campaigns, despite the absence of almost all its field officers. Stonewall Jackson praised the 12th in January 1863 as "a distinguished regiment," and the well-known and respected newspaper correspondent Peter W. Alexander referred to it in the fall of 1862 as "the glorious Twelfth, which has endured more hardships, suffered greater losses and engaged in more battles, than any regiment in the service."[43]

The bloody campaigns of the summer and fall of 1862 not only sustained the reputation of the 12th Georgia; they also delayed the courts-martial of its colonel and major. On July 23 Stonewall Jackson forwarded to Robert E.

Lee's chief of staff Robert H. Chilton the charges and specifications drawn up against Z. T. Conner. Five days later Jackson sent Chilton a list of officers from whom to select a court for Conner, who desired "to be tried speedily by a minimum number" of members.[44]

Almost two and a half months later, following the Second Manassas and Maryland campaigns, Jackson wrote on October 13 that Conner's trial would "take place any day." The absence of Major Hawkins made it useless to proceed, however, because the charges against Conner had been made on his statements. (Hawkins's willingness to testify for the prosecution is hardly surprising, given the major's apparent earlier participation in the cabal to block Conner's promotion.) According to Shepherd Pryor, who had been summoned to appear as a trial witness, neither Conner nor Hawkins was with the regiment in mid-October, although Pryor theorized that the authorities "may try the cases in their absence."[45]

Two months later, on December 27, 1862, a court found Colonel Conner guilty of violating the 52nd Article of War and ordered that he be dismissed from the army. On the morning of January 15 Conner left the 12th Georgia for good. He returned to his family in Macon and took up farming. He died in April 1866.[46]

Maj. Willis Hawkins, a lawyer from Americus, Georgia, managed to avoid a court-martial. In July 1862 he applied for a leave of absence from Stonewall Jackson. When Jackson refused, informing Hawkins that a court-martial had been prepared to try his case, the major went into Richmond, supposedly on account of sickness. There he obtained a leave of absence and went back to Americus. After a prolonged absence from duty without leave, the Confederate Adjutant and Inspector General's Office dropped Hawkins from the army's rolls on November 5, 1862. Twenty-two-year-old Capt. Edward S. Willis, the popular former adjutant of the 12th Georgia and assistant adjutant general on Stonewall Jackson's staff, took Hawkins's place as major of the 12th.

Two months later, on January 5, 1863, Hawkins had his rank as major restored and received a promotion to lieutenant colonel, having undoubtedly utilized his legal skills in petitioning the War Department for the reversal. Although the details of the case are unknown, the Adjutant and Inspector General's Office stated that the original revocation of Hawkins's commission had been "made under a misapprehension of facts." The letter of appointment promoting Edward Willis to the rank of major was also withdrawn, much to the regret of the officers and men of the 12th.[47]

The promotion of Hawkins to lieutenant colonel, despite pending court-martial charges and his continued absence from the army, prompted an angry letter from Gen. Robert E. Lee to the secretary of war. Lee demanded that if Hawkins were "to be restored to the Regiment I request that he be ordered back for trial though two of the important witnesses against him have been killed in battle." Four days after Lee addressed the secretary of war on the matter, Hawkins resigned his commission on January 15, 1863, citing poor health. Edward Willis supported the resignation, claiming that Hawkins had been "suffering from chronic diarrha & debility" and that there was no prospect for his getting well. Willis, praised by Stonewall Jackson as "a bold, prompt and efficient officer of superior mind" and "an accomplished gentleman," took Hawkins's place as lieutenant colonel and on March 26, 1863, replaced Conner as colonel of the 12th Georgia.[48]

Thirty-eight years after the remnants of the 12th Georgia Infantry disbanded at Appomattox, veteran Henry W. Thomas chronicled the unit's history in a well-received book titled *History of the Doles-Cook Brigade*. Thomas devoted several pages to the battle of McDowell, quoting laudatory statements about his regiment from the official reports of Stonewall Jackson and Edward Johnson. In a section at the rear of the volume titled "The Negro," Thomas affectionately related the story of various "negroes who acted as body-servants for the officers and men," including Capt. William Furlow's slave Peter. Slaves such as Peter, explained Thomas, "were, as a rule, kind, gentle, and considerate, and with few exceptions would have remained the same obedient and trusting people if it had not been for the teachings of the adventurers who came South after the surrender and fired their hearts with hatred for their best and truest friends."

Although Thomas wrote in great detail about most of his regiment's battles, he remained completely silent about the May 30, 1862, engagement at Front Royal (where between one-third and one-half of his regiment had been captured) and the subsequent arrests and controversy surrounding Colonel Conner and Major Hawkins. Zephaniah Conner's biographical sketch in *History of the Doles-Cook Brigade* mentions only his bravery at McDowell, his subsequent resignation from the army (with no supporting details), and his skills as a businessman. Willis Hawkins's sketch also mentions McDowell and

Veterans of Calhoun Rifles, Company D, 12th Georgia Infantry, standing on the steps of the Thornton House Hotel in Morgan, Georgia, ca. 1890s. Three of the veterans can be identified, including David D. Peden (far left in first row), Andrew J. Bell (second from left in back row), and Ebenezer Fain (middle man in middle row). Courtesy Tom E. Sanders.

notes his distinguished postbellum legal career in Georgia, including a term as associate justice of the state supreme court.[49]

The contemporary newspaper coverage of the 12th Georgia's role in the 1862 Valley campaign clearly illustrates an assertion made by J. Cutler Andrews in his fine study of Confederate journalism, *The South Reports the Civil War*. The conflicting aims of news and propaganda, he wrote, "made it difficult if not virtually impossible for a Southern correspondent to tell the whole truth about the military situation." Many southern newspaper editors were clearly uncomfortable commenting on or running articles or letters about incidents that reflected poorly on hometown soldiers. Years later, aged Confederate veterans such as Henry Thomas were also unwilling to mention unpleasant topics in print, especially given the dictates of polite Victorian society and the pervasive influence that Lost Cause mythology held over the former Confederacy at the turn of the century.[50]

ACKNOWLEDGMENTS

The author wishes to thank the following individuals for their assistance in the preparation of this article: John P. Ackerly III, Gregory Coco, Robert E. L. Krick, Robert K. Krick, William J. Miller, Eric J. Mink, Michael P. Musick, Johnnie P. Pearson, and George M. Smith.

NOTES

1. Virginia Conner diary, May 9, 1862, Conner Family Collection, Middle Georgia Archives, Macon.

2. J. Cutler Andrews, *The South Reports the Civil War* (Princeton: Princeton University Press, 1970), 517, 529; J. Cutler Andrews, "The Confederate Press and Public Morale," *Journal of Southern History* 32 (November 1966): 448, 453–54.

3. Henry L. Thomas, *History of the Doles-Cook Brigade* (Atlanta: Franklin Printing and Publishing, 1903), 194; Frederick A. Bode and Donald E. Ginter, *Farm Tenancy and the Census in Antebellum Georgia* (Athens: University of Georgia Press, 1986), 76, 78, 80, 163; Joseph C. G. Kennedy, *Agriculture of the United States in 1860 Compiled from the Original Returns of the Eighth Census* (Washington, D.C.: GPO, 1864), 23, 27; Louise F. Hayes, *History of Macon County, Georgia* (Atlanta: Stein, 1933), 261; Conner diary, May 9, 1862.

4. Thomas, *History of the Doles-Cook Brigade*, 59, 230, 233, 235; Martin W. Brett, *Experiences of a Georgia Boy in the Army of Northern Virginia, 1861–1865* (Gainesville, Ga.: Magnolia Press, 1988), 2; obituary of David D. Peden, *Confederate Veteran* 21 (January 1913): 34; Robert K. Krick, *Lee's Colonels: A Biographical Register of the Field Officers of the Army of Northern Virginia* (Dayton, Ohio: Morningside, 1991), 56, 349, 401; folder titled "Conner Family Collection, 1859–1900," Conner Family Collection. For details of the early-war training of several companies of the 12th Georgia, see Richard T. Davis to Joseph E. Brown, May 1, 1861, box 28, loc. no. 3335-01, and James W. Patterson to Joseph E. Brown, May 9, 1861, box 42, loc. no. 3335-08, Georgia Governor's Incoming Correspondence, Georgia Department of Archives and History, Atlanta (repository hereafter cited as GDAH).

5. Thomas, *History of the Doles-Cook Brigade*, 195–98. For descriptions and praise of the 12th Georgia's performance at Greenbrier River and Alleghany Mountain, see "The

Battle of Valley Mountain," *Macon Daily Telegraph*, December 24, 1861; John M. Stubbs, "Correspondence of the Telegraph," *Macon Daily Telegraph*, December 24, 1861; "Ned," "The Battle on the Alleghany," *Macon Daily Telegraph*, January 8, 1862; "Parson Parker" [signed "Bloody 12th Ga. Reg't—Co. I"], *Sufferings of the Twelfth Georgia Reg't in the Mountains of Virginia* (n.p., n.d.); "The 12th Regiment," *Macon Daily Telegraph*, October 1, 1861; James W. Atkins diary, December 13, 1861, Civil War Miscellany, Personal Papers, drawer 283, box 16, GDAH; U.S. War Department, *The War of the Rebellion: A Compilation of the Official Records of the Union and Confederate Armies*, 127 vols., index, and atlas (Washington, D.C.: GPO, 1880–1901), ser. 1, 5:224–29, 462–65, 468 (hereafter cited as *OR*; all references are to ser. 1).

6. Although a member of the 12th told Conner's family on March 6, 1862, that "all the privates love him dearly," this was unquestionably not the case. Henry T. Davenport informed his sister in the fall of 1861 that "old Conner" was "nothing but an arrogant fop." See Atkins diary, December 31, 1861, January 2, 1862; "12th Georgia Regiment," *Macon Daily Telegraph*, January 12, 1862; Henry T. Davenport to "Dear Sister Josie," October 30, 1861, Sarah S. Pfeiffer Collection, Atlanta History Center, Atlanta, Ga.; Charles R. Adams Jr., ed., *A Post of Honor: The Pryor Letters, 1861–1863. Letters from Capt. S. G. Pryor, Twelfth Georgia Regiment, and His Wife, Penelope Tyson Pryor* (Fort Valley, Ga.: Garrett, 1989), 126.

7. Conner diary, March 6, 9, 10, 1862; Zephaniah T. Conner, 12th Georgia Infantry Compiled Service Records (hereafter cited as CSR), M 266, National Archives, Washington, D.C. (repository hereafter cited as NA). On the reasons for Conner's furlough, see Z. T. Conner to Judah P. Benjamin, March 5, 1862, Letters Sent to the Confederate Secretary of War, RG 109, M 437, NA.

8. William Allan, *History of the Campaign of Gen. T. J. (Stonewall) Jackson in the Shenandoah Valley of Virginia. From November 4, 1861, to June 17, 1862* (Philadelphia: Lippincott, 1880), 66, 71; Adams, *Post of Honor*, 51–170.

9. *OR* 12(1):471, 482–83; Allan, *History of the Campaign*, 73; Thomas J. Gibson, "The McDowell Reunion," *Highland Recorder*, May 20, 1898.

10. James G. Rodgers, "The 12th at McDowell," *Macon Daily Telegraph*, June 24, 1862; "H. A. C." [Hiram A. Crittenden], "Letter from Virginia," *Sumter Republican*, May 16, 1862; Henry T. Davenport to father, May 12, 1862, Pfeiffer Collection.

11. Rodgers, "12th at McDowell"; [Shepherd G. Pryor], "Communicated," *Sumter Republican*, May 23, 1862; Henry T. Davenport to father, May 12, 1862, Pfeiffer Collection; "The 12th Georgia at McDowell," *Columbus Daily Enquirer*, May 23, 1862; S. Boykin, "Battle Pictures: Three Glimpses of the 12th Georgia," *Central Georgian*, August 9, 1862; Robert L. Dabney, *Life and Campaigns of Lieut.-Gen. Thomas J. Jackson* (New York: Blelock, 1866), 348; *OR* 12(1):472, 481, 483. The most detailed wartime map of the battle of McDowell, drawn by Jedediah Hotchkiss, shows the 12th Georgia occupying an advanced position before retiring to the center of the main Confederate line. Edward Johnson stated that the regiment occupied the crest of Sitlington's Hill, while William B.

Taliaferro noted that the 12th's position was "well advanced toward the front" (George B. Davis. et al., comps., *Atlas to Accompany the Official Records of the Union and Confederates Armies* [Washington, D.C.: GPO, 1891], plate 5, no. 1). See also Land and Community Associates, *McDowell Battlefield Master Plan* (n.p., 1995), fig. 8.

12. "Requisition for Ordnance and Ordnance Stores, 1st Quarter 1862," in William D. Ivey, 12th Georgia CSR, and "Requisition for ammunition for the use of the 12th Geo Vols," August 13, 1862, in William F. Brown, 12th Georgia CSR, M 266, NA; Jane B. Peacock, ed., "A Foot Soldier's Account: Letters of William Batts, 1861–1862," *Georgia Historical Quarterly* 50 (March 1966): 94; "A Virginian Private Soldier," "The 12th Georgia," *Macon Daily Telegraph*, May 28, 1862; Rodgers, "12th at McDowell"; "H. A. C.," "Letter from Virginia"; Editors of Time-Life Books, *Voices of the Civil War: Shenandoah 1862* ([Alexandria, Va.]: Time-Life, [1997]), 80; Allan, *History of the Campaign*, 76; Robert G. Tanner, *Stonewall in the Valley: Thomas J. "Stonewall" Jackson's Shenandoah Valley Campaign, Spring 1862* (Garden City, N.Y.: Doubleday, 1976), 195; Richard L. Armstrong, *The Battle of McDowell: March 11–May 18, 1862* (Lynchburg, Va.: H. E. Howard, 1990), 67.

13. Rodgers, "12th at McDowell"; Dabney, *Life and Campaigns*, 348; *OR* 12(1):486; obituary of Asa Ernest Sherwood, *Macon Daily Telegraph*, May 23, 1862.

14. "The Battle of McDowell," *Columbus Daily Sun*, May 26, 1862; "H. A. C.," "Letter from Virginia"; [Shepherd G. Pryor], "Communicated"; Boykin, "Battle Pictures"; "Correspondence of the Telegraph," *Macon Daily Telegraph*, May 26, 1862.

15. Allan, *History of the Campaign*, 76; Rodgers, "12th at McDowell"; "Lieut Etheridge: A Remarkable Case," *Countryman*, July 19, 1862.

16. *OR* 12(1):478, 481; Gibson, "McDowell Reunion"; John W. Fravel, "Jackson's Valley Campaign," *Confederate Veteran* 6 (September 1898): 418; Rodgers, "12th at McDowell"; Samuel V. Fulkerson to "Dear Kate," May 16, 1862, Fulkerson Family Papers, Virginia Military Institute Archives, Lexington; Henry T. Davenport to father, May 12th 1862, Pfeiffer Collection. Henry T. Davenport estimated that he fired between 80 and 100 rounds at McDowell.

17. "The 12th Georgia Regiment," *Macon Daily Telegraph*, May 19, 1862; Adams, *Post of Honor*, 181; Rodgers, "12th at McDowell"; "The Battle of McDowell," *Columbus Daily Sun*, May 26, 1862; Irby G. Scott to father, May 12, 1862, Irby H. Scott Papers, Mss. 4706, Duke University Special Collections, Durham, N.C.; [Shepherd G. Pryor], "Communicated"; Conner diary, May 19, 1862; "Captains of the 31st," undated newspaper clipping, copy provided by John P. Ackerly III, Richmond, Va. The figure of 182 casualties at McDowell comes from a newspaper list. Shepherd Pryor, James Rodgers, and an unidentified member of the 12th claimed the regiment lost 183 men, while Irby G. Scott put the number at 185. The 12th Georgia also lost a pet dog, which according to a postwar account "ran from line to line as either army cheered" before being killed.

18. "The Battle of McDowell," *Columbus Daily Sun*, May 26, 1862; "The 12th Georgia at McDowell," *Columbus Daily Enquirer*, May 23, 1862; Henry T. Davenport to father, May 16, 1862, Pfeiffer Collection.

19. *OR* 12(1):484; Conner diary, May 19, 1862; Jedediah Hotchkiss, *Make Me a Map of the Valley: The Civil War Journal of Stonewall Jackson's Topographer*, ed. Archie P. McDonald (Dallas: Southern Methodist University Press, 1973), 46.

20. Conner diary, June 22, 1862; "The Glorious 12th," *Macon Daily Telegraph*, May 21, 1862; *OR* 12(1):484; [Shepherd G. Pryor], "Communicated"; Rodgers, "12th at McDowell"; Henry T. Davenport to father, May 12, 1862, Pfeiffer Collection; "H. A. C.," "Letter from Virginia."

21. "Georgia's Record of Blood," *Columbus Daily Sun*, May 15, 1862; "The 12th Georgia Regiment," *Macon Daily Telegraph*, May 9, 1862.

22. Obituary of Richard T. Davis, *Countryman*, May 27, 1862; "Correspondence of the Telegraph," *Macon Daily Telegraph*, May 26, 1862; "K" [member of Company C, 12th Georgia], "The Departed Brave," *Macon Daily Telegraph*, May 22, 1862.

23. "Senex," "Capt. Samuel Dawson," *Sumter Republican*, May 23, 1862.

24. "Amicus," "Care not for me, Fight on," *Sumter Republican*, May 16, 1862; J. J. Granberry, "Capt. W. L. Furlow," *Sumter Republican*, May 16, 1862; "Peter, a Faithful Servant," *Sumter Republican*, May 23, 1862; "Peter, a Faithful Servant," *Central Georgian*, June 4, 1862; Danny Smith, "Story recounts black man's deeds following Battle of McDowell," *Recorder*, June 1, 1989; Thomas, *History of the Doles-Cook Brigade*, 612–13. William L. Furlow owned $33,400 in real estate and $54,454 in personal estate in 1860; see 1860 Calhoun County, Ga., Census, 46. For other examples of the "faithful servant" genre in Confederate newspapers and the relationship of these stories to the southern defense of slavery, see Drew G. Faust, *The Creation of Confederate Nationalism: Ideology and Identity in the Civil War South* (Baton Rouge: Louisiana State University Press, 1988), 58–61, 63.

25. William L. Furlow to Judah P. Benjamin, January 10, 1862, Letters Sent to the Confederate Secretary of War, RG 109, M 437, NA; William L. Furlow, 12th Georgia CSR, M 266, NA.

26. Allan, *History of the Campaign*, 91, 131.

27. Adams, *Post of Honor*, 190.

28. John Levi Griffin diary, May 27, 28, 1862, Emory University Special Collections, Atlanta, Ga. (note: Emory's accession records identify the author of this diary as John L. Griffin, but this is impossible given Griffin's March 1, 1864, enlistment in Company H, 12th Georgia; internal evidence reveals that the diary was kept by a member of Company D, 12th Georgia); "The Rebel Raid Down the Shenandoah. Curious Rebel Documents Found at Winchester," *New York Herald*, June 16, 1862; Adams, *Post of Honor*, 191. Conner's May 29, 1862, note to Elzey was part of a group of Confederate documents, possibly lost by a member of Stonewall Jackson's staff, found in a partially destroyed railroad car in Winchester.

29. T. J. Jackson to "Colonel," "Hall Town 8.15 A.M. May 30, 1862," Conner Family Collection; Hotchkiss, *Make Me a Map*, 49. Jedediah Hotchkiss confirmed in his May 30 diary entry that Jackson knew that morning about "Shields' approach towards Front Royal."

30. Griffin diary, May 30, 1862; Adams, *Post of Honor*, 193; Hotchkiss, *Make Me a Map*, 49; [member of the 12th Georgia], "Letter from Gen. Jackson's Army," *Augusta Constitutionalist*, June 22, 1862.

31. [Beckwith West], *Experiences of a Confederate States Prisoner, Being An Ephemeris Regularly Kept By An Officer of the Confederate States Army* (Richmond: West and Johnston, 1862), 5–7; Frederic Denison, *The First Regiment Rhode Island Cavalry in the Civil War, 1861–1865* (Central Falls, R.I.: E. L. Freeman, 1876), 86; Lucy Rebecca Buck, *Shadows on My Heart: The Civil War Diary of Lucy Rebecca Buck of Virginia*, ed. Elizabeth R. Baer (Athens: University of Georgia Press, 1997), 91. Beckwith West claimed that there were roughly 100 sick Confederates in the hospital at Front Royal on May 30.

32. Denison, *First Regiment Rhode Island Cavalry*, 86; OR 12(1):682, 722, 727; "W. L. R." [William L. Robinson], "Letter from the 12th Georgia," *Columbus Daily Sun*, June 24, 1862; Allan, *History of the Campaign*, 131. For other Federal accounts of Front Royal, see William Kepler, *History . . . of the Fourth Regiment Ohio Volunteer Infantry in the War for the Union* (Cleveland: Leader Printing, 1886), 67; Franklin Sawyer, *A Military History of the 8th Regiment Ohio Volunteer Infantry* (Cleveland: Fairbanks, 1881), 51.

33. "W. L. R.," "Letter from the 12th Georgia"; G. A. Sargent to "Dear Folks," June 1, 1862, G. A. Sargent Letters, Center for American History, University of Texas, Austin.

34. "W. L. R.," "Letter from the 12th Georgia"; G. A. Sargent to "Dear Folks," June 1, 1862, Sargent Letters; Denison, *First Regiment Rhode Island Cavalry*, 86; Irby G. Scott to "Loved ones at home," "Camp Near Port Republic," June 12, 1862, Scott Papers. Irby G. Scott wrote that "the cavalry charged into our rear shooting and cutting but only wounded 4 men." The 12th Georgia's muster rolls show one man killed and five wounded on May 30.

35. OR 12(1):727, 793; Janet B. Hewett and others, eds., *Supplement to the Official Records of the Union and Confederate Armies*, 100 vols. (Wilmington, N.C.: Broadfoot, 1994), 12(1):664 (hereafter cited as *ORS*); "C," "From Jackson's Army," *Columbus Weekly Sun*, September 2, 1862; Irby G. Scott to "Loved ones at home," June 12, 1862, Scott Papers; "Letter from Gen. Jackson's Army," *Augusta Constitutionalist*, June 22, 1862.

36. OR 12(1):682; "W. L. R.," "Letter from the 12th Georgia"; Adams, *Post of Honor*, 195, 220, 234–35; "History of the Muckalee Guards," *Sumter Republican*, March 20, 1863; Irby G. Scott to "Dear Father," June 19, 1862, Scott Papers. William L. Robinson and Shepherd Pryor both state that the 12th Georgia lost 128 men captured on May 30. Union brigadier general Nathan Kimball claimed that his men captured 155 prisoners on May 30, representing eighteen different southern regiments, and released 20 Union prisoners.

37. OR 12(1):793; Hotchkiss, *Make Me a Map*, 49, 50; Alexander R. Boteler, "Stonewall Jackson in the Campaign of 1862," in *Southern Historical Society Papers*, ed. J. William Jones and others, 52 vols. (1876–1959; reprint, with 3-vol. index, Wilmington, N.C.: Broadfoot, 1990–92), 40:166; G. Campbell Brown memoirs, Brown-Ewell Papers, Tennessee State Library and Archives, Nashville. Although Conner addressed this dispatch to

Ewell, Jedediah Hotchkiss implies in his May 30 diary entry that Jackson saw it prior to meeting Conner that evening. G. Campbell Brown, a member of Richard Ewell's staff, claims in his memoirs that news of the capture of Front Royal prompted Jackson's retreat from Charlestown to Winchester.

38. The author found three versions of the May 30 meeting between Jackson and Conner. Two came from Jedediah Hotchkiss, whose diary suggests that he heard secondhand about the incident. The version in the text is from Wells J. Hawks to Jedediah Hotchkiss, Charlestown, January 17, 1866, box 4, T. J. Jackson Manuscripts, New-York Historical Society, New York. See also Hotchkiss, *Make Me A Map*, 50; Allan, *History of the Campaign*, 131.

39. Hotchkiss, *Make Me A Map*, 49; William Allan to Asher W. Harman, May 31, 1862, box 1, Eldridge Collection, Huntington Library, San Marino, Calif.; John A. Harman to Brother, May 31, 1862, Jedediah Hotchkiss Papers, roll 49, Library of Congress, Washington, D.C. (repository hereafter cited as LC).

40. *OR* 12(1):707–8; "Digest of General Orders and Letters from the Official Order and Letter Books of General T. J. Jackson," Hotchkiss Papers, roll 49, LC; General Orders 136, December 27, 1862, General Orders, Army of Northern Virginia (hereafter cited as GO-ANV), RG 109, M 921, NA; *Regulations for the Army of the Confederate States, Authorized Edition* (Richmond: West and Johnson, 1862), 413–14; *ORS* 12(1):664.

41. "W. L. R.," "Letter from the 12th Georgia"; "Latest from the Valley," *Macon Daily Telegraph*, June 12, 1862; "Jackson's Prisoners Not Re-captured," *Columbus Daily Enquirer*, June 17, 1862. An article in the *Richmond Enquirer*, reprinted in at least one Georgia newspaper, stated only that "a company of the 12th Georgia Regiment fell into the enemy's hands by some blunder on the part of an officer."

42. Conner diary, June 16, 1862.

43. Adams, *Post of Honor*, 200–201; [Member of Co. A, 12th Ga.], "Col W A Hawkins," *Sumter Republican*, July 25, 1862; General T. J. Jackson, "Hd. Qrs 2d Corps ANVa Jany 10th 1863" [a January 9, 1863, petition requesting that Edward Willis be appointed lieutenant colonel of the 12th Georgia], Edward Willis, 12th Georgia CSR, M 266, NA; Peter W. Alexander, "The Georgians in Maryland," *Columbus Enquirer*, October 10,1862. The 12th saw little additional action in the 1862 Shenandoah Valley campaign. At Cross Keys on June 8 it supported artillery batteries near the center of the Confederate line. For details on the 12th at Cross Keys, see Robert K. Krick, *Conquering the Valley: Stonewall Jackson at Port Republic* (New York: Morrow, 1996), 223–26.

44. T. J. Jackson Official Letter Book, no. 246, July 23, 1862, and no. 249, July 29, 1862, Hotchkiss Papers, roll 49, LC.

45. Conner was present with the army during the 1862 Maryland campaign but did not exercise field command of his regiment. See Zephaniah Conner to "My Darling," September 19, 1862, box 1, folder 2, Conner Family Collection; T. J. Jackson Official Letter Book, no. 274, October 13, 1862, Hotchkiss Papers, LC; Adams, *Post of Honor*, 267.

46. General Orders 136, December 27, 1862, GO-ANV, RG 109, M 921, NA; Assistant

Surgeon William H. Hodnett diary, January 15, 1863, U.D.C. Typescripts, vol. 4, GDAH; Georgia Adjutant General's Office, Militia Enrollment Lists, Bibb County, drawer 245, box 4, GDAH; folder titled "Conner Family Collection, 1859–1900," Conner Family Collection.

47. Special Orders No. 259, November 5, 1862, paragraph 11, and Special Orders No. 3, January 5, 1863, paragraph 9, Confederate Adjutant and Inspector General's Office, NA; Hodnett diary, January 10, 1863; William B. Williford, *Americus through the Years* (Atlanta: Cherokee, 1975), 52.

48. Robert E. Lee to C.S. Adjutant and Inspector General, "Head Qrs ANVa Jan 11th 1863," Edward Willis, and Willis Hawkins to Samuel Cooper, January 15, 1863, Willis Hawkins, 12th Georgia CSR, M 266, NA; Gen. T. J. Jackson to Samuel Cooper, "Hd Qrs V Dist Nov 13th 1862," item 45 in *The Confederates: A Price List of Historical Civil War Memorabilia Collected by Gary Hendershott*, June 1998, sale 97.

49. Thomas, *History of the Doles-Cook Brigade*, 198–206, 230, 607–15. For a favorable contemporary review of this book, see "History of the Doles-Cook Brigade," *Confederate Veteran* 12 (September 1904): 446.

50. Andrews, *South Reports the Civil War*, 506. For studies that examine the role of Union veterans' memories, see Earl J. Hess, *The Union Soldier in Battle: Enduring the Ordeal of Combat* (Lawrence: University Press of Kansas, 1997), 158–90; Stuart McConnell, *Glorious Contentment: The Grand Army of the Republic, 1865–1900* (Chapel Hill: University of North Carolina Press, 1992), 166–205. On Confederate veterans and the Lost Cause, see Gaines M. Foster, *Ghosts of the Confederacy: Defeat, the Lost Cause, and the Emergence of the New South* (New York: Oxford, 1987).

PETER S. CARMICHAEL

Turner Ashby's Appeal

In the spring of 1862, stories of Turner Ashby's reckless bravery captivated a young southern nation. His daring exploits during "Stonewall" Jackson's Valley campaign became a popular topic around the campfire and parlor. By all accounts Ashby appeared invincible, a man destined to lead the Confederacy to final victory. After hearing of Ashby's many close calls with death, southerners were shocked that his life ended at Harrisonburg, Virginia, on June 6, 1862, when a Pennsylvania rifleman caught Ashby in his sights. The entire Confederacy mourned his loss. A woman from Front Royal, Virginia, wrote shortly after Ashby's death, "Dear Ashby, I fear his place can never be filled. I grieve for the loss of such a man. I never saw him but I revere him." Mary Boykin Chesnut confided to her diary, "Drop a tear for Turner Ashby. The hero of the Valley. They say he is killed! All things are against us." Many felt his death so keenly that they needed tangible reminders of the general, taking hair and bones from Ashby's horse as treasured keepsakes. By the end of the year, some Valley residents had stacked rocks on the spot where Ashby had been killed as a temporary memorial to their fallen hero.[1]

Death had brought Ashby instant martyrdom in the public memory. He died as a Confederate hero but was remembered as the finest representation of the Old South's cavalier tradition. Glowing tributes, including a front-page article on the cavalryman on October 18, 1862, in the *Southern Illustrated News*, emphasized his pure, chivalrous nature. An engraving of Ashby accompanied the story. It pictured him sitting rigidly on his famous white horse with a fluffy plume sticking out of his hat, striking an aristocratic pose. He looked more like a knight, fresh from a jousting tournament, than a partisan ranger who fought a vicious form of irregular warfare. Virginia artist William H. Caskie, a Confederate officer, sketched the general from memory. He thought the likeness more accurate than could "have been obtained even from the Camera itself."[2] Caskie's drawing, however, sacrificed authenticity for romanticism, truth for propaganda, reality for myth. He successfully turned Ashby into a caricature of the cavalier tradition, a set of values, although authentic to most southerners, that was hopelessly romanticized during the war. Confederates used the chivalric tradition to idealize southern manhood. Fallen heroes such as Ashby became Christlike figures, men of stainless character and fierce bravery who showed the world that southerners were a superior people, fighting a miscreant, depraved Yankee race.[3]

As a Confederate symbol, Ashby projected the values of male honor, Christianity, and aristocratic ease, traits that white southerners claimed as distinctively their own. In a typical pronouncement after the cavalryman's death, the *Richmond Whig* lauded Ashby as the embodiment of the "purest type of pristine chivalry." This same writer could not imagine another Confederate officer of "higher religious sentiments." His "winning and gentle manners grew out of the grand traits of his character most naturally; hence women admired and children loved him and brave men chose him as their champion."[4]

It is true that Ashby stood for key aspects of the cavalier tradition, especially the trait of individual courage, but his life did not conform to the vision of radical innocence and purity that was crucial to the chivalric model. Although descended from English cavaliers, Ashby could not claim forebears who were planters. Moreover, his immediate family had suffered severe financial reverses before the war. He was respected in the community not as a prominent slaveholder or a model Christian, but as a champion rider and local merchant who pursued interests in mines, railroads, and politics. He lived and associated with small slaveholders and ordinary folk.[5] From this experience he must have gained a deep understanding of the yeomen, their fierce independence, their love of home, and their hostility to outsiders. In fact, he secured the allegiance of the Shenandoah Valley residents with a

A postwar engraving showing Turner Ashby in a Confederate uniform. Ashby never posed for such a portrait during the war, though a photographer took a picture of him in death shortly after the battle of Harrisonburg. Lew Wallace and others, *The Story of American Heroism* (Chicago: Werner, 1898), 495.

distinctively homespun, populist appeal. As a cavalry officer Ashby played the rural leader by acknowledging and protecting the rights of his soldiers, most of whom came from small, nonslaveholding farms.[6]

Transforming the fallen cavalryman into a medieval knight obscures the real Ashby, but the process offers valuable insights into the making of an early

Confederate hero. The cavalier myth helped unify white southerners during and after the Civil War by providing them with a collective identity based on the antebellum idea of the superiority of the South. Southerners of all classes drew emotional sustenance from this compelling message. The wartime re-membrances of Ashby, although sincere expressions of mourning, drew from this antebellum idea while foreshadowing many of the key themes that would later define the Lost Cause. Ashby represents an early prototype of the Lost Cause hero, the model Christian gentleman, honorable but forgiving, brave but gentle, whose morals were beyond reproach. He also was presented as having an aristocratic bearing and an elitist view that upheld the Old South's hierarchical ideas about women, poor whites, and African Americans. Al-though Ashby was active in mass politics, seeking the votes of ordinary white men, his comrade and first biographer, James B. Avirett, claimed that the general felt "a perfect detestation" for "unbridled Democracy." "He did not think," Avirett added, "that all men were to be intrusted with the right to vote, but that universal suffrage was the certain precursor of universal misrule or anarchy." Ashby came to represent this cultural and political chivalric tradi-tion in death. After the war, for instance, John Esten Cooke referred to Ashby as "a veritable child of chivalry"; Avirett described him as "a living reality in all that constitutes the peerless cavalier"; and T. C. De Leon wrote, "true knight-doughty leader-high hearted gentleman . . . Chivalric-lion-hearted-strong armed." Lost Cause writers commonly used such language to describe Ashby and a host of other Confederate heroes, to elevate these men and their cause to almost religious greatness. The white South, in turn, embraced this "moonlight and magnolias" view of the Civil War because it soothed south-ern male honor by portraying Confederates as the last defenders of the chival-ric tradition.[7]

A closer inspection of Ashby's background reveals that his prewar career did not conform to the cavalier model. Many of those who wrote about Ashby conveniently sidestepped these contradictions by creating an imaginary pas-toral landscape of the Old South peopled by contented slaves and benevolent masters. This world represented a unique civilization of social harmony, re-finement, and Christianity. Avirett typified writers who placed Ashby in this utopian setting. After comparing northern factory workers to Virginia slaves, Avirett concluded that the "pale, haggard faces of the factory operatives" reflected their degraded condition, while "the gay, careless, and happy ser-vants on the Piedmont estates" proved the superiority of slavery. "No man,"

Avirett concluded, "bore more indelibly impressed upon his character the peculiar influences imparted to Southern society by slavery than did young Ashby."[8]

Avirett was right about Ashby's commitment to slavery, but the evidence suggests that Ashby also embraced aspects of free labor. Like most Virginians in the decade prior to the Civil War, he thought slavery could complement the state's capitalistic development. It is unlikely that he saw himself as a product of an archaic, feudal plantation system. Most southerners believed they had created a modern slave system that looked forward, not backward.[9]

Unlike the ideal cavalier who lived an exemplary Christian life, Ashby never openly professed his faith. He seemed unaffected by the religious awakening that gripped Virginia in the 1850s. While Ashby encouraged the religious training of his troops and occasionally attended services, he lacked that essential piety that characterized Robert E. Lee, Stonewall Jackson, and many other Confederate generals who made public expressions of faith. Ashby's chaplain weakly explained that the demands of his service made it impossible for him to "engage in serious religious conversation," and that an expression of faith, Ashby feared, might not lead to a life consistent with the teachings of the Bible. Although Ashby should not be criticized for failing to proclaim Christ as his savior, his early biographers should be taken to task for trying to turn him into a Christian warrior when events before the cavalryman's death do not support such a claim.[10]

Despite the ahistorical approach of early Confederate writers, they did not have to invent Ashby's gifts as a horseman. Admirers before and after the Civil War emphasized his famed horsemanship as proof that he behaved like a chivalrous knight. During the antebellum years his neighbors and friends considered him one of Fauquier County's finest horseman, a rider of unmistakable talent. He routinely dazzled crowds with his fearless jumps and swift rides. At local jousting tournaments in Virginia and North Carolina he usually left with highest honors.[11]

Ashby's passion for horses, however, does not mean that he envisioned himself as a cavalier. Jousting events were social gatherings, not fantasy events where southerners pretended they were feudal lords. Recreational activities such as fox hunts, tournaments, and hurdle races do not define a person's identity. There is nothing to suggest that Ashby patterned himself after medieval knights or had delusions that he descended from a line of great cavaliers.[12]

Ashby's defenders have twisted his love for horses and his superior equestrian talents into a shallow defense of the Old South. Emphasizing Ashby's amazing gifts as a horseman supported claims by former Confederates that southerners were more courageous, civilized, and chivalrous than their Yankee foes. With this key component of the Lost Cause firmly in place, defeated southerners celebrated Ashby, as well as other horsemen such as Jeb Stuart and John Hunt Morgan, in an effort to redeem their lost sense of honor. They attributed military defeat to the industrial might of the North while taking solace in the belief that the Confederacy produced leaders of Ashby's virtue and manliness.

Ironically, Turner Ashby spent his youth in a time when the cavalier tradition came under attack in Virginia. Born on October 23, 1828, in Fauquier County, he grew up on a modest family farm, "Rose Bank." His father's death and his mother's extravagance nearly impoverished the family. Ashby, consequently, never enjoyed the privileges of the planter class. Like so many old Virginia families, Ashby's parents could not sustain a lifestyle in keeping with their social standing and prestigious ancestry. But unlike many slaveholders' sons, young Turner never received university training. Even his admirers commented on his limited intellectual world. The state's failing economy further curtailed his opportunities as a young man. Exhausted lands, falling prices, and overproduction had forced more than 300,000 white Virginians to leave for the Deep South or the West by 1850, including Ashby's younger brother, Richard, who emigrated to Texas.[13]

A number of complex factors accounted for the state's decline, but many Virginians pointed to the cavalier tradition with its emphasis on aristocratic ease as the source of economic malaise. Virginians of Ashby's generation called for a new set of values that would turn the state into a progressive land blessed by material prosperity, technological advancement, and scientific inquiry.[14] Ashby must have been influenced by this social context. He supported the Whig Party and its agenda of internal improvements, believing so strongly in the party's principles that he ran, although unsuccessfully, for public office in 1859. In his private affairs he entered an agreement with his brother to mine coal deposits in southwest Virginia. His main source of income, however, came from a mercantile business near Markham, a depot along the Manassas Gap Railroad. Neither of these endeavors was the occupation of a Virginia gentleman, nor did either adequately pay the bills. Financial entanglements brought Ashby into court on a regular basis. Whether or not

Ashby was a good businessman is not the point. His endeavors reflected a personal willingness to merge capitalism and slavery, a process that was occurring across the state in the 1850s. A new economic order had gained strength in Virginia, based on a growing class of merchants, small manufacturers, and commercial farmers. These men welcomed the scientific and mechanical improvements of the day, firmly convinced they lived in a modern slave society committed to republicanism, Christianity, and economic development. Although a slaveholder, Ashby aligned with this new class and its ethos, which more closely resembled the dominant ideology of the New South than the insulated world of the old planter elite.[15]

The cavalier image does its greatest damage by sanitizing Ashby's wartime experience, obscuring the bitter fighting that he witnessed and encouraged in the Shenandoah Valley. Stories of Ashby and his band of cavaliers chasing befuddled Yankees across the countryside, as if on a fox hunt, have a charming appeal. Such exploits have contributed to a romantic mystique that still surrounds Jackson's 1862 Valley campaign. Most historians have played on the David and Goliath story of the campaign, emphasizing the great odds that Stonewall Jackson's men overcame against three Federal armies. Ashby's bold escapades, especially his breathtaking escapes from would-be northern captors, reinforce the tendency to focus on the drama of Jackson's movements, to see the Confederates as underdogs at the expense of the campaign's social and political context.[16]

War in the Shenandoah Valley had a brutal dimension. Confederates routinely persecuted Unionists, slaves, free blacks, and southern dissenters. The region's mixed loyalties encouraged abuses by both armies, which had difficulty discerning friend from foe. Frustration led to abuses. In the lower Valley, Union and Confederate soldiers needlessly slaughtered livestock, burned crops, and destroyed mills. In early 1862 Jackson bitterly complained about the "reprobate Federal commanders" in Hampshire County whose track from Romney to Hanging Rock "was one of desolation." "The number of dead animals lying along the road-side, where they had been shot by the enemy," he added, "exemplified the spirit of that part of the Northern Army."[17]

Like their Union counterparts, Ashby's troopers routinely violated that "civilized" line between civilian and soldier. To describe their actions as atrocities would be grossly inaccurate; most amounted to petty vandalism. On June 3, 1862, Ashby's men went on a plundering spree in Martinsburg.

"Adventure of Ashby at Winchester," an illustration in John Esten Cooke's heavily romanticized postwar memoir *Wearing of the Gray*. The caption explains how Ashby, chased by ranks of U.S. troopers, turned on one of his closest pursuers and "seized him by the throat, dragged him from his saddle, and putting spur to his horse, bore him off." Few images convey more graphically the ideal of Ashby as bold cavalier. John Esten Cooke, *Wearing of the Gray: Being Personal Portraits, Scenes, and Adventures of the War* (New York: E. B. Treat, 1867), plate following p. 64.

According to one northern officer, the Confederate cavalrymen "took everything they could lay their hands upon in the way of clothing and food, especially salt, sugar, and coffee, but in other respects did not misbehave."[18] On occasion Ashby's troopers lost their sense of restraint and severely punished their enemies. During a sharp fight near Harpers Ferry on October 16, 1861, they stripped four Union dead, leaving them in "perfect nudity." Union brigadier general John W. Geary described the grim scene: "One was laid in the form of a crucifixion, with his hands spread out, and cut through the palms with a dull knife. This inhuman treatment incensed my troops exceedingly."[19]

Ashby's role in the Harpers Ferry incident is impossible to determine, and he certainly did not give his men free license against the Federals. Nonetheless, he was no gentleman warrior who restricted his actions to the battlefield. The blurred loyalties of a border region often demanded harsh actions against civilians, and Ashby acted accordingly. John H. Boltz was one of many Shenandoah Valley Unionists harassed by Ashby. While asleep in his lower Valley home, Boltz awoke when two soldiers from Ashby's command barged into his house. They arrested the dazed Boltz and escorted him to Ashby's headquarters the next morning. When he discovered that Botlz was a constable and collector for Virginia's loyal Governor Francis H. Pierpont, Ashby became infuriated. He ordered his men to "shoot the infernal Scoundrel or hang him to the first limb you come to and don't fetch him here."[20] He repeated the order a second time and walked away. To Boltz's relief, Ashby eventually calmed down and countermanded the order. Ashby not only used such scare tactics against civilians, but he also routinely sanctioned the seizure of goods, horses, and property of loyal citizens. The mixed political loyalties of the region forced Ashby to practice a harsher view of war.[21]

When it came to conventional warfare, he fought with a vengeance, displaying an almost maniacal desire to kill Yankees. In an 1861 letter to his sister he reported that one of his men had been wounded in skirmishing along the Potomac. For this single casualty he exacted a heavy price from the Yankees, boasting that he had "good [cause?] to believe that I have killed twenty or thirty of them" in return.[22]

Personal reasons also help explain Ashby's vengeful spirit. He became sullen, bitter, and desperate after the death of his younger brother and close companion, Richard. In June 1861 both brothers served in the 7th Virginia Cavalry under Col. Angus W. McDonald. They guarded the border counties of the lower Shenandoah Valley, where they assisted pro-Confederate Marylanders across the Potomac. In their spare time they hunted down suspected Unionists. Given independent command by McDonald, Ashby took a part of the regiment, including his brother's company, to a camp near Cumberland, Maryland. On June 26 Richard Ashby led ten men to a cabin of a local Unionist, but as his patrol closed in on the elusive spy, enemy cavalry suddenly slashed into Ashby's column. With remarkable selflessness he ordered his men to retreat while he blocked the Federal charge. In no time he was surrounded, and a bitter hand-to-hand fight ensued. Most likely Richard refused to surrender. A saber blow to the head cleaved off part of his skull and knocked him out of his saddle. While Ashby lay helpless on the ground, a Federal soldier asked him if he was a Union man or a secessionist (as if the preceding struggle had not confirmed Richard's loyalties). With no hesitation Ashby replied that he was a secessionist. The Union interrogator promptly jabbed a sword into Richard's abdomen before stealing his spurs and horse. The Federals then rode off, leaving Ashby to die.[23]

Reports of gunfire reached Turner Ashby's headquarters, and he quickly led a mounted party to the scene. He found Richard in blood-soaked clothes, slowly dying; his breathing was labored, and his words were barely audible as he pleaded for water. Using some blankets as a makeshift stretcher, Confederates carried Richard to Camp Washington, where he suffered for another week before he died on July 3. His death devastated Turner Ashby. "Mine has been the heaviest loss," he wrote four days later. "I lose the strength of his arm in the fight as well as the companion of my social hours." A witness to the funeral recorded that Ashby stood near his brother's casket, "pale, agitated and trembling."[24]

Ashby reminded his loved ones that Richard's death would be in vain if they did not reaffirm their commitment to the Confederacy. "I mean to bear it as a soldier, and not as one who in this time for sacrifices regards only his own loss. You must all try to bear it in the same way," he advised his sister. "Let it be your boast that you have given a brother for the safety of your country and the preservation of your homes, and Ma that she has give a son for such a cause as ours. When men die as he has died, (and as he prepared to die), for liberty, it shows our enemies that we cannot be conquered. It saves the lives of many."[25]

The cruel manner of Richard's death must have fueled Turner Ashby's passion for hunting down Yankees. If he had not been heartlessly abandoned on the field, Turner believed, his brother would have recovered. To honor Richard's memory, he attacked the Federals at every opportunity, sometimes at great personal risk. Northerners called his relentless desire to "wreck a dire revenge" for Richard's death the "Ashby Oath."[26]

Turner Ashby's spirit of revenge cannot be reduced to Richard's death but must be understood within the context of border warfare in the Civil War. Similar to the fighting in Missouri, Kentucky, Kansas, eastern Tennessee, and western North Carolina, the 1862 Valley campaign also witnessed elements of partisan warfare.[27] A divided civilian population contributed to the unorganized, highly personal fighting in the lower Valley. Although Ashby was not a bushwhacker like William Quantrill or "Bloody Bill" Anderson, he did face an unpredictable civilian population, and he terrorized suspected Unionists while seeking reprisals for his brother's death. In comparison with most Confederate officers in Virginia, Ashby was one of the first to move away from a conciliatory policy toward the North. He did not confine violence to the battlefield, nor did he believe in showing compassion to the enemy. He took a harder view of war, one that resembled the practical thinking of Stonewall

Jackson rather than some romantic vision of a fanciful cavalier who considered war a contest between gallant knights charging across a well-manicured lawn while a group of belles watched from a distance.[28]

Ashby served as Jackson's unofficial cavalry chief during the 1862 Valley campaign, although he received his orders directly from the Confederate War Department. By March 1862 he had command of the 7th Virginia Cavalry, a unit that had ballooned into twenty-seven companies, nearly three times the size of a typical regiment. He used his troopers to screen the army's movements, protect its rear guard, and gather intelligence. In these assignments Ashby performed competently and ranked among the finest Confederate cavalrymen for such operations. He succeeded in large part because he stayed close to the front lines, always made his presence felt, and never missed a skirmish no matter how minor. Even the Federals came to admire his tactical skill and conspicuous bravery, although they were frustrated by their failure to bag the elusive cavalryman. With some irritation Union staff officer David Strother admitted that "a gull would stand as good a chance to catch a fox, as our force to catch Ashby." Not everyone was so impressed. "You have probably read the many accounts of Ashby's career," wrote Robert Gould Shaw a few weeks after Ashby's death. "For my part," added the young officer who later would command the famous 54th Massachusetts Infantry, "I can't understand where he got his reputation from, and am inclined to think there is a good deal of newspaper humbug about it." Although Shaw's regiment had been in the advance of Banks's force, it rarely encountered Ashby's men. "When seen," Shaw noted, "they have always been out of riflerange, and the few prisoners I have seen myself were wretched 'white trash,' poorly mounted."[29]

The poor organization and lack of discipline in the 7th Virginia often overshadowed Ashby's accomplishments in the field. At critical junctures during the Valley campaign, Ashby's men forgot they were soldiers and abandoned their posts. With good reason, Jackson considered Ashby's cavalry unruly and unreliable. He wanted Ashby to govern his men with West Point professionalism, not like some militia captain. In May 1862 he summed up his long-standing criticisms of Ashby to friend and political supporter Congressman Alexander R. Boteler of Shepherdstown, Virginia (who, ironically, also served as Ashby's advocate in Richmond). "With regards to Col. Ashby's promotion," Jackson explained, "I would gladly favor it, if he were a good disciplinarian, but he has such bad discipline and attaches so little importance to drill, that I would regard it as a calamity to see him promoted. I desire so soon as he gives proper attention to these matters (which are so essential to success in operating with large masses of troops) to see him promoted."[30] Most of Stonewall's subordinates agreed that Ashby gave his men too many liberties. For example, on April 24, 1862, Lt. Col. Edward T. H. Warren denounced Ashby as a "humbug" whose command was in "perfectly disorganized and inefficient condition." Fellow cavalryman and admirer Thomas T. Munford offered the opinion, which might be taken more than one way, that Ashby "could handle a mob better than other officers could handle a well drilled corps."[31]

Ashby's lax style of leadership nearly resulted in his dismissal. On three occasions in April 1862 he failed to execute Jackson's orders with sufficient vigilance. As the weather started to clear on April 15, Jackson anticipated a Federal advance into the upper Valley. He instructed Ashby to prevent any military property at Mount Jackson from falling into enemy hands. The next morning Union cavalrymen raced into Columbia Furnace, where they captured an entire company of Ashby's cavalry, some sixty men, asleep in a church. Ashby had not ensured that a picket line had been posted, and now the Federals were only seven miles from Mount Jackson.

Federals caught Ashby off guard again the following morning. His main line at Mount Jackson collapsed under a combined infantry and artillery attack. Contrary to Stonewall's orders, Ashby's men did not destroy the supplies and equipment in town, a lapse that the commanding general would not tolerate. They worried instead about their own safety and fled the scene. Union troopers followed close on the Confederates' heels and managed to save much of the equipment and military stores in town, including several locomotives. To slow the Federal advance, Ashby tried to burn the bridge over the North Fork of the Shenandoah River. Before he could ignite a pile of combustibles, the enemy nearly surrounded him. He emerged from the bridge with the Federals close behind, creating the impression to some Confederates that he was leading the Union regiment in pursuit. After his dramatic ride, in which he lost his famous white charger, he formed his broken ranks at Rude's Hill. Ashby's individual heroics added to the cavalryman's ever growing folklore but did not earn him redemption at headquarters. Jackson could not understand why Ashby's men were so unprepared, further proof that Ashby could not be trusted with a significant command. With the loss of Mount Jackson and the important river crossing, the Federals could pressure the Confederate flanks. Ashby's critical mistakes forced Jackson to retreat southward with the Valley army.[32]

Two days after the Mount Jackson debacle, portions of Ashby's command lost contact with Jackson's headquarters. Stonewall wanted to destroy three bridges over the South Fork of the Shenandoah (Columbia Bridge, Red Bridge, and White House Bridge) in order to restrict enemy movements in the Luray Valley. Ashby's recent blundering convinced Jackson to give this critical assignment to his incomparable mapmaker, Jedediah Hotchkiss. Before he could carry out his assignment, Hotchkiss had to locate Ashby's cavalry. It took some time before he found two companies inside an old foundry. To his horror the troopers, who had consumed too much applejack, were lounging around rather than vigilantly guarding the rear of the army. Their picket line resembled a sieve, and before Hotchkiss could burn the spans, Federal cavalry poured through, catching Ashby's men in their drunken state. The hungover cavalrymen offered little resistance. Most scurried away, seeking shelter in the Blue Ridge Mountains. Many of the men did not reappear in camp for ten days. An angry Hotchkiss considered the incident a "perfect stampede" and a "disgraceful affair."[33]

The unwieldy size of Ashby's command, coupled with his disdain for drill and discipline, had troubled Jackson from the onset of the campaign. Moreover, the string of disasters in mid-April demonstrated the immediate need for reorganization. On April 24 Stonewall effectively stripped Ashby of his cavalry by dividing his companies between two infantry brigades. In the future Ashby would only control the advance and rear guards. If necessary he could use other portions of his command. The proud cavalryman considered Jackson's order intolerable, a flagrant violation of his authority, and he promptly submitted his resignation. Moments later Hotchkiss found the cavalryman "sitting before the fire in a very moody humor." He turned to Hotchkiss and explained that "Jackson was treating him very badly in desiring to divide his command into two regiments and requiring him to drill them." From their brief conversation Hotchkiss believed that Ashby "seemed to think that although he had so many companies he could easily manage them all himself and that it was unnecessary to have them drilled."[34]

The rupture between Jackson and Ashby rattled a fragile Confederate command system that tottered on collapse. This incident seemed to support the growing belief among Stonewall's subordinates that their superior suffered from an acute mental disorder. They openly criticized his brusque manner and secretive ways. Quartermaster John Harman wrote, "I have just seen Col. Ashby and he is determined not to remain any longer." Harman blamed this "great calamity" on Jackson, proof that "we are in great danger from our cracked-brained General." "I do not know what the cause of the difficulty is," Harman added, "but they have had a muss. Do not speak of it, it will hurt us bad enough anyway."[35]

Ashby also made his case outside army channels, asking Boteler to present his position to the secretary of war. The cavalryman described his loss of authority as an "indignity" that came "without any apparent failure to do my duty [and] leaves me in utter astonishment at the cause of my command being taken from me." In what must have been a temporary lapse of memory, Ashby claimed "that for the last two months I have saved the army of the Valley from being utter destroyed." He had accomplished these amazing feats "without the aid of Gen. Jacksons command and embarrassed by the want of such information from him which I considered myself entitled to." Ashby thought the War Department should know "that while I send my unconditional Resignation, that I do not desire to shrink from any of the danger or sacrifice which my countrymen must make in this her darkest hour."[36]

Jackson understood that he plied dangerous waters. A hasty move would send Ashby overboard and with him the rest of the Valley cavalry. He decided to meet his unhappy subordinate, an opportunity he granted few other disgruntled lieutenants during the war. Gen. Charles S. Winder, who spoke at length with Ashby about withdrawing his resignation, probably arranged the meeting. During this tense encounter, Ashby bluntly told Jackson that "he would hold him to a personal account for the indignity he had put upon him." He then raised the stakes, threatening to organize an independent partisan command and operate in the lower Valley. Word of this proposal was already gaining support among the cavalry's lower-ranking officers. Ashby's only field-grade officer, Maj. Oliver R. Funsten, also backed this tough stance against Jackson by tendering his resignation. Jackson's attempt to rein in his cavalry had backfired. He faced a potential mutiny. Ashby's popularity far exceeded what loyalty, if any, the Valley cavalry felt for Stonewall.[37]

With his options exhausted and in no position to bargain, Jackson restored Ashby to full command. It must have been a bitter pill for Stonewall to swallow. He later explained that "Colonel Ashby's influence over his command" was so great "that I became well satisfied that if I persisted in my attempt to increase the efficiency of the cavalry it would produce the contrary effect." Stonewall even feared that Ashby would turn his men against him. The only concession Ashby made was a promise to discipline his troopers. With some relief, Harman informed his brother that "the difficulty between Jackson and Ashby has been settled for the present by General Jackson backing square down; I am glad of it, but I am afraid there will be no good feeling in the future." Hotchkiss agreed that Jackson had lost the dispute, writing in his journal that Ashby "is left at liberty to dispose of his force as he deems best."[38]

The crisis had passed, but the fundamental problems between the two men persisted. Even the temporary loss of his command did not prompt Ashby to change his ways. He continued to ignore the cavalry's organizational problems, never drilled his troops, and refused to punish his men for their habitual disregard of military protocol. As his organizational and disciplinary problems spiraled out of control, Ashby further incurred Jackson's wrath by accepting new recruits from the infantry. Stonewall had strictly prohibited such reenlistments, insisting that "men should continue in that arm in which they have been serving." A frustrated Jackson wanted to drop the hammer on Ashby. Behind the scenes he encouraged the War Department to take decisive action. On May 5, 1862, he explained why his previous attempts at reorganization had failed. The situation, he admitted, had deteriorated since then. To avoid another showdown with Ashby and a possible mutiny among his horsemen, he pleaded with Richmond authorities to take immediate action and organize the cavalry "into regiments at the earliest practicable moment."[39]

Before the War Department could intervene, the two men locked horns again. When Nathaniel Banks decided to abandon Strasburg on May 24 and withdraw northward to Winchester, Ashby's troopers rode to Middletown to scout the enemy's movements. For three hours Jackson waited to hear from Ashby before sending Hotchkiss and sixteen cavalrymen to make a reconnaissance. They quickly sent word back that Banks had abandoned Strasburg and was in full retreat to Winchester. After a difficult march, Jackson reached the high ground overlooking Middletown, where he saw an artillerist's dream on the Valley Turnpike. Bracketed between two stone walls rolled a column of Union wagons. Jackson pitched into the inviting target with two batteries. The sudden explosion of shells sparked a wild retreat. Wagons careened out of control, soldiers sprinted for safety, and the entire column came unhinged.

Jackson yelled for his cavalry chief to lead the pursuit. With a handful of companies, Ashby's troopers swept across the field, but the colonel quickly lost control of his command. The booty of war proved too alluring for his men. Many broke ranks to loot and gather discarded equipment. Any semblance of organization disappeared in a frenzy of pillaging. A few men even detached horses from wrecked Union vehicles and took them to their farms. Only fifty cavalrymen remained from a unit that carried more men on its rolls than a regiment. Jackson had feared such a scenario all along, and he blamed Ashby for squandering an opportunity to destroy at least a portion of the Federal army. "I was pained to see," Stonewall wrote in his official report, "that so many of Ashby's command, both cavalry and infantry, forgetful of their high trust as the advance of a pursuing army, deserted their colors, and abandoned themselves to pillage to such an extent as to make it necessary for that gallant officer to discontinue farther pursuit."[40]

When Jackson drove Banks's army from Winchester the following day, he wanted Ashby to slash at the disorganized mass of retreating Federals fleeing toward the Potomac River. Stonewall frantically searched for Ashby, but he could not find the colonel or any of his twenty-seven companies. Another opportunity was slipping away, and the cavalry's absence had given Banks a critical head start. A frustrated Jackson complained that "never was there such a chance for cavalry; oh, that my cavalry were in place." In his official report Jackson made the exaggerated claim that "there is good reason for believing that, had the cavalry played its part in this pursuit . . . but a small portion of Banks' army would have made its escape to the Potomac."[41]

The plundering of the preceding evening largely explains Ashby's disappearing act at Winchester. Although a few of his companies were elsewhere in the Valley, Ashby's lack of discipline explained the dispersion of his command. The night march to Winchester made matters worse. When the fighting started early the next morning, Ashby lacked sufficient time to reorganize his troopers. Jackson was astonished that he did not see a single cavalryman during the Winchester fighting. Near dusk, when an agitated Stonewall finally located Ashby, he asked the cavalryman why he never reached the field. The colonel replied "that he had moved to the enemy's left, for the purpose of cutting off a portion of his force."[42] This might explain Ashby's absence, but it does not exonerate him. He knew that the bulk of the southern cavalry already opposed the enemy's left and that his movement would unmask the Valley army's other flank. In the end, it remains unclear as to why Ashby did not appear at the close of the battle. It is clear that he had lost control of his command. Jackson does not bear responsibility for the cavalry's disappearance.

After the war, Jed Hotchkiss recalled that Jackson relieved Ashby for his poor performance at Winchester. No extant wartime correspondence supports this claim. It seems unlikely that Jackson would have taken such draconian steps. His attempt to ease Ashby out of command the preceding April nearly wrecked the cavalry. Whatever the truth of Hotchkiss's assertion, Ashby achieved redemption during the first week and a half of June, when he slowed General Frémont's advance into the lower Valley. At Woodstock on June 1, the Federals overran the Confederate rear guard, but Ashby, after hearing the gunfire, raced to the scene, rallied some stragglers, and launched a surprise counterattack. When he triumphantly returned to Jackson's headquarters, Stonewall supposedly restored him to command. Ashby continued to frustrate Frémont's movements in the main valley, performing some of his finest work of the campaign. On June 6, two miles south of Harrisonburg, Ashby drove back a hasty Union cavalry attack. In the pursuit an infantry battle developed. Ashby had dismounted to lead some Maryland foot soldiers when a bullet from a Pennsylvania Bucktail pierced his heart and killed him instantly.[43]

Without Ashby the Valley cavalry became virtually worthless. Thomas Munford recalled that "it was several days before his old command could be counted on." Hotchkiss had observed the preceding April that "when Ashby's men are with him they behave gallantly, but when they are away from him they lack the inspiration of presence and being undisciplined they often fail to do any good." In Richmond, Robert E. Lee worried that no one, including his nephew Fitzhugh Lee, could control the cavalry after Ashby's death. Ashby's troopers were so demoralized after Harrisonburg that they proved incapable of performing the basic task of picket duty. They shamefully abandoned their posts on June 8, leaving the road to Port Republic open to some Union troopers who nearly captured Jackson at his headquarters.[44]

Jackson's near-capture must have given him just cause to reappraise Ashby's talents as a cavalryman. Late in the evening, when Jackson learned of Ashby's death, he "walked the floor of his room, for some time, in deep sorrow, greatly moved by the sad news." Typically, Jackson never strayed from the bare facts in his official reports, but he made an exception with Ashby. "As a partisan officer I never knew his superior," he wrote. "His daring was proverbial; his powers of endurance almost incredible; his tone of character heroic, and his sagacity almost intuitive in divining the purposes and movements of the enemy."[45]

The blow of Ashby's death fell hardest on his men. When one of his troopers learned of Ashby's demise, he admitted, "I could scarcely keep back a gush of tears!" Another soldier wrote that within hours of the event, "a gloom was cast over the whole army. . . . I consider that we lost more by his fall than we had gained during the whole campaign." At Ashby's funeral in Charlottesville, an observer noted that his "old company all came down to pay the last tribute of respect to him." She thought it "was very touching to see such bold Warriors weep like women over his grave." Another Confederate officer went so far as to claim that "at that time Ashby was deeper down in the affections of the Valley army than Jackson."[46]

How did Ashby obtain the fierce devotion of his men when he had achieved so little on the battlefield? His military record was mixed, filled with spectacular highlights of individual bravery but short on meaningful contributions to the army. His contempt for drill and organization dulled the fighting abilities of his cavalry. The lack of preparedness, as already discussed, hurt the army at critical junctures during the campaign. When he was not neglecting his command, he squabbled with Jackson. Ashby's reputation, however, survived his well-publicized clashes with Stonewall, arguably the most popular Confederate general at that stage of the war. Disputes with "Old Jack" and a mediocre war record failed to diminish the men's love for Ashby, who seemed to possess mystical powers over his troopers. They followed him with unequivocal devotion. When one of Ashby's horses was killed, his men surrounded the dead creature and plucked the hair out of its tail and mane. They also clipped Ashby's whiskers for keepsakes just before his funeral.[47] Few Confederate officers were ever worshiped so fervently. If Ashby did not achieve the loyalty of his men exclusively through the cavalier image and his battlefield gallantry, what explains his appeal?

Ashby emerged as a Confederate hero because he understood the rural background of the Shenandoah's residents while drawing from the same cultural language that defined male conduct. Like most white southerners, he was committed to the values of honor and courage. By fighting with unrestrained bravery on the battlefield, he forged an indestructible bond with his troopers. According to one man, Ashby "never said 'Men, go on' but it was 'men, follow me.'" Another soldier in the Valley army observed, "I have seen him in battle and he seemed to possess a magnetic influence over his men. They would follow wherever he would lead, and he was always foremost." Ashby epitomized the ideal fighter because he seemed oblivious to danger. While riding the picket lines, Ashby explained to a comrade that "when the Yankee pickets fire at him . . . he stops and sits on his horse right still, without dodging or moving in the least." He instructed his men that they should also evince a similar calm demeanor in the face of danger.[48]

Ashby's battlefield heroics would have been irrelevant if he had been a martinet in camp. His soldiers cherished their freedoms as white men. As civilians before the war, they resented any violation of their liberties, especially if it came at the hands of a haughty slaveholder.[49] Most of Ashby's men had prewar militia experience where they had enjoyed a degree of equality with their officers. Those antebellum views shaped their expectations of military life. Confederate enlisted men, consequently, would not tolerate a domineering officer who ran roughshod over their freedoms. They demanded a voice as to who would lead them, where they would serve, and what branch of service they would join. On May 5, 1862, for instance, one of Ashby's captains sent him a list of companies that had selected their own commanders. They would not wait for instructions from above, and Ashby approved of the arrangement. Unlike Jackson and other professional military officers who wanted to strip their soldiers of their civilian sensibilities, Ashby acknowledged his men's rights and sought to protect them. One of his subordinates captured the essence of his populist style, writing after the war that Ashby "did not believe in machine-made soldiers."[50]

Ashby opened a dialogue with his men that almost never would have been allowed in professional armies. One of his soldiers appreciated Ashby's command style and described the cavalryman as "a man before he was a soldier." Ashby did not parade around camp like some dandy, nor did he rule with an iron fist. He always treated his men as equals while looking out for their welfare. In this way he gained their allegiance. An Ashby trooper remembered that on the picket line, "he would laugh and talk with the men, with great urbanity and freedom, & made himself most agreeable too."[51]

The camaraderie and freedom of the cavalry gave Ashby's command an undeniably romantic appeal. Their mobility also made it easier for his men to make those crucial but short visits home. "On horseback, I felt like a new man," wrote a Confederate trooper, "and contemplated the war from a much more favorable standpoint." Even Gen. Richard Ewell, Jackson's outspokenly disgruntled subordinate, admitted to cavalryman Thomas Munford the night after Ashby had been killed that "he would rather have an independent cavalry regiment than the best division of infantry in the army." "You fellows have some fun," Ewell added, "but I am no better than a darned tin soldier."[52]

Ashby's image as a bold cavalier leading a freewheeling tribal band across the valley might have lured a handful of recruits into his ranks. But Ashby's appeal was more complex and geared toward the interests, needs, and fears of independent farmers and small slaveholders. From the onset of the war, the white residents of the Shenandoah Valley contended with a serious manpower shortage. As residents of a wheat-producing area, Valley farmers did not rely as heavily on slave labor as did their Piedmont and Tidewater neighbors. Valley residents, consequently, protested to Confederate authorities that they lacked a reserve pool of labor to replace valuable artisans lost to war. Their pleas, as least initially, had little effect. Local economies nearly collapsed under the crushing manpower demands of the Confederacy. Farmers desperately needed the services of millers, tanners, and shoemakers. Without these basic services, so essential to the daily existence of rural people, many struggled to survive.[53] Members of the 7th Brigade, Virginia Militia, presented the Valley's difficult case to Jefferson Davis.

> We desire, first, to say that no portion of Virginia has been more loyal to the South and her interest than the militia of this valley, [but] the Valley of Virginia is a wheat-growing country, in which slave labor is scarce; consequently the larger proportion of the labor must be performed by white men between the ages of eighteen and forty-five years. The time for sending the wheat crops has arrived, and unless at least a considerable proportion of the men now here can be returned to their homes to attend to putting that crop in the ground we will be unable to raise supplies sufficient for our own subsistence.[54]

The controversial Conscription Act passed on April 16, 1862, exacerbated the Valley's manpower problems. The legislation drafted white males between ages eighteen and thirty-five years for a period of three years, unless the war ended sooner.[55] Although reactions were mixed across Virginia, many people resented the intrusion of national authority and the exemptions that favored the wealthy. Requiring an additional three years of service also agitated those already in the ranks who believed they had fulfilled their duty. Resistance to the draft was strongest in the Valley. In April several hundred members of the Rockingham County militia mutinied and sought refuge in the mountains. Jackson sent Confederate troops under Col. John R. Jones to quell what the papers called the Blue Ridge Rebellion. Some heavy shelling flushed the malcontents out of the hills, and their leader surrendered. Such open protest was rare, but a general dissatisfaction infected the Valley army that spring, explaining why Confederate units from the area suffered their highest desertion rates during the war.[56]

Ashby grasped the political turmoil and deteriorating social conditions that plagued the Valley in the spring of 1862. He properly feared that Jackson's by-the-book approach would only intensify the troops' dissatisfaction, further undermining morale at home. On April 25 he informed Boteler that "such has been the constrictions of the new conscript Law here that I deem Gen. Jackson's Army in the worst condition it has been in since it came to the Valley." He blamed Stonewall for failing to appreciate "the condition of his Army and its daily diminution." Ashby understood that the rank and file faced unrelenting pressures at home, exacerbated by the army's manpower demands and its refusal to liberally grant furloughs to soldiers who were needed on the farm. Jackson, on the other hand, seemed oblivious to the special needs of his soldiers, rural men who were trying to ensure that their families did not starve. They were feeling the growing pains of becoming soldiers, rebelling against Jackson, who played the part of the overbearing father. He showed little patience, refused to compromise, and demanded that his troops mature into professionals overnight.[57]

Unlike Stonewall, Ashby should be credited for having a better grasp of the political and social realities of the Valley. He was also more astute in compromising with small farmers and the yeomanry as a way to improve the military efficiency of the Confederacy. He succeeded in promoting a democratic spirit in his command based on the local interests of his men. Like that of his own soldiers, Ashby's world centered on his small, tightly knit community in Fauquier County. If his men were to become loyal Confederate soldiers, Ashby must have understood that it depended on their ability to reaffirm local attachments. Based on this assumption, Ashby granted a liberal "French Furlough" system, even though the practice violated military protocol at the most fundamental level. The constant presence of Ashby's cavalry in the Shenandoah Valley contributed to this phenomenon, resulting in a fluid relationship between camp and home front. Jackson always operated in the backyard of Ashby's men, where they faced the conflicting demands of family and nation. When there was a lull in active campaigning or they did not feel their presence was necessary, Ashby's troopers saw no reason to remain with the Valley army. They believed the urgent needs of their families required short trips home. If a wayward soldier returned to the ranks within a reasonable amount of time and offered a legitimate excuse for his truancy, Ashby and his officers generally looked the other way.[58]

This laxity was the main source of Ashby's discipline problems. Ashby's subordinate Albert C. Lincoln complained that the men sometimes took advantage of the French Furlough system. On February 18, 1862, he was "sorry to report so many absent without leave." "That portion of the Company that are now at home have left three or four times in the same manner," he added. "Some of them had not been back more than three weeks since the retreat from Romney." Lincoln warned that more would leave if they were not granted furloughs and given their bounties. "They are becoming dissatisfied & in fact they can not be blamed for it, for they have not been treated as they should be." Lincoln's letter reveals the strong bargaining position of the rank and file. If government officials did not address local needs or the soldiers failed to receive the necessary compromises from senior officers such as Ashby, the men protested with their feet. Desertion did not always mean a rejection of the Confederacy.[59]

While Ashby might have been too liberal in granting absences without leave, his leadership style made sense during the first two years of the war when soldiers were adjusting to the realities and restraints of army life. They might have looked like soldiers, but they still had a civilian outlook and a strong attachment to home. Ashby's loose organizational system also gave company-grade officers more freedom in dealing with their men. One of Ashby's staff members endorsed the company organization as "most excellent." "This was entirely satisfactory to the men," he added.[60]

Jackson and other military officials condemned Ashby's unwieldy company system and policy of French Furloughs. Had Ashby followed Stonewall's stern measures of discipline, however, he probably would have ignited a rebellion in the ranks. Ashby's open command system might be viewed as a sign of weakness or even negligence, but his men appreciated his gestures as an acknowledgment of their rights. This also helps explain why the Valley's civilians championed Ashby as their protector. He not only defended them from the Yankees, but he also supported civilian demands by allowing men to assist loved ones on the farm. In this way Ashby gained the unyielding support of his soldiers and civilians. Furthermore, he recognized local interests as a way to secure his command's commitment to the Confederacy. When the women of Shepherdstown felt threatened by Yankee raiders, they sent a petition directly to Ashby rather than to the Confederate War Department. He emerged as the protector of the Valley, not because of a provincial outlook, but because he had a surprisingly sophisticated view of war that did not reduce nationalism to simple allegiance to Richmond's central government.[61]

In death, Ashby's populist image gave way to that of the cavalier. Such a transformation required southerners to use selective memory and at times to induce amnesia. Early in the war, artillerist Charles W. Trueheart had criticized Ashby for his limited intellectual powers and his general lack of refinement, but just a few weeks after the cavalryman's funeral, all imperfections were forgotten. He "fell [as] one of the Noblest & bravest of Va[']s sons," Trueheart wrote: "He was strictly moral and temperate; read & revered the Bible which he always carried with him. He seldom if ever, made use of profane language; was highly polished in his manners, & admired & respected by everyone." During Ashby's eulogy, Avirett admitted that Ashby had not professed his faith, but he assured the audience that the cavalryman was headed for the pearly gates. He wanted southerners to remember Ashby as a Christian soldier who gave his life on the altar of the Confederacy.[62]

Not only did Ashby suddenly become pious and sophisticated in death, but his physical appearance also changed. During the war many of his comrades thought Ashby resembled an Arab fighter with his dark face, black eyes, heavy black beard that grew close to his eyes, and nontraditional uniform. He was even mistaken for a mulatto. Another observer believed he looked like Lucifer. Because of his swarthy complexion, he rode as the Knight of the Black Prince or Knight Hiawatha before the war. According to the cavalier myth, dark skin always signified a baseness, while whiteness signified nobility. In remembering Ashby, Confederates often spoke less of his dark features and more of an Anglo-Saxon appearance. Newspapers overlooked his casual attire and emphasized his soldierly bearing, plumed hat, and immaculate dress. Although he rode a number of animals of different colors, he was most often described as riding his famous white charger. The white steed served the purposes of Ashby admirers, symbolizing purity and gallantry and accentuating Ashby's new image as the quintessential cavalier. The *Southern Illustrated News* described the animal as "beautiful" and "noble," giving Ashby a "bold and picturesque appearance."[63]

Confederates resurrected Ashby as the perfect southerner to ease the psychological trauma of war. In doing so, Virginians returned to the ideal of the cavalier, a cultural myth that had lost much of its influence during the 1850s. The death and destruction of war, however, left them searching for a way to define themselves as superior, virtuous people, even if the Yankees were winning on the battlefield. The making of Ashby into a Confederate hero also served white southerners during the postwar years when they knew they would stand judgment before the world court. Just a few months after Appomattox, a Front Royal resident thought that the Ashby legacy had become even more important to the Valley's public memory. The cavalryman, she wrote, had raised an "enduring monument . . . for himself in the hearts of the people of the Valley." "His memory," she added, "is cherished thus above all others that have fought in the struggle." Ashby's rebirth as a cavalier reminds us that the principles of the Lost Cause were not a postwar construction. They originated in the Confederacy's sincere attempt to memorialize its dead.[64]

By propagating the cavalier myth, southerners retreated into a dreamy world of chivalrous cavaliers and genteel aristocrats, avoiding an honest appraisal of the Old South and Confederate defeat. In 1866 more than 1,000 Winchester women filed into the Stonewall Cemetery, the final resting place of Turner Ashby. The Charlestown paper reported that the day was set aside to commemorate "the fall of the chivalrous ASHBY." Speeches were delivered by a number of ex-Confederates, including Jackson staff officer Henry Kyd Douglas, who believed that Ashby carried himself "like a knight of the olden time." Similar ceremonies were enacted across the South to pay homage to fallen Confederate patriots. Although filled with sincere emotions of grief, these events did injustice to the historical memory of countless Confederate heroes, including Ashby, who is unfortunately remembered as the "Knight of the Valley."[65]

Until recently every generation of white southerners since the war has learned, like some catechism, that all Confederates were gallant and moral, that they fought for a Christian nation, and that they protected the honor of their women against barbaric Yankee hordes.[66] Those who strayed from this dogma often became social outcasts. Postwar southerners, consequently, came to rely on chivalry as an explanatory device to give meaning to and understanding of the Confederate cause. No matter how poor their region had become after the Civil War, or how repressive against black people, white southerners could tell themselves that they came from a noble breed. In June

The *Southern Illustrated News* placed this equestrian portrait on its cover in the autumn following Ashby's death. Based on a work by William H. Caskie, it depicts Ashby as a plumed cavalier astride a prancing white charger. *Southern Illustrated News*, October 18, 1862.

1865, Valley residents gathered at the Harrisonburg battlefield to mark the spot of Ashby's death. One woman rejoiced that the little boys wore Ashby's name on their collars. These lapel pins came from the hair of the cavalryman's dead horse. This same woman considered the entire gathering inspiring, an irrefutable sign that future generations would never forget the gallant Ashby and the noble lessons of his life. "I found evidence that he yet lived in the hearts of a grateful people—that the sacrifice had not been made in vain—no false step imparted to him, but a high honorable & noble career."[67]

If postwar southerners had examined Ashby as a rural leader who engaged in brutal partisan warfare, they would have overthrown the cavalier tradition and the basic tenets of the Lost Cause. Few people are capable of stepping outside their experience and critiquing the assumptions of their world. Over time, however, it should be easier to move away from the mythical Ashby, to look at his military career within the social context of the Shenandoah Valley, and to see through the romantic haze of the past. By doing so, one finds a much different war in Virginia, a place where white society was badly divided, where fighting was often uncivilized, and where Confederate leaders lived not as saints but as regular people who possessed the virtues and faults of all humans. For whatever reason, this perspective has too seldom been embraced. Most Americans, instead, have followed the romantic trail blazed by Ashby's admirers, a well-worn historical path that leads to a make-believe land of gallant cavaliers, women in hoop skirts, and contented slaves.[68]

ACKNOWLEDGMENTS

The author would like to thank Ashby experts Patricia Walenista and Stephen L. Ritchie. Although neither agrees with my interpretation of Ashby, each was extremely generous in providing me with vital information. Jon Berkey, Keith S. Bohannon, and William J. Miller also alerted me to important Ashby material.

NOTES

1. Letitia A. Blakemore diary, June 17, 1862, in Laura Virginia Hale Archives, Warren Heritage Society, Front Royal, Va.; Mary Chesnut diary, June 13, 1862, in *Mary Chesnut's Civil War*, ed. C. Vann Woodward (New Haven: Yale University Press, 1981), 385–86; Susan Shacklett to Dora [?], June [?], 1862, Turner Ashby Papers, Special Collections, James Madison University, Harrisonburg, Va. The best modern study of Ashby is Paul Christopher Anderson, *Blood Image: Turner Ashby in the Civil War and the Southern Mind* (Baton Rouge: Louisiana State University Press, 2002). See also Charles L. Dufour, "Gen. Turner Ashby," in *Nine Men in Gray* (New York: Doubleday, 1963), 41–73. For other, generally worshipful, accounts, see Clarence Thomas, *General Turner Ashby, the Centaur of the South: A Military Sketch* (Winchester, Va.: Eddy Press, 1907); Millard K. Bushong, *General Turner Ashby and Stonewall's Valley Campaign* (Verona, Va.: McClure, 1980); Frank Cunningham, *Knight of the Confederacy: Gen. Turner Ashby* (San Antonio: Naylor, 1960). The earliest Ashby monograph came from the pen of his chaplain, James B. Avirett, who offered a comprehensive examination of Ashby's prewar and wartime career in *The Memoirs of General Turner Ashby and His Compeers* (1867; reprint, Gaithersburg, Md.: Olde

Soldier Books, 1987). The book is vintage Lost Cause propaganda that seeks to promote Ashby's image as the great cavalier.

2. "General Turner Ashby," *Southern Illustrated News*, October 18, 1862, 1. For more wartime tributes to Ashby, see "Ashby's Grave," *Richmond Daily Whig*, October 15, 1862; "The Last Day of Gen. Ashby," *Southern Confederacy* (Atlanta, Ga.), June 21, 1862; J. A. VIA., "The Death of Ashby," *Southern Literary Messenger* 34 (May 1863): 315; "Iris," "In Memory of Ashby," *Southern Literary Messenger* 35 (November and December 1863): 718.

3. For an overview of the Lost Cause and its varied purposes in southern culture, see Gaines M. Foster, *Ghosts of the Confederacy: Defeat, the Lost Cause, and the Emergence of the New South* (New York: Oxford, 1987); Charles R. Wilson, *Baptized in Blood: The Religion of the Lost Cause, 1865–1920* (Athens: University of Georgia Press, 1980); Gary W. Gallagher and Alan T. Nolan, eds., *The Myth of the Lost Cause and Civil War History* (Bloomington: Indiana University Press, 2000).

4. "The Late General Ashby by One Who Knew Him," *Richmond Daily Whig*, July 24, 1862. Discussions of the cavalier image can be found in William R. Taylor, *Cavalier and Yankee: The Old South and American National Character* (New York: George Braziller, 1961); Rollin G. Osterweis, *Romanticism and Nationalism in the Old South* (New Haven: Yale University Press, 1949).

5. Although Ashby came from a distinguished Virginia lineage, his immediate family had hit hard times, preventing him from securing the financial or social status of a prominent slaveholder. Ashby's mercantile business prospered for much of the 1850s until 1857, when he overextended credit. The insurance agent for R. G. Dun & Company reported in 1858, "Is supposed to have done well, but like many has given too much credit & indulgence so that he cannot meet his liabilities promptly. Is now settling up & paying off. Speaks of discontinuing." A year later Ashby sold his business and was in liquidation. See Turner Ashby entries for January 15, July 29, 1853, August 24, 1854, September 1, 1855, April 18, August 22, 1856, February 10, August 4, 1857, January 27, August 6, 1858, and January 27, 1859, in Virginia Volume 13, Fauquier County, Va., and R. G. Dun & Co. Collection, Baker Library, Harvard University Graduate School of Business Administration, Cambridge, Mass.

6. The yeoman's fierce commitment to liberty and independence has been widely discussed in the secondary literature. For the best treatment of this issue, see Elizabeth Fox-Genovese and Eugene D. Genovese, "Yeomen Farmers in a Slaveholders' Democracy," in *Fruits of Merchant Capital: Slavery and Bourgeois Property in the Rise and Expansion of Capitalism* (New York: Oxford, 1983), 249–64.

7. Avirett, *Memoirs*, 21, 25; John Esten Cooke, *Wearing of the Gray: Being Personal Portraits, Scenes, and Adventures of the War* (1867; reprint, Bloomington: Indiana University Press, 1959), 70; T. C. De Leon, *Belles, Beaux, and Brains of the 60's* (New York: G. W. Dillingham, 1909), 202. After Jeb Stuart's mortal wounding at Yellow Tavern on May 11, 1864, Confederates immediately turned him into the quintessential cavalier. Stuart's historical

image was shaped to meet the emotional needs of a southern people at war, a process that resembled Turner Ashby's transformation into a cavalier in 1862. See Paul D. Escott, "The Uses of Gallantry: Virginians and the Origins of J. E. B. Stuart's Historical Image," *Virginia Magazine of History and Biography* 103 (January 1995): 47–72. On the tradition of chivalry, see Maurice Hugh Keen, *Chivalry* (New Haven: Yale University Press, 1984).

8. Avirett, *Memoirs*, 26.

9. The literature on the slave South and its place in an expanding capitalistic world is extensive. Recent historiography has emphasized the modern, progressive outlook of antebellum southerners. For some representative works, see James Oakes, *Slavery and Freedom: An Interpretation of the Old South* (New York: Knopf, 1990); Eugene D. Genovese, *Freedom and Progress in Southern Conservative Thought, 1820–1860* (Columbia: University of South Carolina Press, 1992); Michael O'Brien, *Rethinking the South: Essays in Intellectual History* (Athens: University of Georgia Press, 1993), 112–28.

10. Avirett, *Memoirs*, 45, 46.

11. On Ashby's riding prowess, see Dufour, "Ashby," 43–44; "The Late General Ashby by One Who Knew Him," *Richmond Daily Whig*, July 24, 1862; "Glimpses of Turner Ashby," Holmes Conrad Papers, Virginia Historical Society, Richmond (repository hereafter cited as VHS).

12. Ashby did not leave a large body of personal papers, especially from the prewar years. Limited evidence makes it difficult to determine whether he saw himself as a product of mainstream southern values. Most of the primary sources that describe him as a courtly knight come from the postwar years, far removed from the economic and intellectual conditions of antebellum Virginia. A closer examination of Virginia in the 1850s reveals a state trying to shed the image of a land of knightly squires who enjoyed the life of aristocratic ease. Ashby must be viewed as a product of this environment. For the best treatment of Virginia in the 1850s and its emerging progressive ethos, see Beth Barton Schweiger, *The Gospel Working Up: Progress and the Pulpit in Nineteenth Century Virginia* (New York: Oxford, 2000).

13. On Ashby's early years, see Avirett, *Memoirs*, 15–48. Virginia's economic woes sparked an exodus of its white citizens. On this phenomenon, see Virginius Dabney, *Virginia: The New Dominion* (Garden City, N.Y.: Doubleday, 1971), 275–76.

14. Men who spent at least a portion of their twenties in the 1850s typically called for their fellow Virginians to reject the aristocratic values of the past, which they blamed for the state's economic decline. They called for a new set of values that stressed social improvement for the individual and the society as a whole. Hard work, getting an education, frugality, and piety formed a crucial part of this new message. No longer did they want the rest of the country to see the Old Dominion as a place where people lived off the glories of past. See Peter S. Carmichael, "The Last Generation: Sons of the Virginia Slaveholders and the Creation of a Southern Identity, 1850–1865" (Ph.D. diss., Pennsylvania State University, 1996), esp. chap. 1.

15. An overview of Ashby's prewar business and political activities can be found in Dufour, "Ashby," 43–44. Ashby was a middling slaveholder who lived modestly for most of the 1850s until 1860; his personal property taxes skyrocketed from $250 in 1859 to $1,043 the following year. It appears that once Ashby sold his mercantile business in 1859, he profited handsomely from investments in sheep and cows. He might have sold horses on the side as well. See Turner Ashby's "Personal Property Tax Roles from Fauquier County" for the years 1853–61, Virginia State Library, Richmond. Ashby owned ten slaves in 1860, but six were under age eighteen and two were over age sixty. See Turner Ashby, Virginia Census Slave Schedules, 1860, reel 226D, Virginia State Library, Richmond. For a sample of Ashby's legal woes, see Fauquier County Circuit Court Law order book, F 1854–1860 (reel 87), 71, 294, 295, 296, 419, 453, and Law order book, G 1860–1872 (reel 87), 36, Fauquier County Court House, Warrenton, Va. On the dynamic changes to Virginia's antebellum economy, see Steven Elliott Tripp, *Yankee Town, Southern City: Race and Class Relations in Civil War Lynchburg* (New York: New York University Press, 1997); Kenneth W. Noe, *Southwest Virginia's Railroad: Modernization and the Sectional Crisis* (Urbana: University of Illinois Press, 1994).

16. Robert G. Tanner's study of the 1862 Valley campaign tends to exaggerate the odds against Stonewall. This problem stems from its focus on the Confederate high command at the expense of understanding the context within which Union armies operated. Nor does Tanner connect military operations to the social and political conditions of the Valley (he should not be criticized for this oversight because he intended to write a traditional campaign study). References to civilians' diaries and letters almost always reflect the growing popularity of Jackson and a deep affection for the Valley troops. Unfortunately, Tanner never probed deeper to convey the complex needs and demands that civilians placed on the Confederate army. He does offer a solid overview of the economic and social conditions of the Shenandoah Valley on the eve of the Civil War. See Tanner, *Stonewall in the Valley: Thomas J. "Stonewall" Jackson's Shenandoah Valley Campaign, Spring 1862* (Garden City, N.Y.: Doubleday, 1976; rev. ed., Mechanicsburg, Pa.: Stackpole, 1996), 3–23. Robert K. Krick also contributes to the mythical view of Jackson as the master of the Valley, a man who overcame the most desperate odds. He concludes a magnificently detailed study of the fighting at Cross Keyes and Port Republic with the sentimental but popularly appealing statement that "the Valley and the River remain a perpetual memorial for Stonewall Jackson" (Robert K. Krick, *Conquering the Valley: Stonewall Jackson at Port Republic* [New York: Morrow, 1996], 503).

17. U.S. War Department, *The War of the Rebellion: A Compilation of the Official Records of the Union and Confederate Armies*, 127 vols., index, and atlas (Washington, D.C.: GPO, 1880–1901), ser.1, 5:395 (hereafter cited as *OR*; all references are to ser. 1).

18. David Hunter Strother [Porte Crayon, pseud.], *A Virginia Yankee in the Civil War: The Diaries of David Hunter Strother*, ed. Cecil D. Eby Jr. (Chapel Hill: University of North Carolina Press, 1961), 55.

19. *OR* 5:242. For additional examples of bitter fighting in the lower Valley in 1861–62, see "More Vandalism," *Rockingham Register and Advertiser*, January 24, 1862; "Important from Harper's Ferry," *Baltimore Sun*, February 8, 1862; "The Late Affair at Harper's Ferry," *Baltimore Sun*, February 11, 1862.

20. John H. Boltz, "Allowed Claims," RG 217, National Archives, Washington, D.C.

21. For examples of Ashby's men harassing Unionists in the Shenandoah Valley, see *OR* 5:520, 858; Oliver Ridgway Funsten to Turner Ashby, August 21, 1861, Ashby Family Papers, VHS; Strother, *Virginia Yankee*, 55. On the mixed loyalties of the Valley, see *OR* 5:394, 661, 733–34, 735, 943, 1004.

22. Turner Ashby to Dorothea Farrar (Ashby) Moncure, September 6, 1861, Ashby Family Papers.

23. On Richard Ashby's mortal wounding, see J. B. A., "Full and Authentic Account of the Daring Exploits of the Two Ashbys," *Daily Richmond Whig*; John T. O'Toole, "The Revenge of Turner Ashby," in *Civil War: The Magazine of the Civil War Society* 58 (August 1996): 40–44; J. R. Rust, "Address of Captain J. R. Rust Delivered on November 6, 1897, to the Turner Ashby Camp of Confederate Veterans Describing [the] Death of Capt. Richard Ashby, Brother of Gen. Turner Ashby," in *Diaries, Letters, and Recollections of the War between the States* (Winchester, Va.: Winchester-Frederick County Historical Society, 1955), 3:16–19; Charles D. Walker, "Richard Ashby," in *Memorial, Virginia Military Institute: Biographical Sketches of the Graduates and Eleves of the Virginia Military Institute Who Fell During the War Between the States* (Philadelphia: Lippincott, 1875), 36–40; Avirett, *Memoirs*, 107–16.

24. Turner Ashby to Dora Ashby, July 7, 1861, in Avirett, *Memoirs*, 115; Amanda Virginia Edmonds diary, July 8, 1861, in Amanda Virginia Edmonds, *Journals of Amanda Virginia Edmonds: Lass of the Mosby Confederacy, 1859–1867*, ed. Nancy Chappelear Baird (Stephens City, Va.: Commercial Press, 1984), 52.

25. Turner Ashby to Dora Ashby, July 7, 1861, in Avirett, *Memoirs*, 115. For a similar expression of grief, see Turner Ashby to Mary Green (Ashby) Moncure, July 19, 1861, Ashby Family Papers.

26. "The Ashby Boys," *New York Tribune*, June 12, 1862.

27. On guerrilla warfare, see Michael Fellman, *Inside War: The Guerrilla Conflict in Missouri during the American Civil War* (New York: Oxford, 1989); Benjamin Franklin Cooling, *Fort Donelson's Legacy: War and Society in Kentucky and Tennessee, 1862–1863* (Knoxville: University of Tennessee Press, 1997); Noel C. Fisher, *War at Every Door: Partisan Politics and Guerrilla Violence in East Tennessee, 1861–1869* (Chapel Hill: University of North Carolina Press, 1997). For an overview of the subject, see Daniel E. Sutherland, "Sideshow No Longer: A Historiographical Review of the Guerrilla War," *Civil War History* 46 (March 2000): 5–23.

28. On Stonewall Jackson's hard view of war, see Charles Royster, *The Destructive War: William Tecumseh Sherman, Stonewall Jackson, and the Americans* (New York: Knopf, 1991), esp. chap. 2.

29. Strother, *Virginia Yankee*, 16; Robert Gould Shaw to his father, June 29, 1862, in Robert Gould Shaw, *Blue-Eyed Child of Fortune: The Civil War Letters of Colonel Robert Gould Shaw*, ed. Russell Duncan (New York: Avon, 1992), 213.

30. Thomas J. Jackson to Alexander R. Boteler, Alexander R. Boteler Papers, William R. Perkins Library, Duke University, Durham, N.C.

31. Edward T. H. Warren to his wife, April 24, 1862, Warren Papers, Special Collections, Alderman Library, University of Virginia, Charlottesville; Thomas T. Munford to Jedediah Hotchkiss, August 19, 1896, Jedediah Hotchkiss Papers, roll 49, Library of Congress, Washington, D.C. (repository hereafter cited as LC).

32. Ashby's movements and mistakes in the Valley campaign have been well chronicled by historians. For a concise treatment of the subject, see James I. Robertson Jr., *Stonewall Jackson: The Man, the Soldier, the Legend* (New York: Macmillan, 1997), 355–56. Also see Dufour, "Ashby," 61–62; Tanner, *Stonewall in the Valley*, 154–60. For a defense of Ashby in the Valley, see Thomas T. Munford, "Reminiscences of Jackson's Valley Campaign," in *Southern Historical Society Papers*, ed. J. William Jones and others, 52 vols. (1876–1959; reprint, with 3-vol. index, Wilmington, N.C.: Broadfoot, 1900–92), 7:523–25 (hereafter cited as *SHSP*).

33. Jedediah Hotchkiss to his wife, April 20, 1862, in Jedediah Hotchkiss, *Make Me a Map of the Valley: The Civil War Journal of Stonewall Jackson's Topographer*, ed. Archie P. McDonald (Dallas: Southern Methodist University Press, 1973), 28.

34. Jedediah Hotchkiss to his wife, April 24, 1862, in Hotchkiss, *Make Me a Map*, 33. On Jackson's dismissal of Ashby, see Avirett, *Memoirs*, 176; Tanner, *Stonewall in the Valley*, 160–62; Robertson, *Stonewall Jackson*, 361–62.

35. John Harman to A. W. Harman, April 25, 1862, Hotchkiss Papers, roll 39, LC.

36. Turner Ashby to Alexander R. Boteler, April 25, 1862, Simon Gratz Collection, Historical Society of Pennsylvania, Philadelphia.

37. R. P. Chew to Clarence Thomas, March 3, 1907 in Thomas, *General Turner Ashby*, 195; Robertson, *Stonewall Jackson*, 362.

38. *OR* 12(3):880; John Harman to A. W. Harman, April 26, 1862, Hotchkiss Papers, roll 39, LC; Jedediah Hotchkiss diary, April 25, 1862, in Hotchkiss, *Make Me a Map*, 33.

39. *OR* 12(3):880.

40. *OR* 12(1):704. On Ashby's actions at Middletown, see Tanner, *Stonewall in the Valley*, 269–73; Robertson, *Stonewall Jackson*, 400–402.

41. Robert L. Dabney, *Life and Campaigns of Lieut.-Gen. Thomas J. Jackson* (1865; reprint, Harrisonburg, Va.: Sprinkle, 1983), 381; *OR* 12(1):707.

42. *OR* 12(1):706–7. For a critical assessment of Ashby's actions at Second Winchester, see Tanner, *Stonewall in the Valley*, 287–88, 317–20; Robertson, *Stonewall Jackson*, 409–10.

43. Jedediah Hotchkiss to Holmes Conrad, September 8, 1896, Hotchkiss Papers, roll 34, LC. For the best account of the fight at Harrisonburg and Ashby's death, see Krick, *Conquering the Valley*, 25–32. Also see Richard Ewell to John Esten Cooke, February 10, 1864, in Case Western Reserve Historical Society, Cleveland, Ohio; W. W. Goldsborough,

"How Ashby Was Killed," *SHSP*, 21:224–26; Bradley T. Johnson, "Memoir of the First Maryland Regiment: The Battle of Winchester," *SHSP*, 10:104–5.

44. Thomas Munford to Jedediah Hotchkiss, August 19, 1896, Hotchkiss Papers, roll 49, LC: Jedediah Hotchkiss to his wife, April 20, 1862, in Hotchkiss, *Make Me a Map*, 29. For Lee's comments about Ashby's cavalry, see OR 11(3):580, 907. A detailed account of Jackson's near-capture in Port Republic can be found in Krick, *Conquering the Valley*, 39–111.

45. Jedediah Hotchkiss diary, June 6, 1862, in Hotchkiss, *Make Me a Map*, 53; *OR* 12(1):712.

46. Both quotations are from Krick, *Conquering the Valley*, 31; Nannie Thompson (Bayne) Clark to Aunt Dollie, June 9, 1862, Ashby Family Papers.

47. Charles W. Trueheart to his sisters, April 22, 1862, in Edward B. Williams, ed., *Rebel Brothers: The Civil War Letters of the Truehearts* (College Station: Texas A&M University Press, 1995), 54; John E. Roller, "Our Heroes, the Leaders of a New Reformation" (n.p., 1907), 9.

48. Charles W. Trueheart to Henry Trueheart, July 7, 1862, in Williams, *Rebel Brothers*, 63; William L. Jackson to [?], June 8, 1862, William L. Jackson Papers, Special Collections, West Virginia University, Morgantown; George M. Neese, *Three Years in the Confederate Horse Artillery* (1911; reprint, Dayton, Ohio: Morningside, 1988), 41. For a discussion of the concept of courage among Civil War soldiers, see Gerald F. Linderman, *Embattled Courage: The Experience of Combat in the American Civil War* (New York: Free Press, 1987), esp. chap. 1.

49. On the importance of liberty among nonslaveholding Confederates, see James M. McPherson, *What They Fought For, 1861–1865* (Baton Rouge: Louisiana State University Press, 1994), 9–11, 12–14, 25, 49–52; William A. Blair, *Virginia's Private War: Feeding Body and Soul in the Confederacy, 1861–1865* (New York: Oxford, 1998), 36–37, 62, 65. Commenting on the reelection of his captain in 1862, George M. Neese describes the essential qualities of leadership necessary to govern volunteer soldiers. Ashby exhibited these same characteristics. See Neese, *Three Years in the Confederate Horse Artillery*, 53–54.

50. James Edward Marshal to Turner Ashby, May 5, 1862, Ashby Family Papers; T. L. Settle to Clarence Thomas, [undated], in Thomas, *General Turner Ashby*, 177.

51. N. G. West to Clarence Thomas, [undated], in Thomas, *General Turner Ashby*, 175; Charles W. Trueheart to Henry Trueheart, July 7, 1862, in Williams, *Rebel Brothers*, 64.

52. George Baylor, *Bull Run to Bull Run* (Richmond: B. F. Johnson, 1900), 1; Thomas Munford to Jedediah Hotchkiss, August 19, 1896, Hotchkiss Papers, roll 49, LC.

53. William A. Blair offers an excellent examination of the Shenandoah Valley as part of his study of Virginia during the Civil War. One of the first scholars to show how conflicting local and national demands on the Valley shaped Confederate loyalty, he demonstrates that civilians tried to strike a balance between local issues and the interests of Richmond authorities. See Blair, *Virginia's Private War*, 17–18, 19, 22, 50–51, 57, 105–6.

54. *OR* 5:820–21.

55. On the 1862 Confederate Conscription Act, see Albert Burton Moore, *Conscription and Conflict in the Confederacy* (1924; reprint, New York: Hillary House, 1963), 12–26; Emory M. Thomas, *The Confederate Nation, 1861–1865* (New York: Harper and Row, 1997), 152–55.

56. In a perceptive analysis of desertion among Virginia units, William A. Blair discovered that "the records also fail to lend credibility to the impression that desertion increased steadily through the war, escalating after 1863 and becoming a torrent by 1864." "Desertion in Virginia regiments ballooned early in the war," he concluded, "and slowed as time went on before probably escalating in 1865" (Blair, *Virginia's Private War*, 61). On the Blue Ridge Rebellion and the social dislocation of war in the Valley, see ibid., 51; Strother, *Virginia Yankee*, 24, 27. Three pacifist denominations opposed the war and thereby challenged Confederate authority in the Valley. See *OR* 12(3):835.

57. Turner Ashby to Alexander R. Boteler, April 25, 1862, Gratz Collection. For additional examples of protest against Jackson's policies in the Valley, see *OR* 5:1040–42, 1046–47; 12(3):841–42. Jackson's difficulties with subordinates were legendary and continued after he left the Shenandoah Valley. All of Stonewall's biographers have dealt with his heavy-handed tactics and rigid leadership style. See Robertson, *Stonewall Jackson*, xiii–xvi; Royster, *Destructive War*, 44–45, 47, 50–51, 71–73; Frank E. Vandiver, *Mighty Stonewall* (New York: McGraw-Hill, 1957), 211–13, 248, 273, 375, 377, 382, 407–9, 440–42.

58. On the French Furlough system in the Confederate army, see Blair, *Virginia's Private War*, 62–64.

59. Albert C. Lincoln to Turner Ashby, February 18, 1862, Ashby Family Papers.

60. N. G. West to Clarence Thomas, [undated], in Thomas, *General Turner Ashby*, 175.

61. "Petition to Turner Ashby from the Ladies of Shepherdstown, Jefferson County, Virginia," in Ashby Papers, Special Collections, JMU. Other examples of Ashby's popularity among the Valley's civilians include A. R. Boteler's letter to the Secretary of State, [undated,] in Laura Virginia Hale, *Four Valiant Years in the Lower Shenandoah Valley, 1861–1865* (Strasburg, Va.: Shenandoah Publishing, 1973), 89–91; *OR* 12(1):418.

62. Charles W. Trueheart to his mother, December 26, [1861], and to Henry Trueheart, July 7, 1862 in Williams, *Rebel Brothers*, 38, 63; Avirett, *Memoirs*, 255–58.

63. Perceval Reniers, *The Springs of Virginia: Life, Love, and Death at the Waters* (Chapel Hill: University of North Carolina Press, 1941), 159; "General Turner Ashby," *Southern Illustrated News*, October 18, 1862, 1. For a comparison of Ashby to a mulatto, see "The Ashby Boys," *New York Tribune*, June 1862; Henry Kyd Douglas, *I Rode with Stonewall* (Chapel Hill: University of North Carolina Press, 1940), 81–82; "Cavalry Officers," *Richmond Enquirer* [1861 or 1862?], in Scrapbook 1861–1986, unidentified compiler, Mss5:7 Un3:15, VHS.

64. Susan Shacklett to Mrs. [?] Ashby, [undated, but the content indicates that it was written in June 1865], Ashby Family Papers. Turner Ashby's 1866 reinterment in Winchester intensified the memorial activities associated with the cavalryman and solidified his standing as the Valley's great war hero. See "A Labor of Love: The Reinterment of the

Brothers Ashby," *Staunton Valley Virginian*, September 9, 1866; "Funeral Obsequies at Winchester," *Shepherdstown Register*, October 27, 1866. Gary W. Gallagher has called for historians to connect the Lost Cause to its wartime origins rather than viewing it as a postwar creation without roots in the Confederate experience. See Gallagher, "Early, the Lost Cause, and Civil War History," in *Lee and His Generals in War and Memory*, ed. Gary W. Gallagher (Baton Rouge: Louisiana State University Press, 1998), 199–226.

65. "Wednesday in Winchester," *Virginia Free Press* (Charles Town, W.Va.), June 7, 1866; Douglas, *I Rode with Stonewall*, 82. For other ex-Confederates who also described Ashby as the epitome of southern knighthood, see Cooke, *Wearing of the Gray*, 60–71; John Esten Cooke, "Humors of the Camp," in *Camp-Fire Sketches and Battlefield Echoes* (Springfield, Mass.: King, Richardson, 1869), 565; J. William Jones, "Reminiscences of the Army of Northern Virginia: How Frémont and Shields 'Caught' Stonewall Jackson," *SHSP*, 9:278–89; Richard Taylor, *Destruction and Reconstruction: Personal Experience of the Late War* (1879; reprint, New York: Longmans, Green, 1955), 80–81; John O. Casler, *Four Years in the Stonewall Brigade* (1893; reprint, Dayton, Ohio: Morningside, 1971), 85; Harry Gilmor, *For Years in the Saddle* (New York: Harper and Brothers, 1866), 13; Dabney Herndon Maury, *Recollections of a Virginian in the Mexican, Indian, and Civil Wars* (New York: Scribner's, 1894), 47–49.

66. Educators used Turner Ashby's life to instill in young people the "proper" values as well as a "correct" understanding of the past. In her popular *Stories from Virginia History for the Young* (Lynchburg, Va.: J. P. Bell, 1897), 184–85, H. Mary Tucker Magill wrote, "The great soldiers, called knights, used to make vows, when they went to war, that they would protect the weak, particularly women; that they would be noble and brave; that they would rather die than turn their backs on an enemy; and that they would fear God and honor their country and be generous to their enemies. There were a good many soldiers in the Confederate army who had all the spirit of these knights of old, but one es-pe-cial-ly I want to tell you about, because I think he was one of the most interesting men I ever knew. This was General Turner Ashby."

67. Susan Shacklett to Mrs. [?] Ashby, [undated but the content indicates that it was written in June 1865], Ashby Family Papers.

68. On the resiliency of the Lost Cause and its influence today, see Tony Horwitz, *Confederates in the Attic: Dispatches from America's Unfinished Civil War* (New York: Pantheon, 1998).

ROBERT E. L. KRICK

Maryland's Ablest Confederate

GENERAL CHARLES S. WINDER OF

THE STONEWALL BRIGADE

When thirty-one-year-old Charles S. Winder arrived at Charleston, South Carolina, on April 8, 1861, he found a city bracing for war. Reporting to Gen. P. G. T. Beauregard, he received orders that eventually directed him to Morris Island. Writing in his diary on April 8, Winder speculated sadly on "the horrors of Civil War" that stood "in bold relief ever before me." Four days later he watched the firing on Fort Sumter and wrote of the "thrill it sent to my heart." The small garrison at Fort Sumter soon surrendered, triggering a somber passage for the diary: "No one rejoiced here." Those reflective and often sober comments, written by an eyewitness at one of the most explosive moments in American history, were the fruit of experience. Charles Winder knew better than most what the events at Charleston portended. As a professional soldier from a family of soldiers, Winder could recognize some of what lay ahead. In the preceding decade he had survived a ghastly shipwreck and three hard-fought battles on the frontier. Few men around Charleston harbor that week were as well seasoned in the fields of suffering and soldiering. The doleful diary entries foreshadowed their author's future in the forthcoming war. Less than eighteen months later Winder would be dead on the battlefield. In that short span he forged a military record that placed him highest on the list of all Marylanders who fought for the Confederacy.[1]

Charles Sidney Winder came from a gently aristocratic background. One of eight children born to Edward S. and Elizabeth Tayloe Lloyd Winder, Charles first saw light on October 18, 1829. The Winders lived in Talbot County, a section of Maryland far removed from the better-known parts of the state. As residents of the Eastern Shore, they were separated by the Chesapeake Bay from both Baltimore and Washington, D.C. Charles had an almost unbeatable pedigree. His grandfathers had been successive governors of the state, and his Aunt Anne Catherine Lloyd married Franklin Buchanan, one of the more prominent naval officers in the country before and during the Civil War. Charles also was related in two different ways to Francis Scott Key.

His mother's family had wealth, while his father's side provided a long, if generally undistinguished, record of military service. Charles's grandfather Governor Edward Lloyd was among the richest men in Maryland, with an enormous estate called "Wye" in Talbot County. Among the fighting Winders, Charles could point to (but probably did not) Gen. William H. Winder, his father's cousin. William had commanded the routed American forces at the battle of Bladensburg in 1814, a low point in the War of 1812. Charles's father, Edward, served in the 2nd U.S. Dragoons in the Florida War, where he acquired a disease from which he died in 1840. Two of Charles's older brothers saw military service as well, including James Murray Winder, who was mortally wounded in 1847 during a Mexican War battle. John H. Winder, notorious provost marshal of Richmond during the Civil War, was a distant relation.[2]

The particulars of Winder's youth are not of record. The early death of Edward Winder threw the family under the responsibility of the Lloyds, and Charles seems in most ways to have been more closely connected to his mother's side of the family. He was shipped off to Annapolis at an early age for study at St. John's College. Developing solidly there, he was described in 1846 by one of his professors as "well advanced" in his studies. "I am happy to add," continued the mentor with some unction, "that his morals are correct." Senator J. A. Pearce from Maryland, writing a year earlier, contented himself in calling Charles "a fine promising lad."

The Winder family's ill fortune with military affairs did not deter young Charles from pursuing a career in that field. Commencing in 1845 he brought influence to bear in the proper quarters to secure an appointment to the U.S. Military Academy. His genealogy probably helped, as the authorities often proved sensitive to applicants whose close relations had died in service. Uncle

General Charles S. Winder

Charles S. Winder as a captain in the antebellum U.S. Army. There is no known Civil War view of the general. Robert Underwood Johnson and Clarence Clough Buel, eds., *Battles and Leaders of the Civil War*, 4 vols. (New York: Century, 1887–88), 2:457.

Franklin Buchanan wrote vigorous endorsements. So did several members of the state legislature. Charles received the appointment, apparently without much trouble, on March 5, 1846. That gave him just a few months to prepare for the dramatic change in his life. He reported to West Point in the summer of 1846, hard on the heels of the departing members of the subsequently famous class of 1846.[3]

Winder's term at the academy exposed two of the salient features of his subsequent career: perpetual poor health and an affinity for discipline and order. Even at sixteen years of age Charles Winder was not a robust young man. The dispensary records for the academy show that he checked in frequently with a variety of complaints ranging from "obstipatio" to tonsillitis. "Cephalalgia" (headache) proved to be his most common grievance, and on one occasion in February 1848 Winder spent a week in the hospital suffering from an unspecified contusion. Between October 1846 and Christmas of 1848 the sickly cadet logged thirty separate visits to the post hospital that encompassed ninety-one different days. Perhaps the rigors of life at West Point accounted for some of Winder's ill health, because his number of visits to the sick room for 1849 and 1850 dropped dramatically, suggesting that he had adapted to the way of life by then.[4]

Consistently feeble health did not impair Winder's academic performance. He stood in the upper quarter of his class in 1847 and 1848 and directly in its middle during 1849 and 1850. Drawing was his bane, while he excelled at French. During his final year in New York, Winder gave clear evidence of the sort of officer he was to become. In a class of forty-five young men, he finished first in Infantry Tactics (though twenty-first in artillery) and did not accumulate a single demerit. He finished his cadet career with a total of 107 demerits. His generally good conduct and apparent military aptitude earned Winder the appointment as captain in one of the cadet companies, a prized assignment.[5]

Winder graduated from the academy in the summer of 1850 and entered service in a U.S. Army that was between major wars. The rapidly expanding western frontier stretched the army dangerously thin. In addition to conducting campaigns against the Indians in nearly every corner of the country, the army bore responsibility for manning dozens of widely scattered forts and outposts. In consequence, unpolished officers such as Charles Winder (still only twenty years old when he graduated) often assumed immediate and weighty responsibilities. Although the Marylander would see an inordinate amount of action in the Old Army, he was fortunate to duck frontier duty in his first assignment. As a brevet second lieutenant in Company M, 4th U.S. Artillery, Winder received orders posting him to Fort Hamilton in New York City. An extended postgraduation vacation kept him from reporting until November 30, 1850. After a short stay at Fort Hamilton, he received promotion in July 1851 to second lieutenant in Company H, 3rd U.S. Artillery. His new position required duty at Fort Adams in Rhode Island—certainly one of the least hazardous assignments anywhere in the country during those turbulent times. Winder spent almost precisely two years there, a stay softened by frequent short leaves of absence. For most of his final year in New England, Lieutenant Winder commanded his company, learning the art of leading soldiers. Fort Adams was to be the last dull posting of his career. Except for long stretches of sick leave, Winder would spend the final nine years of his life in very active assignments, with the menacing prospect of combat or death his daily escort.[6]

The first crisis of Winder's military career came not on the battlefield but on the high seas. He was one of nearly 20 officers and more than 500 enlisted men from the 3rd Artillery who received orders directing them to California. A new steamer, the *San Francisco*, was engaged for transportation. In addition to six companies and assorted headquarters personnel, the *San Francisco* carried the families of some officers, a few sutlers and laundresses, and a herd of cattle. The vessel sailed on December 22, 1853, bound for Rio de Janeiro and ultimately California. Two and a half days later, steaming off the East Coast near Cape Hatteras, the ship ran into a brutal winter storm. Violent northwesterly winds struck the *San Francisco* at 9:00 P.M. while it progressed at a brisk 8½ knots. Despite valiant efforts to keep the ship from drifting broadside to the waves, disaster struck. The overworked engine failed, leaving the vessel helpless. Increasingly large waves pounded it, tearing away planking, railings, and sails. Winder probably was near the fore end of the ship, where the troops had been placed during the emergency. Officers organized bailing parties that fought to keep the *San Francisco* buoyant.

Conditions worsened on Christmas Day. The foremast snapped off near the deck, and about 8:00 A.M. a giant wave ruined the ship. Arriving as a black wall of water, it tore off the paddlewheel box, both smokestacks, and the entire upper saloon. Three feet of water instantly invaded the lower cabin. "The horror of this moment cannot be described," remembered a survivor. Some accounts estimate that 150 people were swept overboard, including a number of the more senior officers onboard, and "it was only by the greatest exertions the ship was kept afloat." Charles Winder escaped the killer wave, probably by good luck, and almost immediately began to assume a disproportionate share of the responsibilities in the struggle to save the rest of the passengers.

Most subsequent testimony mentioned Lieutenant Winder as one of the heroes of the story. During the next four days he labored tirelessly to keep the ship afloat. A witness reported seeing Winder in the engine room "nearly all the time," working among the men on the bailing parties. He and Lt. John G.

Chandler alternated supervising the process on one side of the engine room. They acted on their own initiative, without advice or orders from their superiors. Winder also went toward the bow of the ship and helped with the endless chore of heaving provisions and supplies overboard to lighten the load. A civilian passenger, writing only days after the event, mentioned Winder by name and praised him for "great courage and energy." The ordeal dragged on for days. A succession of other ships steamed by, remarkably stumbling upon the *San Francisco* despite the poor visibility. The captain of one ship reported seeing the crippled vessel with "everything swept above deck, and the spray making a complete breach over her." Persistently wretched weather prevented rescue operations long enough for discipline to collapse on the foundering ship. Soldiers and civilians alike broke into the storeroom, "determined to enjoy themselves before the ship went down." Revelers feasted on unlimited food and followed their indulgence by "copious and undiluted draughts" from the bar. Within hours many of them died and were thrown overboard, their deaths being attributed to an outbreak of cholera.[7]

The weather finally quieted enough to permit the rescue of passengers. Col. William Gates, the regimental commander, was among the first to transfer from the *San Francisco* to the *Kilby*. Another ship, the *Three Bells*, took off more of the weary survivors on New Year's Eve, but Winder remained aboard the *San Francisco* until the very end. When the transfer commenced, he approached Lt. S. L. Fremont, the regimental quartermaster, and remarked, "I will remain with my company until the last." Lieutenant Winder commenced a diary during these trying scenes, a journal he was to keep haphazardly until a few hours before his death in 1862. The very first entry tersely explained his plight: "On wreck of San Francisco. Drank a bottle of champagne to celebrate the New Year's coming in. Stormy & chances bad." Another diarist still aboard did not mention the champagne but observed, "Many of the people sick, and dying fast." Two days later one more ship, the *Antarctic*, arrived to carry away the survivors. It was greeted by Winder and the others with "three hearty cheers." On January 4, his tenth day adrift, Winder left the *San Francisco* permanently. His relief likely dimmed when he learned that the *Antarctic* was not headed for the United States but, rather, to Liverpool, England.[8]

As the senior soldier aboard the *Antarctic*, Winder faced renewed responsibility. Roughly 200 bedraggled survivors (30 of whom were women and children), looked to the twenty-four-year-old lieutenant to get them home. "The suffering since our wreck has been intense," Winder wrote from Liverpool. Thirty-one of his charges had died aboard the *Antarctic* during the passage from "exposure, fatigue, and want of proper nourishment." For one of the few times in his career, discipline in Winder's command flagged. While he was ashore in Liverpool attempting to find provisions and arrange transportation back to the United States, sixteen of his soldiers jumped ship and deserted. Despite poor morale and a long series of impediments, Winder successfully returned to Boston the following month with the balance of his people.[9]

The details of Winder's role in the *San Francisco* disaster began to emerge in February 1854, when a court of inquiry chaired by Gen. Winfield Scott convened to examine the performance of Colonel Gates. Although Winder did not appear before the court, extensive testimony by fellow officers uniformly praised his conduct. Capt. Francis O. Wyse of the 3rd Artillery spoke forcefully, crediting Winder and two others with good behavior: "I candidly believe that their untiring exertions, night and day, in superintending and encouraging the men to bail under the most fatiguing circumstances, saved that wreck from going to the bottom."[10]

After a short furlough at home in Maryland, Winder tried again to reach the West. He had received news of his appointment as regimental adjutant on April 5, 1854, and left shortly thereafter to join his unit in California. Although there were several problems with the ship, this trip proved safer, and Winder arrived at San Diego on May 29. A few days later he reached Benicia, about halfway between San Francisco and Napa. Despite being so near to San Francisco, Winder's temporary new home hardly could be called an urban posting. Long stretches of boredom and unrefined surroundings made Benicia resemble a typical frontier billet. The only combat Charles Winder saw there was with the local wildlife, which he slew in great numbers. Even his diary entries from 1854 and 1855 were monotonous. He seems to have fallen into a pattern of sleeping, reading, smoking cigars, hunting, pining for home, and conversing with fellow officers. The particulars of his military duties are not apparent, and the highlights of his time at Benicia were the occasions when he left the area to visit other sites in California.[11]

After a long year in the salubrious climate of central California, Winder took passage on a ship that would carry him home by way of Acapulco and Panama. A new unit was forming in the East, and Winder had been promoted to captain and assigned the command of a company. His first duty was to lure recruits into the nascent 9th Infantry. Upon reaching Maryland, Captain Winder immediately attempted to parlay his new rank into a romantic conquest. For some years he had been courting his first cousin, Alice Lloyd. Back in 1850 Alice's father, Edward (Winder's uncle), had quashed the idea of their marriage. In April 1852 young Winder had renewed his campaign, but again Uncle Edward had failed to endorse the union. Having waited fully five years from start to finish, Charles Winder sallied forth again in June 1855. On April 16 he "tried to persuade" his cousin to let him ask her father's permission. She refused, changed her mind, asked her father herself, and received his consent, all within a matter of hours. Charles was "too happy" at the result. The pair pondered the date of the wedding and, after consulting an almanac, decided on August 7, 1855.[12]

The 9th U.S. Infantry included a cadre of officers destined to achieve prominence during the Civil War. Its colonel, George Wright, flourished for decades in the Old Army but was beyond his prime by the 1860s. Silas Casey was the lieutenant colonel, and other officers serving in the regiment simultaneously with Winder included future Confederate generals George E. Pickett and James J. Archer. After his recruiting stint, Winder spent two months in Virginia at Fort Monroe with his Company E, preparing it for service on the frontier. The captain and his company steamed off in December 1855, bound for Washington Territory. They moved among several different forts and outposts in 1856, including Fort Vancouver, Fort Cascades, and Bellingham Bay. These assignments, mostly in the coastal sections of the territory, kept Winder away from the volatile Palouse country in what now is eastern Washington. He saw some action in scattered skirmishes with local Indians, but his primary combat experience lay several years distant.

In the autumn of 1856, before he could participate in any large actions, Winder fell sick and began a long stretch of ill health that really defined his antebellum career. It may have been some strain of fever acquired during one of his frequent passages through tropical latitudes as he traveled to and from the frontier, or perhaps it was a reemergence of the chronic feebleness shown in his youth at West Point. Whatever its origin, the sickness kept Winder from his command for an incredibly long time. He left Washington Territory in November 1856 and returned to Maryland. Thanks to frequent extensions of his sick leave, Winder managed to spend all of 1857 and the first part of 1858 at home. Writing on February 1, 1858, he professed to be "not only ready but anxious to join my company without delay" on the Pacific Coast. After the long westward journey, he found his men on April 26, 1858, having missed seventeen months of active service. They were stationed at Fort Walla Walla. A fellow officer at the fort that summer described it as being "in a beautiful spot . . . well wooded and with plenty of water."[13]

Winder's arrival at the fort proved most timely. Fractious Indians from the Yakima, Spokane, Palouse, and Couer d' Alene tribes had been doing their best to ward off settlers bent on developing the Snake River country. The murder of two miners brought matters to a crisis, and less than three weeks after Winder's return, he and his company formed part of an expedition that set out from the fort to investigate. Lt. Col. Edward J. Steptoe, a middle-aged Virginian, led a force that consisted of 160 soldiers and assorted wranglers. Winder's company provided the only infantry support, and it bore responsibility for protecting two mountain howitzers. Versatile dragoon companies filled out the rest of the column. Steptoe's command hardly could be called a strike force. Most of the men carried antique musketoons, while some toted Mississippi Jaeger rifles. Winder's small company, which traveled on horseback, counted a few carbines in its armament, but poor staff work at Fort Walla Walla meant that each man in the column had no more than forty rounds of ammunition. Clearly Steptoe did not anticipate any sizable encounter, and indeed his superiors hoped to avoid violence by using "judicious and generous appliances."[14]

Leaving the fort on May 6, the column struck northward toward the scene of unrest. It crossed the Snake River on a ferry provided by a friendly Nez Percé and by May 16 found itself in dangerous territory. The various tribes, learning of the incursion, angrily united and blocked Steptoe. Charles Winder wrote two weeks later how "in a few seconds as if by magic" the Indians "appeared all around us." He thought that 1,000 to 1,200 warriors opposed the column, which is a fairly typical estimate. Although the army men saw some bows and arrows, most of the Indians brandished rifles that made them at least as well armed as Steptoe's men. May 16 passed in parleying and taunting; Steptoe explained to a delegation of Indians that his aims were peaceful and that he wished to get transportation across the nearby Spokane River. When he observed the strength and intransigence of the opposition, Steptoe decided to retreat toward Walla Walla, commencing the movement on the evening of May 16. Captain Winder found the appearance of his foes especially interesting. The Indians were heavily painted and were "charging around us, yelling, whooping, shaking scalps and such things over their heads,

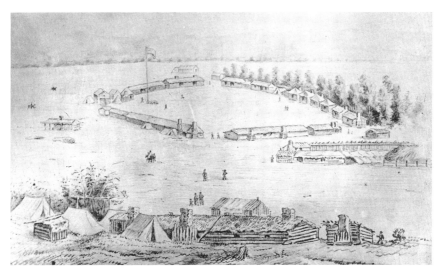

Sketch of Fort Walla Walla, Washington Territory, in 1857, the year before Winder arrived at the post. Photo by UW, neg. no. 18600, Special Collections Division, University of Washington Libraries, Seattle.

looking like so many fiends." After much noise but no fighting, Steptoe's men made camp for the night, alarmed at their prospects for the following day. Winder was officer of the day and bore responsibility that evening for the defense of the camp against an expected night attack. Most of the other officers were lieutenants, and Winder probably was second in command of the expedition.

Early the next morning, as Steptoe's badly outnumbered force began to march back toward Fort Walla Walla, the assembled Indians attacked the rear of the column. At first the fighting swayed back and forth, with the terrain favoring the attackers and discipline saving the defenders. The dragoons saw the most action, primarily heavy skirmishing, and "although very gallant, showed themselves not at all proficient." Two of the company commanders died in the fight, and at one point Lieutenant Colonel Steptoe began "to fear the most serious consequences to us." In a remarkably defeatist postbattle report, Steptoe commented that after the death of the two officers, the men "were becoming discouraged & not to be relied upon with confidence." If Charles Winder agreed with that assessment, he kept the observation to himself. "The scene beggars description," he wrote home, with Indians "charging in all directions, yelling, and whooping, and firing on us." The soldiers managed to secure a prominent hill and conducted their defense from that spot. Winder was proud of his men and felt gratified by their "cool and courageous" behavior during the long day.

After dark the officers convened, and they all agreed that a forced march to the Snake River was their best option. Steptoe gave orders to abandon all equipment—including the mountain howitzers—and to march as rapidly as possible. His decision to bury the artillery, Steptoe reported to his superior, "will give you . . . a conception of the strait to which we believed ourselves . . . reduced." Afterward he entertained doubts about the sagacity of that decision and admitted, "What distresses me is, that no attempt was made to bring them off." The hasty retreat was quite a feat by any standard. The column, now lightened considerably and traveling by horseback, made eighty-five miles in twenty-two hours without sleeping or eating. "It was a hard march and exhausted all of us," reported Winder.[15]

The survivors reached Fort Walla Walla on May 22, "rather the worse for wear and tear," in Winder's opinion. This affair, known as the battle of Steptoe Butte, produced fewer casualties than the chilling accounts from participants would suggest. The army lost only 19 men, 3 of whom were from Winder's company. Estimates of Indian losses generally range between 30 and 50. This close and personal combat, with the issue in doubt, was a new experience for Winder and not one he relished. Steptoe Butte was "the first fight of any importance I have participated in," he wrote two weeks later, "and [I] must say in candor I should be satisfied were my fate so changed as to prevent my ever going into another . . . though I'll do my duty under all and any circumstances." It took several days after May 17, he admitted, for the sound of the battle to stop ringing in his ears.[16]

The official report from Steptoe is such a self-serving, rambling document that it makes no mention of good work by any of his subordinates. Perhaps one of those junior officers felt tweaked by it, for Steptoe awkwardly submitted a corollary to his report on May 28, reminding the authorities that Winder and others were with the column and "displayed, throughout, the greatest zeal, cheerfulness, & coolness."[17]

As a direct result of the miserably unsuccessful Steptoe affair, the army began to accumulate troops in the region and brought in a more confident commander to face the Indians and, "if possible, chastise them severely." Winder accompanied this second column into the Spokane River country, in the process absorbing the sort of field experience few others could claim when the Civil War commenced three years later. George Wright was the colonel of Winder's 9th Infantry and a man with extensive credentials. Two years earlier he had extinguished a similar alarm in the Washington Territory. Despite being in his mid-fifties in the rugged frontier environment, Wright demonstrated considerable energy and foresight. His column numbered nearly 700 soldiers, about 400 mules, and some 200 packers and herders. It carried 30,000 rations for nearly six weeks of campaigning and was thought to be "the largest operation ever conducted in the Pacific Northwest." By late August 1858 Wright was in position to strike. The ensuing battle of Four Lakes, fought on September 1, was a decided victory for the soldiers. Winder's company of forty-three men formed part of a rifle battalion commanded by Frederick T. Dent, brother-in-law of Ulysses S. Grant. The foot soldiers stormed a wooded area defended by the Indians. A few blasts from mountain howitzers demoralized the defenders. "Sweeping through the woods," Dent's two infantry companies cleared the field. More reliable rifles gave the soldiers an advantage, and Colonel Wright reported no casualties at all in his command. Winder received passing mention in the official reports of the fight. Erasmus D. Keyes, E. O. C. Ord, and Robert Ransom were among the other heroes of the story.[18]

The relatively bloodless victory at Four Lakes was insufficient for Colonel Wright. He continued chasing the Spokane Indians and their allies and overtook them on September 5 in the battle of the Spokane Plains. Winder found himself supporting the mountain howitzers again, but in this case Wright ran Winder and the little guns up to the skirmish line. From there they pursued fleeing Indians into a body of woods and assisted in another complete victory. The colonel praised the work of Winder's company, thanking it for "bravely advancing with the Howitzers, and pouring in a fire with their rifles, whenever an opportunity offered, until the close of the Battle." Several days later the primary Yakima chief and his son came to parley with Wright. The chief's son was seized and hanged as the murderer of the two miners back in April, and the chief was shot while attempting to escape. Not surprisingly, on September 17 Wright executed "a Treaty of Peace and Friendship" with the Couer d' Alene. Charles Winder's name appears fifth on the list of witnesses to that event.[19]

Now a toughened veteran, Winder was back at Fort Walla Walla on September 23, having marched 597 miles since August 10. He immediately applied for a leave of absence "for the purpose of visiting my family in the east and attending to private business of importance to myself." The application was approved after some initial confusion, and Winder left for home on November 19. Almost inevitably, he wrangled extensions to the vacation and did not rejoin his company until July 1, 1859. His trip westward from Maryland was the eighth time he had boarded a ship to make the long journey from one coast to the other. On this occasion Winder embarked at New York City with a few other officers. They stopped and spent "a delightful day in Havana, and another as charming when crossing the Isthmus of Panama." The party reached San Francisco and immediately took passage for Portland, Oregon, whence they continued inland to their posts.[20]

Winder managed to hold out for only nine weeks before he departed on sick leave once again on September 11, 1859. The degree to which Winder truly was incapacitated will never be known. He had demonstrated sufficient personal courage on several occasions to deflect any insinuations on that front. Likewise he had proved, with some consistency, that he was chronically unwell. The pattern would continue up to the day of his death, when he rose from a sickbed to join his men at the front. Nonetheless in 1859 he may have been exploiting the privileges available to officers of that era by taking enormous leaves of absence. His surviving diary entries reveal how deeply homesick Winder was, a condition worsened by the incredible distance (in both miles and time of travel) between the Pacific Coast and Maryland. During the busy summer of 1858 Winder glumly wrote about his family, "I feel too keenly that I am separated from mine by a long long way and God alone knows if I am ever to see them. 'Tis a terrible thought and almost maddens me."[21]

Whatever ailment plagued Winder apparently could not be cured by home cooking. Thanks to certificates from army surgeons, he was able to celebrate his next two birthdays at home in Maryland. In 1860 the census taker found the Winders living in Talbot County with Edward Lloyd, the captain's father-in-law. The couple had produced two sons by then. Winder was listed as "Capt. in Navy," a dire insult in some circles. The family may have forgotten the particulars of his occupation after nearly two years at home, or perhaps the census taker was so shocked to learn Edward Lloyd's net worth (close to a million dollars) that he bungled the rest of the paperwork.[22]

Winder never served again in the U.S. Army. His illness kept him in Maryland into 1861. The approach of sectional hostilities found him squarely on the side of the South. He left no surviving account to document his views that stormy spring, and strong political feelings seem not to have been a prominent

part of his daily life. Yet his actions prove that he was unequivocally sympathetic to the South. He resigned his hard-won rank in the U.S. Army on
April 1, and on the same day left for Montgomery, Alabama, to seek an
audience with Confederate authorities. A passenger on Winder's southbound
train made his acquaintance and claimed never to have met "with a more
modest and charming man, or one who bore more decidedly the stamp of
high breeding, purity of character, and chivalrous courage." In Montgomery,
Winder spoke with Adj. Gen. Samuel Cooper, President Jefferson Davis, and
the secretary of war. He carried a letter of recommendation to the president
from kinsman Charles Howard. The referral pointed out that the climate in
the Northwest had been disagreeable to Winder, but not surprisingly "he has
considered himself quite fit for any duty in this part of the country, and is quite
confident that your Southern atmosphere will perfect his entire restoration to
continued good health." Winder had a "pleasant interview" with each of the
officials, and the Confederate government quickly accepted his services. His
credentials certainly were well known to Cooper and Davis, both of whom
had been prominent in military affairs in the 1850s.[23]

If they had time to ponder such things, the president and his military
deputies must have been overjoyed to secure Winder's allegiance. Just thirty-
one years old, Winder had been one of the youngest captains in the Old Army.
His incredible adventure with the wreck of the *San Francisco* in 1853–54 gave
him experience in dealing with a life-threatening crisis. Participation in three
large battles with the Indians in the Northwest placed him among the most
veteran officers of his age anywhere in the country. Winder was in every way
a desirable addition to the armies of the Confederate States of America.

The secretary of war commissioned him a major in the Corps of Artillery
on April 5, 1861, a position to rank from March 16. Winder went at once to
Charleston, South Carolina, where he reported on April 8, full of dark predictions for the fate of the country as it approached civil war. He assumed
command of Castle Pinckney, in Charleston Harbor, on April 10, but the
following day he was sent to Morris Island for staff duty. From there he
watched the first shots fired at Fort Sumter on April 12. The following day he
wrote about Robert Anderson and the Federal garrison inside the fort, admitting in his diary that he "felt deeply for himself & command." Those private
opinions contrasted with his public mien. Writing officially that same day,
Winder referred to "the glorious contest now going on." Although he played
no part in the drama at Fort Sumter, the Maryland major threw himself at

once into the business of defending the harbor and organizing troops. Within days his patience wore thin. Winder grumbled on April 17 that the soldiers around him were "rather insubordinate and unreasonable. Rather tired of these Militia Troops." The old discord between professional officers and volunteer soldiers certainly applied in Winder's case, and his rigorous adherence to discipline subsequently became one of his defining traits as a Confederate general.[24]

When he was not engaged in stifling the exuberant volunteers, Winder represented Josiah Gorgas as an ordnance officer at Charleston. He commanded the arsenal there beginning on May 24 and simultaneously was appointed the recruiting officer for the city. He spent most of May in Charleston and left a lengthy trail of paperwork as proof of his industry. One example survives from June 7, when he reported that he had signed a receipt for 20,000 rounds of .69-caliber ammunition—but upon counting them discovered there only were 19,670 rounds present. This duty probably was helping the war effort somehow, but Winder could not be blamed if he wondered whether this represented the best use of his military education. He also assumed responsibility for fabulous sums of money to be used "For the Armament of Fortifications, Purchase of Ordnance & Ordnance Stores & Infantry accoutrements." He eventually received $56,000 of government money for those purposes without ever being bonded.[25]

Within a few weeks he left South Carolina for the active front in Virginia. It is not known whether he petitioned the government to stimulate the transfer or if the authorities merely recognized the advantages of having him command soldiers in the field. Major Winder departed for Richmond on July 8, the same day he received a commission as colonel in the Provisional Army of the Confederate States. He was given command of the 6th South Carolina Infantry, a unit that arrived at Richmond in the third week of July. "I shall never forget Colonel Wynder's first appearance," recalled a veteran of the 6th nearly fifty years later. "The evening of the day we reached camp, we were formed in line of dress parade. Colonel Wynder rode in front of our line on his small mouse colored pony, being introduced to us as our new colonel." Winder led his green troops immediately toward the sound of the guns at Manassas, probably before he even had time to learn the names of his officers. The regiment arrived in midafternoon and handed around ammunition, but it failed to see action in the famous battle of July 21.[26]

Having just missed the only sizable fight of the year in Virginia, Winder

View of the Charleston arsenal with various types of ordnance in the foreground. Winder commanded this installation for part of the summer of 1861. Francis Trevelyan Miller, ed., *The Photographic History of the Civil War*, 10 vols. (New York: Review of Reviews, 1911), 5:189.

and his Carolinians settled into the equivalent of winter quarters in midsummer. They drilled, picketed, skirmished, and played. The soldiers respected their colonel and may even have been fond of him, though they quickly learned he was not the loquacious sort. On July 27 their band commenced a serenade, and the men clamored for a speech, which Winder delivered, he told his diary, "much to my disgust. I returned thanks and retired." Apart from instilling discipline in his volunteers, Winder spent a good deal of time hanging around headquarters. He got on well with army commander Joseph E. Johnston, but he had several ugly episodes with his brigade commander, Brig. Gen. David R. Jones. The brigadier bore the quaint nickname of "Neighbor," reportedly because of his genial disposition, but Winder and Jones quarreled repeatedly. In the first week of December, Winder demonstrated an unlovely side when he wrote a long, churlish letter to army headquarters insisting that General Jones had conspired to deprive him of his rightful position as senior colonel in the brigade. Winder explained in a self-righteous phrase typical of many Civil War officers that his complaint was submitted "in justice to myself." The army commander replied that Jones bore the authority of President Davis in the matter, and Winder's pleas apparently ended in failure. Seven weeks later, just after another spat in which he described Jones as "cross & ill natured," Winder found the brigadier unexpectedly cheerful and friendly. Such inconsistency offended the Marylander most of all, and the warm reception caused Winder to observe that he was "fast loosing all respect" for Neighbor Jones.[27]

The winter dragged along with little excitement. Colonel Winder occupied himself filling out requisitions, sitting on court-martial cases, and supervising regimental elections. Once he mediated in a dispute, hoping to block a duel. Very few clues survive about Winder's political feelings; most that do come from that autumn and winter of 1861. He periodically received intelligence from Maryland and presumably from his family. After learning of some episode in Baltimore in October, Winder jotted in his diary, "Oh, how my blood boiled to avenge the outrages committed." Two months later he wrote to a friend that he could not seek duty away from the front "until my poor down trodden state and family are freed from the Despot's grasp." He felt compelled "to strike a blow for the cause & punish a few Yankees, for their vile conduct." One of his staff officers confirmed later that Winder fought "for his own dear Maryland of which he was constantly speaking, and whose deliverance was his greatest ambition."[28]

As the war approached its first anniversary, events elsewhere in Virginia influenced Winder's subsequent course. Some commanders began to weed out inept subordinates, while other officers drifted away from the army as hopes faded for an easy victory or a short war. When Gen. P. G. T. Beauregard left Virginia for new duty in a different theater, he boldly asked the authorities to provide him with several promising young officers to command his new brigades. Charles Winder was at the top of Beauregard's list, just ahead of A. P. Hill, Samuel Garland, John Pegram, and George H. Steuart. "I am but slightly acquainted with these officers," Beauregard admitted, "and have been induced to present their names from the confidence they have inspired . . . in those who know them well." Adjutant General Cooper ignored every part of Beauregard's request, but evidently Winder already enjoyed a favorable reputation in some circles.[29]

Only five weeks after the endorsement from Beauregard, Winder received his promotion to brigadier general. The appointment occurred on March 7, 1862, to take rank from March 1. It was not until March 21, however, that Winder learned the good news. A week of confusion and official indecision followed. An order issued on March 25 announced that he would assume command of the brigade then led by Col. George B. Anderson. At the same time, army gossip had Winder taking command of D. R. Jones's old brigade, from which Neighbor had just been promoted. If the Marylander had joined one of those brigades, his war record and ultimate reputation likely would have been different. Unexpected events in the Shenandoah Valley pushed Winder toward a different opportunity and into a fateful association with Thomas J. "Stonewall" Jackson.[30]

For some months Richard B. Garnett had led the famous Stonewall Brigade of Jackson's Valley army. On March 23 at the battle of Kernstown, Garnett's actions on the battlefield so enraged Jackson that the army commander pressed charges, relieved Garnett from duty, and notified the government in Richmond that he needed a replacement at once. General Winder was handy (being in Richmond at the time) and made a logical choice. He learned of his assignment to Jackson on March 28 and hastily rode toward the Valley to meet his new chief. It is unclear whether this was their first encounter, though it is very likely that Winder was aware of Jackson long before the Civil War. Jackson had left West Point the same summer that the youthful Winder had arrived, and the Marylander's first assignment upon graduating in 1850 was at Fort Hamilton, a post Jackson had left only weeks earlier. When Charles Winder reached the Valley on April 1, he entered new territory both geographically and professionally. Few men could boast of having been present at both Fort Sumter and First Manassas, yet Winder truly had seen no significant action in the first year of the war. He had waited in northern Virginia, hoping for a chance, watching with his brigade "until our

General Charles S. Winder

hearts grew sick for the Yankees to advance." His assignment with Stonewall Jackson would change all that. Never again would Winder complain about insufficient opportunity.[31]

Those who knew Winder in 1862 or who saw him during the ensuing campaigns fell under the spell of his military bearing and professional appearance. Henry Kyd Douglas at army headquarters recalled Winder as "handsome and attractive in person, graceful on horseback or off, polished in address, [and] dignified and courteous in manner." Another of Jackson's aides termed Winder "a model of knightly beauty and grace," though "rather slight in stature." A North Carolinian who saw Winder took special notice of his attire and later described the general as "faultlessly dressed, even to his unsoiled garments." Even on the march General Winder projected a military attitude. Although he often wore a drab overcoat while riding, he "looked very soldierly in it, as in everything," wrote his aide-de-camp.[32]

Richard Garnett's Stonewall Brigade consisted of five regiments of Virginia infantry, the 2nd, 4th, 5th, 27th, and 33rd. The 27th was the smallest unit, with only eight companies, and the whole brigade numbered forty-nine companies. Of that figure, thirty-nine had been raised in the Shenandoah Valley, including all eleven companies of the 5th Virginia Infantry. For the next ten weeks those men, with an unproved Maryland general at their head, would tramp on familiar roads up and down Virginia's interior. Their reputation, earned at First Manassas, would be buttressed by weeks of good work as the keystone in their namesake's legendary Valley campaign.[33]

The relationship between Winder and the Stonewall Brigade commenced inauspiciously. Before he ran afoul of Jackson, Richard B. Garnett had been popular in the brigade, and his eviction from command created anger among the troops. The men bridled at the arrival of Winder and viewed him as an unwelcome replacement. "The brigade is in a very bad humour," confirmed Jackson's staff officer Sandie Pendleton on April 3. "Had it not been that our cause was too sacred to jeopardize there would have been considerable commotion made amongst us," wrote one soldier. Another of Jackson's staff indicated that there was, in fact, some "commotion." "General Winder was received in sulky and resentful silence," and the regimental officers in the brigade vowed not to visit Winder at his camp as a silent and silly tribute to Garnett's memory. McHenry Howard of Winder's staff noted that the men in the ranks were aggressively hostile, too; on one occasion in April they even hissed at the general as he rode past. "The boys all took a dislike to him from the start," confirmed the contumacious John Casler of the 33rd, "and never did like him afterwards." They thought he was a "fancy general," and his stiff-necked style of discipline won him few friends in a brigade noted for the fierce autonomy of its members. Within days of assuming command, for example, Winder approached the camp of the Rockbridge Artillery (the battery assigned to the brigade) and, according to one of the cannoneers, "hauled our captain over the coals for the way he allowed the horses to be picketed." The battery's officers quickly learned that "our new brigadier required the regulations of war to be carried out in every particular." Even if Winder was correct—as he probably was—his incorrigible Old Army style of management played poorly in the ranks of the Stonewall Brigade.[34]

Winder could point to a good relationship with other generals in the army as an offset to the strained relations with his subordinates. Henry Kyd Douglas of Jackson's staff said that Stonewall's dealings with Winder were not "pleasant," elaborating that the pair "were in some respects, determination and wilfulness, very much alike; in personal appearance and bearing the exact opposite." But most sources are silent on the subject of hard feelings between Winder and Jackson for most of their relationship, and the Marylander's diary frequently reported cordial consultations with his superior. Winder also cultivated friendships with two key officers in the Valley army: Richard Taylor and Turner Ashby. The former was Winder's frequent companion on the march. Similar social and intellectual backgrounds may have drawn Taylor and Winder together, as might their joint status as rookies in Jackson's army. It is harder to discern what built the bonds with Ashby. Winder must have abhorred the bushy-bearded cavalry wizard's indolent nature and proud disregard for discipline, yet the two got along famously. When Ashby threatened to leave the army after an episode with Jackson in April, Winder acted as mediator. He met with Ashby at least twice during the crisis and repaired the cavalier's feelings sufficiently to retain his services for the army.[35]

Winder's arrival on April 1 coincided with a long period of recuperation for the Valley army. Although it allowed the Garnett controversy to simmer, the lull also gave the new commander time to become familiar with his command. When Jackson started to push the army westward into the mountains to deal with John C. Frémont's Federal force, Winder and his brigade were rested and ready. Their role in the subsequent battle of McDowell on May 8 was minor. They formed the rear of Jackson's column and marched hard all day to catch up. Stonewall himself came in the twilight to hasten the brigade

General Charles S. Winder

up Sitlington's Hill as reinforcements, but it arrived too late to be of service. That night Winder entered in his diary an estimate of the distance marched by his men on May 8: an astounding thirty-five miles. During the long march the brigade came among some of the boys from the Virginia Military Institute who had been called out for the emergency. One weary cadet approached Winder and said, "Mister, won't you take me up behind?" The general shared his horse for a time, and when the youngster asked what cavalry company Winder rode with, he was horrified to learn he had begged a ride from a general.[36]

Unharmed in the battle, Winder's brigade led the advance northward toward Franklin in the following days. Winder displayed energy and good judgment on several occasions, and McHenry Howard wrote later that some men of the brigade had thawed so much they "spontaneously cheered" Winder during the march. That same week he had his first recorded angry moment with General Jackson. Some misunderstanding had occurred between them over a technicality, and Winder heard he had been placed under arrest by the short-fused Jackson. An apprehensive McHenry Howard watched Winder, "saw the color rise in his face," and cringed when Winder chided Jackson that he "intended to have his rank as second in command of the army respected by everybody." Nothing came of the episode.[37]

The next four weeks of the campaign threw the Stonewall Brigade into several tight places. In each instance the brigade acquitted itself well, and that period must be considered the apogee of Winder's Civil War career. After slowly traveling through the central part of the Valley in mid-May, Jackson's army suddenly surged eastward across Massanutten Mountain and descended on the Federal garrison at Front Royal on May 23. The Stonewall Brigade marched twenty-six miles that day but arrived too late to participate in the fight. After a brief rest Winder led it toward Winchester, a trip that took twenty-four hours of intermittent walking and nighttime skirmishing. The brigade was the army's van, and Winder, accompanied by Jackson, paced along the Valley Turnpike urging the men forward through the darkness and toward the outskirts of the town. The regiments were allowed only one hour to doze just before dawn on May 25. They found themselves at first light just south of Winchester, with Yankees blocking their path. Jackson ordered Winder to develop the Federal position, which he did by bringing up several batteries of artillery and personally supervising their fire. It was a hot place with heavy casualties, but Winder relished his temporary role as an artillerist.

He "always had a liking for that arm of the service," recalled Lieutenant Howard of his staff, "and now remained for the most of the time on this part of the field, directing the fire of our guns, and being much exposed." Perhaps Winder's thoughts drifted back to the distant Washington Territory, where four years and one week earlier his infantry company had been surrounded by Indians, supporting the army's mountain howitzers in the disastrous battle at Steptoe Butte.[38]

Winder did more than play at chief of artillery at the battle of First Winchester. He acted as site supervisor, feeding fresh brigades into the line and directing the initial course of the action. He also had some role in selecting the route of Richard Taylor's Louisiana brigade as it climbed around the base of the hill occupied by the Federals and eventually delivered the decisive attack. By the end of the fight at Winchester, the Stonewall Brigade and its commander were feeling the cumulative effects of constant marching and fighting. "All exhausted," wrote Winder in his diary that night. He added that it had been forty-eight hours since he had eaten.[39]

Hard marching and continuous skirmishing often were a Civil War soldier's lot, as was fighting. Winder's brigade had its full share of the former without much of the latter in late May. It had avoided the combat of Front Royal and First Winchester, leaving the perception that it was more "fresh" than other brigades in Jackson's army. When the march down the Valley toward Harpers Ferry commenced, the Stonewall Brigade (temporarily reduced to four regiments) resumed its familiar place in the front. In fact it moved alone, pressing northward all the way to Charlestown on the road to Harpers Ferry. On May 28 Winder unexpectedly encountered a small force of Federals there and seized the initiative at once, driving it out of town. His self-sufficiency and vigor in this little affair impressed the men in the brigade and may have raised Jackson's estimation of his worth as well. An artillerist traveling with the brigade wrote that evening that General Winder with his staff constituted the advance of the whole army, since no cavalry was on hand to clear the way.[40]

After pushing forward all the way to Bolivar Heights at Harpers Ferry, Jackson discovered that Winder's brigade—and indeed the entire army—was in danger of being cut off by Union brigadier general James Shields, who was marching with a Federal column from the east toward Front Royal. Simultaneous pressure from the west and north meant that Jackson's force faced disaster on three fronts. The solution was quick marching, always an

General Charles S. Winder

effective weapon in Jackson's arsenal. It is about forty miles from Bolivar Heights to the bottleneck at Strasburg, where the Federal columns were converging. Jackson detailed cartographer Jedediah Hotchkiss, an especially reliable member of his staff, to carry the retreat orders to Winder. Before leaving, wrote Hotchkiss, he met with Jackson, who "impressed me with the gravity of the situation." Hotchkiss found Winder long before dawn on May 31 and alerted him to the danger. At 4:30 A.M. the Stonewall Brigade commenced an epic march toward safety. Moving through Middleway and Bunker Hill, the four regiments struck the Valley Turnpike and turned south, making all speed toward Winchester. When a frightened staff officer spread a story that Federals were blocking the column's route, Winder dismissed the false rumor quickly and handled the episode like a veteran general. His brigade camped very late that night "in an exhausted condition" at Bartonsville, south of Winchester, having tramped about twenty-eight miles. Winder was up at 3:00 the next morning, and the column was on the march by 5:30 on a "rainy disagreeable morning." Thanks to collaboration from Turner Ashby's cavalry, Winder's brigade sneaked through the closing jaws of the Union trap and camped that evening five miles south of Strasburg. "All worn out" in the brigade, wrote Winder, but the press of anxiety and imminent action prevented him from sleeping at all on the night of June 1. He had squeezed an extraordinary performance from his men. The march demonstrated Jackson's "foot cavalry" at its finest and renewed the Stonewall Brigade's reputation as a top-flight unit.[41]

The army continued up the Valley at a more leisurely pace, though the Stonewall Brigade did walk another twenty-one miles on June 5, prompting Winder to observe that "Jackson is insane on these rapid marches." Fast marching had saved the army, yet illustrations of its negative influence on the constitutions of the men abounded. J. K. Edmondson of the 27th Virginia Infantry wrote his wife that he "never saw the Brigade so completely broken down and unfitted for service" as it was that first week in June. He estimated that Winder had lost nearly 1,000 men who, unable to meet the brutal pace, had dropped out along the way during the speedy marches of May 31 and June 1. Professional straggler John Casler of the 33rd placed the number at 500. Most of them wandered through the mountains and rejoined the army at a later date, but in the interim the brigade was horribly depleted.[42]

Lack of sleep, the erosion of his brigade, and the death of his friend Turner Ashby on June 6 probably frayed Winder's nerves and perhaps contributed to

A stretch of the Valley Turnpike just above (south of) Winchester. Winder's brigade traversed this part of the pike during its remarkable march southward from Harpers Ferry on May 31–June 1. U.S. Army Military History Institute.

another unhappy episode with Stonewall Jackson. Its specific origin is not entirely certain. Winder's diary for June 7 included an abrupt phrase without elaboration: "growing disgusted with Jackson." The next day, mixed together with details about his peripheral role in the Federal raid at Port Republic, is another offhand sentence: "Wrote note to Genl. Jackson requesting to leave his command." Nothing more appears in Winder's diary, nor did the army commander leave any record of the dispute. Richard Taylor, on good terms with both men, mentioned in his reminiscences an affair that he timed as occurring in mid-June, after the battle of Port Republic. He remembered that Jackson had refused to grant a leave to Winder and that the aggrieved Marylander had resigned. Taylor wrote that he interceded with Jackson and repaired the breach. Whether this crisis was the same as the one alluded to in Winder's diary for June 7 and 8 may never be known. Whatever the facts, they did not seem to impair cooperation between Jackson and Winder at the battle of Port Republic on June 9.[43]

On the morning of June 9, when Jackson launched attacks northeast of

Port Republic, the Stonewall Brigade numbered about 1,300 men. Winder's day began at 3:45 A.M. He gathered his units and crossed the South River to form part of Jackson's opposition to Shields's advance. The ensuing action on the river plain tested both the brigade and its commander. With three of his five regiments detached on various chores, Winder supervised only the 5th and 27th Virginia during the battle—a total of approximately 500 soldiers. The opening minutes of the engagement were reminiscent of First Winchester, two weeks earlier. Winder was the first general on the field (with Jackson) and again found himself supervising artillery, this time four pieces engaged in a futile duel with the menacing Federal position on a high knob known as the Coaling. Always an able tactician, Winder soon separated the guns in order to create a more dispersed target, reducing the effectiveness of the Unionist artillery. He stayed there in flat farmland as an obvious target, purposely being pounded by the cannon at the Coaling, while two of his other regiments disappeared into the woods in an ill-managed attempt to flank the enemy's guns. It is not clear why General Winder did not accompany this maneuver element of his brigade, and perhaps his absence explains why the flankers failed to drive home an effective attack.[44]

Shortly thereafter Winder pressed forward his two regiments, scuffling with Union infantry on the right bank of the South Fork of the Shenandoah River. Blistering small arms fire drove the 5th and 27th back toward Port Republic and ignited a crisis. Winder's horse was shot three times during the melee, and for a long pause it was uncertain whether the general would be able to halt the retreat of the two regiments. "Tried to rally my men but failed," Winder wrote in his diary; but the arrival of other Confederate infantry provided a backstop, and he was able to knit together the remnants of the regiments before they fell back too far. He then daringly seized the initiative, driving forward with his two regiments and two others he had absorbed into his organization. The bold rush belied his force's small numbers and predictably ended in failure. With his attack blunted, Winder recoiled as Federals retaliated by launching their own attacks. The resulting disaster drove most of the Virginians from the field and left Winder holding a thin line east of Port Republic. From there he observed the back and forth fighting at the Coaling, and as usual attempted to direct some artillery to assist the Confederate efforts there. A tally at day's end showed 160 casualties in the two regiments Winder personally had commanded during the long hours on the plain at Port Republic.[45]

The battle of Port Republic proved to be the capstone to Jackson's Valley campaign. Its triumphant conclusion produced a few days of rest that Winder failed to use to his advantage. On June 11 he complained of being "really worn out." He labored over his battle reports and saw to the reconstitution of his jaded brigade. All too soon the entire army moved eastward, toward Richmond. R. E. Lee needed Jackson's troops to assist in the salvation of the capital city. The brigade alternated between marching and riding the rails. The evening of June 25 found the army near Ashland, just north of Richmond. It had been a frustrating trip, with much standing around punctuated by long, muddy marches. The Stonewall Brigade at this time belonged to Jackson's old division, an entity that had no commander. In the forthcoming battles around Richmond, Jackson would supervise the division himself without offering any real explanation about why Winder or some other subordinate was not given temporary command of the force. Perhaps Winder's recent mysterious encounter with Jackson had cost him the assignment; more likely, Stonewall was wary of entrusting so significant a post to an officer with only nine weeks of experience as a general. Events during the next seven days would show that Winder's strong personality and willingness to bear responsibility all but made him the division commander anyway.[46]

Jackson's entire column awoke early on June 26 to make up time lost earlier in the week. General Winder arose at 1:15 A.M., expecting to march forty-five minutes later. In fact, his brigade did not leave Ashland until about 6:00 A.M., having delayed in order to prepare rations. Its experience was typical of the malaise that plagued the Valley army that week. Long hours of laborious marching ended late that afternoon without any action for Jackson's men, though everyone could hear the boom of battle at Mechanicsville. "God give us the victory & spare me from the dangers of battle," was Winder's evening wish.[47]

The next morning he was awake at 3:00 and by midday was not far from Old Cold Harbor. The battle of Gaines's Mill roared to the south, and Jackson's wing of Lee's army occupied the far Confederate left. Confusion seemed to dominate that end of the battlefield. The Federals occupied a long, low ridge on which sat the McGehee House. Between their line and Jackson stretched a flat, boggy wood utterly unlike anything found in the Shenandoah Valley. The Confederates struggled to bring adequate force to bear on any specific point, and Jackson's brigades disappeared into the trees without much effect. After a long wait in reserve, the Stonewall Brigade received its anticipated attack orders. Struggling through the woods below Old Cold Harbor, Winder's men

General Charles S. Winder

angled toward the McGehee House ridge, some 700 yards beyond the tree line. "The musketry was terrific, never heard such," Winder commented. When the brigade reached the open field, it found troops from other commands scattered around. The chaos and disorganization had reached such magnitude that there was little hope of sorting out the units before dark. Winder vigorously took charge of everyone within earshot, including Georgians of Alexander R. Lawton's brigade and perhaps remnants of at least two brigades from D. H. Hill's division. He saw familiar faces in the ranks of the 1st Maryland Infantry, which was preparing to launch a charge. Winder ordered it to wait until he could bring up his own brigade, and eventually he led this peculiar conglomeration up the incline toward the McGehee House, reaching it in triumph just at dark. The brigade delivered "a wild yell" when it started its charge, and when Jackson was told that it was Winder's men making the noise, he predicted, "We shall soon have good news from that charge. Yes, they are driving the enemy!" In this instance the enemy was the U.S. Regulars, including men from Robert Buchanan's brigade. Winder knew some of the officers on the other side of the firing line, especially Buchanan himself, who had married Winder's sister. Although casualties in the Stonewall Brigade did not amount to much at Gaines's Mill, Winder lost the services of Col. James W. Allen of the 2nd Virginia, who was killed in the charge in front of the McGehee House.[48]

After two days of rest, Jackson's divisions pursued the retreating Federal army south toward the James River. Pushing through Savage's Station on June 30 ("road strewn with dead and evidences of the rout," noticed Winder), the column pulled up short at White Oak Swamp, where a burned-out bridge and unprecedented lethargy in Stonewall Jackson's constitution ended the day's movements. The next morning Jackson pressed on through Riddell's Shop and up to the base of Malvern Hill, fifteen miles south of Richmond. Once again Jackson's soldiers anchored the left of the Confederate position, and for most of that July 1 afternoon the infantry had little to do. Toward evening Winder received orders to take his brigade forward in support of Maj. Gen. D. H. Hill's division, then occupied in a fruitless assault on the Federal batteries atop Malvern Hill. Wandering through the "field, wood, & swamp" that fringed the hill, General Winder became separated from most of his own brigade and failed to locate General Hill. As was his habit, Winder forged ahead anyway, looking for action. He eventually settled into a position on a knob just north of Malvern Hill. From there the parts of the Stonewall

Brigade that had survived the trip through the woods enjoyed an advantageous line of fire into troops from the Union Fourth Corps that had pushed forward onto the front slope of Malvern Hill. Winder managed his own small fight, with about 200 rugged men of his own brigade blasting away in the growing darkness while enduring "a terrific fire." As at Gaines's Mill, disoriented regiments from other commands wandered past, and Winder annexed them to himself for the evening. His personal attention did much to maintain a steady front. Lieutenant Howard remembered that Winder "passed up and down animating the men and endeavoring to form a more regular and orderly line. . . . I remember the General seizing a man by the shoulder and exclaiming, 'Scoundrel, you have shot one of your own friends, I saw you do it.' " Complete darkness ended the battle of Malvern Hill.[49]

The end of the Seven Days campaign energized the Army of Northern Virginia, to which the Stonewall Brigade now was permanently attached. General Winder rested in camp for the next two weeks. On July 3 he had a chance encounter with his old regiment, the 6th South Carolina, and was gratified when the regiment spontaneously cheered him. General Winder told them "he was glad to see them, and to hear of their gallantry." His diary entries during this fortnight were much like those from earlier in the war. They demonstrated over and over again his deep unhappiness at being separated from his family. Scarcely a day passed without his lamenting the absence of his "sweet pets." His thoughts increasingly turned toward religion. Winder's stern personality shielded an extreme piety that only his closest friends could identify. Hapless offenders in the Stonewall Brigade who felt the wrath of Winder's discipline hardly could have pictured him writing in his diary, "Oh that I c'd pass this sabbath day with my darling wife. Truly happy sh'd I be. God grant me patience to bear up under this separation and teach me to trust in his great mercy." Entries of this sort became more common in July 1862 and continued until the day of his death in August.[50]

Winder's last campaign began on July 19 when he boarded a train and headed north. Stonewall Jackson again had received orders that led to independent operations, and Winder's brigade was to form part of an expedition into northern Virginia. The Confederates hoped to achieve a victory over Union forces that had gathered there under Gen. John Pope. It seems likely that Winder had secured the confidence of Stonewall by then, but other concerns plagued the Marylander, especially the enforcement of discipline. Heavy straggling angered him, and to suppress it he reportedly issued orders that offenders would be bucked the next day from dawn until dusk. Bucking was a particularly harsh punishment, and according to John Casler (who predictably was among the victims), about thirty soldiers of the brigade suffered that treatment for a full day. Casler wrote that when Jackson heard of the episode, he ordered Winder not to do it again. From this point on, Casler claimed, some of the men in the brigade could be heard ominously suggesting that the next battle the brigade fought would be Winder's last, as they had him "spotted."

Halfhearted soldiers were not the only offended parties. About the same time as the bucking episode, Winder arrested John Neff, the excellent colonel of the 33rd Virginia, for disobedience of orders. Neff pointed out that he had been following a directive from Jackson and presumed that Stonewall's orders took precedence. General Winder contested Neff's claim and planned a court-martial. The death of both men before the month was out prematurely settled the case. William Poague of the artillery documented a third disciplinary squabble in the first week of August. He wrote that General Winder gave him "stringent orders" on how to define desertion. This put Poague in a difficult position. "I had to place under arrest several men of the battery and prefer charges," recalled Poague with some unhappiness. Winder's version of these cases is not of record, but he seems to have been unconcerned about assuaging the feelings of his subordinates.[51]

In the midst of these leadership problems, Winder's fragile health deserted him. He had been marching great distances and consistently sleeping very little since joining Jackson's army in April, and the accumulated strain finally broke him down. From the end of July until August 9, the general complained almost daily of some malady. On August 5 he offered a typical summary: "Had a very bad night suffering from Headache. C'd not sleep, sent for Dr." The physician failed to improve Winder's health, and for the next several days the general was confined to his tent, unable to march with his brigade as it headed toward a collision with the Federals. Still bedridden on August 7, he celebrated his wedding anniversary by thinking of home. Oppressive heat increased his woes, and the prospect of battle made him restless. He sent his aide McHenry Howard to find General Jackson, asking "if there will be a battle, and if so, when . . . and which way is the army going?" Jackson admitted that action seemed likely but probably not until August 9. Jackson sent Howard back with that message and instructed him to "say to General

Winder that I am truly sorry he is sick." After a sleepless night Winder determined on August 8 to find his brigade, regardless of the consequences. He and his staff rode toward Orange Court House in the hot sun and finally reached the brigade's camp that evening. The heat and noise combined to keep Winder awake yet again. Had he realized it was to be his last night of life, he might have been more appreciative of the sleeplessness.[52]

The next morning, August 9, Winder arose to contemplate the day's duties. Things began happily when he received word that Jackson had left Brig. Gen. A. R. Lawton in the rear of the column on other duty. That made Winder the senior man in his division, and at the battle of Cedar Mountain for a few minutes Charles Winder handled a division as its commander. Jedediah Hotchkiss from Jackson's staff wrote that Winder "looked very pale and badly" that morning, and a friend commented afterward that Winder "could scarcely sit on his horse" from the effects of his illness. When the battle commenced near the foot of Cedar Mountain that afternoon, Winder promptly brought up five pieces of his own artillery to counter Union cannon across the fields in front. As had been the case so often before, he occupied himself in closely managing the guns. Uncharacteristically, the position he had selected was not a sound one for artillery. Converging wood lines formed a right angle that hemmed in the cannons and permitted the Federal batteries to deliver a converging fire on Winder's corner of the field. The general had dismounted and was standing in his shirtsleeves beside a pine tree, using an opera glass to spot the effect of his artillery fire. He was bellowing orders, with his hands cupped around his mouth to project his voice over the noise of the cannonade, when a Federal shell struck him almost squarely.[53]

Artillerist Ned Moore, who was looking at Winder when the shell hit, wrote that the general "fell straight back at full length, and lay quivering on the ground." A shell had passed between his left arm and torso, taking off his elbow and pulverizing the body as far back as the spine. John O'Brien of his staff later informed the general's family that Winder "immediately fell crying out 'My God I'm shot.'" The staff managed to push him onto a stretcher and move him away from the carnage, but he suffered intensely, groaning, "Oh! God how my back pains me." A doctor pronounced the case hopeless and left the general with something to ease his agony. Winder took the news poorly at first, saying "My God, *must* I die? Is there no chance for me?" O'Brien and McHenry Howard stayed with him until the end, carefully responding to his minor requests. He lived for about an hour, praying and talking occasionally about his family, calling them "my little pets," precisely as he had referred to them in his diary for many years. A chaplain materialized and reminded Winder to "lift up your heart to God." The gloomy party moved down the road toward the rear, and McHenry Howard said later that as he held the general's hand, he could feel it growing colder toward the end. For the last ten minutes he was unconscious, and near sundown Charles Winder died so quietly that his staff had difficulty marking the precise time.[54]

It would be some years before the remains could be returned to Winder's beloved Maryland. The extreme heat and total disruption of the transportation patterns in that part of Virginia combined to prevent his body from being shipped immediately to Richmond. He was buried the next day at a Masonic Cemetery just south of Orange Court House, following a quickly planned funeral at the Episcopal Church attended by citizens and a host of wounded officers and acquaintances. Someone (it is not clear who) arranged to have the body removed to Richmond a few days later. It arrived in the capital city via the Virginia Central Railroad on August 17. Capt. Edward S. Gay commanded the Public Guard, a ceremonial unit that escorted the remains to the capitol building. Virginia's Governor John Letcher was part of the crowd, as was Winder's distant cousin, Brig. Gen. John H. Winder. A guard of honor watched over the body that night as it lay in the Old Senate Chamber, the coffin draped with both national and state flags.[55]

The next day Winder was buried at Hollywood Cemetery, a peaceful resting place for thousands of Confederate war dead. He stayed there until the autumn of 1865, when his faithful aide-de-camp McHenry Howard returned to Richmond and removed the general's remains to Maryland. Today Charles Sidney Winder's permanent grave is directly behind the main building at Wye House, the old home of the Lloyd family. The stone for his kinsman Adm. Franklin Buchanan is nearby.[56]

Charles Winder was only thirty-two years old when he died. He never knew the bloody fields of Brawner's Farm, Sharpsburg, Chancellorsville, or Gettysburg, and as an officer in the Stonewall Brigade he might not have survived those contests. He built his reputation at other places and in a variety of ways. A dispassionate inspection of Winder's antebellum credentials clearly marks him as one of the ablest young officers in either army. He achieved a fine record at West Point in matters both military and personal. Confronted with virtually unique opportunities to lead men in times of crisis (the wreck of the

A structure commonly identified as the house in which Winder died of his wound at Cedar Mountain. He more likely died in the front yard of the "school house" near the battlefield, and this *could* be a depiction of that building. Robert Underwood Johnson and Clarence Clough Buel, eds., *Battles and Leaders of the Civil War*, 4 vols. (New York: Century, 1887–88), 2:458.

San Francisco and the battles of Steptoe Butte and Four Lakes), Winder excelled. His presence at Fort Sumter and First Manassas gave him a broad view on the blossoming war, a perspective not shared by most other officers. After promotion, when he was hurled into combat with increasing responsibilities, Winder continued to prosper and grow. Under his leadership the Stonewall Brigade set the standard for hard fighting and even harder marching in the 1862 Shenandoah Valley campaign. The story of the brigade's urgent dash from Harpers Ferry through Strasburg is a classic tale of which Winder could be proud. He had in his makeup many characteristics of a good leader, particularly his desire to handle important tasks. Gathering troops under his wing at First Winchester, Port Republic, Gaines's Mill, and Malvern Hill, Winder made it very clear that he welcomed responsibility and was unafraid of its dangers.

General Charles S. Winder

It is equally certain that the general lacked charisma and flexibility away from the battlefield. No hint of drollness or good humor appears in any of the surviving sources, including even his diaries. He seems not to have tempered his mania for discipline with common sense and may not have been able to reconcile his Old Army habits with the requirements of leading volunteer citizen-soldiers in a war for independence.

Men associated with the Valley army mourned Winder's death with apparent sincerity, nearly always lamenting the loss of a good officer rather than a close friend. When Elisha F. Paxton was promoted to command the Stonewall Brigade in the autumn of 1862, Jackson's chief of staff Sandie Pendleton explained to his family that Paxton was "a first rate officer and every way worthy of the command," though "by no means such a man as Winder." Moxley Sorrel, a staff officer in a different wing of the army, later wrote of Winder as "one of the finest and most promising of the brigadiers." A Georgian who served in Jackson's army in 1862 viewed Winder as "an officer of pre-eminent worth" who "was regarded as one of the very best officers in Jackson's Corps." John Worsham of the 21st Virginia echoed that sentiment, calling the Marylander's death "a great loss to our command and the army." An artillerist who fought beside Winder on several occasions honored him by writing of the Stonewall Brigade that "no commander ever led it so well and effectually . . . except the first—the inimitable, unapproachable, original Stonewall Jackson." The "original" Stonewall Jackson joined the chorus of eulogies, writing to his wife two days later, "I can hardly think of the fall of Brigadier-General C. S. Winder without tearful eyes." Even Winder's great critic, the perpetually dissatisfied John Casler, admitted afterward that his commander "was a good General and a brave man, and knew how to handle troops in battle." But Casler spoiled the praise by adding that "his death was not much lamented by the brigade, for it probably saved some of them the trouble of carrying out their threats to kill him."[57]

Winder's death was a further blow to his mother in Maryland, a woman who already had survived the early loss of her husband and one son in the army. "Alas for his poor mother," wrote a kinsman later that summer, "this is a sad condition for so amiable & christian a lady." The Winder women— Charles's mother, wife, and sisters—could take consolation from the reputation and record of their general. Although Winder served for only sixteen months, his deeds established him as a successful, promising, and honorable officer. Kyd Douglas entertained "no doubt that had he lived he would have been the commander of a corps before the war ended." Such speculation is almost pointless, but it is a reminder of the vast potential never fully developed in Charles Sidney Winder, Maryland's ablest Confederate soldier.[58]

ACKNOWLEDGMENTS

Several friendly historians helped accumulate material for this essay. Brian Pohanka is the original Winder scholar. In addition to providing a great many leads on the general, Brian kindly looked over a draft of this essay and offered his views. Michael P. Musick at the National Archives guided me through piles of arcane Old Army documentation that proved essential in the reconstruction of Winder's early career. My friends Keith S. Bohannon, William J. Miller, and Eric J. Mink also funneled Winder material in my direction. I thank them all.

NOTES

1. Charles S. Winder diary, April 8, 12, 13, 1861, Winder Family Papers, Maryland Historical Society, Baltimore (repository hereafter cited as MHS). Most subsequent references in these notes to Charles S. Winder will be abbreviated into the letters CSW. CSW's lifelong association with Maryland probably has stunted the breadth of his legacy. That state provided the Army of Northern Virginia with many excellent soldiers, but Maryland indisputably falls outside the traditional definition of the South and is less jealous than some other states of its native sons' reputations among Confederates.

2. George A. Hanson, ed., *Old Kent: The Eastern Shore of Maryland* (Baltimore: John P. Des Forges, 1876), 33–39; *Maryland Genealogies: A Consolidation of Articles from the Maryland Historical Magazine*, 2 vols. (Baltimore: Genealogical Publishing, 1980), 1:123–27, 169–82; Edward C. Papenfuse, Alan F. Day, David W. Jordan, and Gregory A. Stiverson, eds., *A Biographical Dictionary of the Maryland Legislature*, 2 vols. (Baltimore: Johns Hopkins University Press, 1979), 2:901–4.

3. Hector Humphreys to Ed Long, January 29, 1846; J. A. Pearce to Randolph Marcy, July 10, 1845; Franklin Buchanan to Randolph Marcy, December 13, 1845, January 14, 1846; and a petition from six members of the Maryland legislature to Ed Long, February 6, 1846, all in "U.S. Military Academy Cadet Application Papers, 1805–1866," RG 94, M688, roll 159, National Archives, Washington, D.C. (repository hereafter cited as

NA). Professor Humphreys's letter states that CSW had been "under my charge for several years." Taken literally, that would mean that CSW was about thirteen years old when he moved to Annapolis.

4. Cadet Hospital Register, book nos. 606 and 607, State of New York, RG 94, NA.

5. *Official Register of the Officers and Cadets of the U.S. Military Academy, West Point, New-York* (New York: W. L. Burroughs, 1850) and similar annual pamphlets dated 1847, 1848, and 1849. CSW placed twenty-second in a graduating class of forty-five in 1850. Gouverneur K. Warren eventually became the best-known officer of the group.

6. "Returns From Regular Army Artillery Regiments," M727, rolls 20 and 27, NA. Roll 27 covers CSW's time in the 4th U.S. Artillery; roll 20 spans the duration of his stint in the 3rd U.S. Artillery.

7. *New York Daily Times*, January 14, 16, February 16, 1854.

8. CSW Diary, January 1–2, 1854, Winder Papers; *New York Daily Times*, January 14, 20, 1854. The *San Francisco* eventually sank after every survivor had been transferred to the rescue ships. The disaster occupied a prominent spot in the national news, and the media enjoyed surprisingly fresh though inaccurate intelligence. Diarist Elizabeth Lomax in Washington, D.C., expressed "great anxiety" over the plight of the *San Francisco* as early as January 4. Five days later she lamented the loss of many Old Army friends, though she mistakenly supposed the event had occurred "off the coast of California" instead of North Carolina. See Elizabeth Lindsay Lomax, *Leaves from an Old Washington Diary, 1854– 1863*, ed. Lindsay Lomax Wood (New York: Dutton, 1943), 14–15.

9. CSW to Lt. Col. L. Thomas, from Liverpool, England, January 24, 1854, and to Col. S. Cooper, from Liverpool, England, January 24, 1854, both in Letters Received, AGO, Main Series, W61 1854, RG 94, NA. The same source contains CSW's letter to Col. S. Cooper, from Fort Adams, Rhode Island, February 17, 1854, reporting his return from England.

10. *New York Daily Times*, February 14, 1854. The testimony from the Gates court of inquiry can be found in "Records of Judge Advocate General's Office," file HH-397 (February 1854), 6W4, row 3, compartment 7, shelf D, box 217, RG 153, NA. Much of the most pertinent testimony was published in the *New York Daily Times* during the investigation and has been cited already in these notes. The report of General Scott's court of inquiry was printed as AGO General Orders #8, a copy of which can be seen at the National Archives in file (pt.) 16G (AGO) 1854. In it CSW is first on a short list of officers who "particularly distinguished themselves."

11. See CSW diary, April 5, May 29, 1851, Winder Papers, as examples. In his diary entry for January 12, 1855, CSW mentioned making "a grand shot, killed 9 ducks at one discharge," and on February 23, 1855, he met Virginian William "Extra Billy" Smith, who like CSW was destined to become a Confederate general under Stonewall Jackson.

12. CSW diary, May 2, 15, June 16, 22, 1855, and CSW to "My dear Uncle" [Edward Lloyd], April 22, 1852, Winder Papers; "Returns from Regular Army Infantry Regiments," M665, roll 102, NA. CSW's wife's given name probably was Alice, but it and

Alicia seem to have been used interchangeably by the family. The couple produced three children in five years: Charles Sidney Jr., Edward Lloyd, and Elizabeth Lloyd. Elizabeth died only three months after her father in 1862. For genealogical data on CSW's immediate family, see Hanson, *Old Kent*, 34.

13. "Returns from Regular Army Infantry Regiments," M665, roll 102, NA; CSW to Col. S. Cooper, February 1, March 1, 1858, both in "Letters Received by the Office of the Adjutant General [Main Series]" [file hereafter referred to as "Main Series"], M567, 1858, 33W, frames 920 and 1022, NA; Lawrence Kip, *Army Life on the Pacific* (New York: Redfield, 1859), 41.

14. E. J. Steptoe to Maj. W. W. Mackall, from Fort Walla Walla, May 2, 1858, in "Main Series," M567, 1858, 165P, frames 379–80, NA; John A. Hemphill and Robert C. Cumbow, *West Pointers and Early Washington* (Seattle: West Point Society of Puget Sound, 1992), 62, 166; N. Clarke to Col. S. Cooper, from San Francisco, California, June 1, 1858, in "Main Series," M567, 1858, 148P, NA.

15. E. J. Steptoe to Maj. W. W. Mackall, from Fort Walla Walla, May 23, 1858, in "Main Series," M567, 1858, 165P, frames 383–87, NA; CSW to "My dear Charley" [Charles H. Key], June 2, 1858, Winder Papers; Edmond S. Meany, *History of the State of Washington* (New York: Macmillan, 1927), 213. Meany is nearly unique in estimating the Indian force at only 600 men. His account is among the earliest overviews written but is unreliable in places. CSW's June 2 letter was published in *Maryland Historical Magazine* 35 (March 1940): 56–59.

16. E. J. Steptoe to Maj. W. W. Mackall, from Fort Walla Walla, May 23, 1858, in "Main Series," M567, 1858, 165P, frames 383–87 and 392–95, NA; CSW to "My dear Charley," June 2, 1858, Winder Papers. One of the company commanders killed in the fight was Oliver H. P. Taylor, part of the celebrated West Point class of 1846.

17. E. J. Steptoe to Maj. W. W. Mackall, from Fort Walla Walla, May 23, 1858, in "Main Series," M567, 1858, 165P, frames 448–49, NA. One of the heroes of the fight was Lt. David McM. Gregg, later a fine division commander in the Army of the Potomac's Cavalry Corps.

18. G. Wright to Maj. W. W. Mackall, August 14, September 2, 1858, in "Main Series," M567, 1858, 249P and 260P, frames 728–29 and 801–10, NA; Hemphill and Cumbow, *West Pointers and Early Washington*, 139–65; Kip, *Army Life on the Pacific*, 44–45, 56; Fred R. Brown, *History of the Ninth U.S. Infantry, 1799–1909* (Chicago: R. R. Donnelly, 1909), 86. The chapter of the unit history dealing with the 1858 campaign was written by E. J. Harvie, who was a lieutenant in CSW's company during that period. Harvie's disappointing account is very superficial and barely mentions CSW.

19. G. Wright to Maj. W. W. Mackall, from Camp on the Spokane River, September 6, 1858, in "Main Series," M567, 1858, 260P, frames 770–75, NA; Meany, *History of the State of Washington*, 215–16; "Preliminary articles of a Treaty of Peace and Friendship between the United States & the Couer d' [A]lene Indians," in "Main Series," M567, 1858, 270P, frames 863–64, NA. Article 7 of the agreement stated, remarkably, "It is agreed by the

chiefs and head men of the Couer d' Alene Nation, that this treaty . . . shall extend also to include the Nez Perce nation of Indians."

20. Brown, *History of the Ninth U.S. Infantry*, 87; "Returns from Regular Army Infantry Regiments," M665, roll 102, NA; CSW to Maj. W. W. Mackall and to Alfred Pleasonton, both from Fort Walla Walla, October 14, 30, 1858, in "U.S. Army Continental Commands, 1821–1920," pt. 1, "Department of Oregon, Letters Received, 1858–1861," box 1, RG 193, NA; memoirs of Gen. Samuel Wragg Ferguson, typescript in Fort Sumter National Monument archives, Charleston, S.C.

21. "Returns from U.S. Military Posts, 1800–1916, Fort Walla Walla, Washington, August 1856–May 1867," M617, roll 1343, NA; "Returns from Regular Army Infantry Regiments," M665, roll 102, NA; CSW to Charles H. Key, June 2, 1858, Winder Papers. The most popular theory on CSW's illness is that he suffered from some type of recurrent tropical fever, perhaps malaria.

22. Population Schedules of the Eighth Census of the United States, 1860, for Talbot County, Maryland, M653, roll 482, RG 29, NA. Edward Lloyd died in August 1861.

23. F. B. Heitman, *Historical Register of the United States Army from Its Organization* (Washington, D.C.: National Tribune, 1890), 705; Edward Warren, *A Doctor's Experiences in Three Continents* (Baltimore: Cushings and Bailey, 1885), 257–58; Charles Howard to Jefferson Davis, April 2, 1861, in CSW's Compiled Service Record (hereafter cited as CSR), M331, roll 271, NA; CSW Diary, April 1, 5, 6, 1861, Winder Papers.

24. CSW's CSR, M331, roll 271, NA; CSW diary, April 8, 10, 12, 13, 17, 1861, Winder Papers; CSW to Allen J. Green, April 13, 1861, Frederick M. Dearborn Collection, folder 1057, Houghton Library, Harvard University, Cambridge, Mass.

25. Department of S.C., Ga., Fla., Special Order #111/2, May 11, 1861; Adjutant and Inspector General's Office, Special Order #58/6, May 24, 1861; CSW to Col. E. Manigault, June 7, 1861, a copy of which kindly was provided to the author by Mike Masters of Clyde, N.C.; "Letters Received by the Confederate Secretary of War, 1861–65," documents 3753-1861 and 5378-1861, M437, NA. The two May 1861 orders cited above are filed under CSW's name in "Unfiled Papers and Slips . . . ," M347, NA. The earlier order states that CSW was assigned to that department, with orders to report to Gen. P. G. T. Beauregard. The May 24 order is more specific. It announced CSW as the new recruiting officer at Charleston and ordered him to "take charge of the arsenal" there.

26. CSW diary, July 8, 15, 21, 1861, Winder Papers; CSW's CSR, M331, roll 271, NA; memoirs of Richard Baxter Ervin, p. 18, typescript in Richmond National Battlefield Park archives, Richmond, Va.

27. CSW diary, July 27, December 8, 1861, January 27, 29, 1862, Winder Papers; CSW to Col. Thomas Jordan, from Centreville, Virginia, December 6, 1861, in "Letters Received by the Confederate Secretary of War, 1861–1865," M437, roll 18, NA. "Loosing" is CSW's spelling.

28. CSW's CSR, M267, roll 212, NA; "Letters Received by the Confederate Adjutant and Inspector General," document 129-W/1862, M474, NA; CSW to Frederick L.

Childs, December 18, 1861; CSW diary, October 27, November 23, 1861; and John F. O'Brien to Edward Winder, October 16, 1862, all in Winder Papers. The CSR in M267 is for CSW's service with the 6th South Carolina. In it one can find records of CSW's mundane daily activities, such as a requisition for 5,000 percussion caps to be used by his regiment.

29. P. G. T. Beauregard to Samuel Cooper, January 30, 1862, in Janet B. Hewett and others, eds., *Supplement to the Official Records of the Union and Confederate Armies*, 100 vols. (Wilmington, N.C.: Broadfoot, 1994–2000), serial 93, pt. 3, 1:638.

30. CSW's CSR, M331, roll 271, NA; CSW diary, March 21, 1862, Winder Papers; U.S. War Department, *The War of the Rebellion: A Compilation of the Official Records of the Union and Confederate Armies*, 127 vols., index, and atlas (Washington, D.C.: GPO, 1880–1901), ser. 1, 12(3):837 (hereafter cited as *OR*; all references are to ser. 1); Mauriel Phillips Joslyn, *Charlotte's Boys: Civil War Letters of the Branch Family of Savannah* (Berryville, Va.: Rock-bridge, 1996), 105.

31. CSW diary, March 28, April 1, 1862, Winder Papers; CSW's CSR, M331, roll 271, NA; CSW to Frederick L. Childs, December 18, 1861, Winder Papers. For a concise treatment of the Richard B. Garnett episode, see Robert K. Krick, "The Army of Northern Virginia's Most Notorious Court Martial," *Blue and Gray Magazine* 3 (June–July 1986): 27–32, and the essay by A. Cash Koeniger in this volume.

32. Henry Kyd Douglas, *I Rode with Stonewall* (Chapel Hill: University of North Carolina Press, 1940), 125; [Robert L. Dabney], "What I Saw of the Battle of the Chickahominy," *Southern Magazine* 10 (July 1872): 10–11; William Ruffin Cox, in *Histories of the Several Regiments and Battalions from North Carolina in the Great War, 1861–'65*, comp. Walter Clark, 5 vols. (Goldsboro, N.C.: Nash Brothers, 1901), 4:446; McHenry Howard, *Recollections of a Maryland Confederate Soldier and Staff Officer under Johnston, Jackson, and Lee* (Baltimore: Williams and Wilkins, 1914), 119. Howard's memoir is cited repeatedly in the following notes. The best source on CSW's Civil War career, it includes even more valuable material than CSW's own diary. McHenry Howard was a distant cousin of CSW.

33. Lee A. Wallace Jr., *A Guide to Virginia Military Organizations, 1861–1865* (1964; rev. ed., Lynchburg, Va.: H. E. Howard, 1986), 83–84, 87–89, 110–11, 116–17.

34. A. S. Pendleton to mother, April 3, 1862, quoted in W. G. Bean, ed., "The Valley Campaign of 1862 as Revealed in Letters of Sandie Pendleton," *Virginia Magazine of History and Biography* 78 (July 1970): 343–44; Margaretta Barton Colt, *Defend the Valley: A Shenandoah Family in the Civil War* (New York: Orion, 1994), 130; Douglas, *I Rode with Stonewall*, 37; Howard, *Recollections*, 83; John O. Casler, *Four Years in the Stonewall Brigade* (Girard, Kans.: Appeal Publishing, 1906), 73; William Thomas Poague, *Gunner with Stonewall: Reminiscences of William Thomas Poague, a Memoir Written for His Children in 1903*, ed. Monroe F. Cockrell (Jackson, Tenn.: McCowat-Mercer, 1957), 19, 21.

35. Douglas, *I Rode with Stonewall*, 38–39; CSW diary, April 3, 7, 20, 25, 28, 1862, Winder Papers; Howard, *Recollections*, 90, 119.

36. Robert G. Tanner, *Stonewall in the Valley: Thomas J. "Stonewall" Jackson's Shenandoah Valley Campaign, Spring 1862* (Garden City, N.Y.: Doubleday, 1976; rev. ed., Mechanicsburg, Pa: Stackpole, 1996), 192–93; CSW diary, May 8, 1862, Winder Papers; Howard, *Recollections*, 94–95.

37. Howard, *Recollections*, 99–100. For most of the Valley campaign, Richard S. Ewell rather than CSW was Jackson's top subordinate.

38. CSW diary, May 23, 24, 25, 1862, Winder Papers; George W. Kurtz, in Garland R. Quarles, Lewis N. Barton, C. Vernon Eddy, and Mildred Lee Grove, eds., *Diaries, Letters, and Recollections of the War between the States* (Winchester, Va.: Winchester-Frederick County Historical Society, 1955), 47; Howard, *Recollections*, 109; Tanner, *Stonewall in the Valley*, 282–83; unsigned letter from member of Company H, 27th Virginia Infantry, May 26, 1862, Mary Kelly Smith Papers, North Carolina Department of Archives and History, Raleigh; *OR* 12(3):735. CSW's mare "Pet" was wounded in this fight. See John F. O'Brien to Edward Winder, October 16, 1862, Winder Papers.

39. Howard, *Recollections*, 109; CSW diary, May 25, 1862, Winder Papers.

40. Tanner, *Stonewall in the Valley*, 327; CSW diary, May 28, 1862, Winder Papers; Howard, *Recollections*, 112; William Humphreys letter, June 14, 1862, typescript in author's possession.

41. Jedediah Hotchkiss to C. S. Arnall, September 5, 1896, frame 210; Jedediah Hotchkiss to Samuel J. C. Moore, September 8, 1896, frame 212; and C. S. Arnall to Jedediah Hotchkiss, September 8, 1896, frame 220, Jedediah Hotchkiss Papers, Library of Congress, Washington, D.C.; all three letters are on roll 34. See also Jedediah Hotchkiss, *Make Me a Map of the Valley: The Civil War Journal of Stonewall Jackson's Topographer*, ed. Archie P. McDonald (Dallas: Southern Methodist University Press, 1973), 50; CSW diary, May 31, June 1, 1862, Winder Papers; Howard, *Recollections*, 116.

42. CSW diary, June 5, 1862, Winder Papers; James K. Edmondson, *My Dear Emma: War Letters of . . .* , ed. Charles W. Turner (Verona, Va.: McClure Press, 1978), 96; Casler, *Four Years in the Stonewall Brigade*, 80.

43. CSW diary, June 7, 8, 1862, Winder Papers; Richard Taylor, *Destruction and Reconstruction: Personal Experiences of the Late War* (New York: Appleton, 1879), 78–79.

44. Robert K. Krick, *Conquering the Valley: Stonewall Jackson at Port Republic* (New York: Morrow, 1996), 291–92, 320; *OR* 12(3):742.

45. CSW diary, June 9, 1862, Winder Papers; *OR* 12(3):741–42; Krick, *Conquering the Valley*, 434. CSW's official report is more delicately phrased than his diary, which bluntly states, "I tried to rally the men. . . . I partially succeeded."

46. CSW diary, June 11, 12, 15, 23, 24, 25, 1862, Winder Papers.

47. Ibid., June 26, 1862.

48. Douglas, *I Rode with Stonewall*, 104; CSW diary, June 27, 1862, Winder Papers; Howard, *Recollections*, 146; Washington Hands, "Civil War Memoirs," Special Collections, Alderman Library, University of Virginia, Charlottesville.

49. CSW diary, June 30, July 1, 1862, Winder Papers; Howard, *Recollections*, 153;

P[eter] W[ellington] A[lexander], "Lawton's Brigade in the Battles Before Richmond," *Milledgeville (Ga.) Southern Recorder*, August 19, 1862.

50. James R. Boulware diary, July 3, 1862, South Caroliniana Library, University of South Carolina, Columbia; CSW diary, July 6, 1862, Winder Papers.

51. Casler, *Four Years in the Stonewall Brigade*, 101–2; John F. Neff to "Dear Parents," August 4, 1862, U.S. Army Military History Institute, Carlisle Barracks, Pa.; Poague, *Gunner with Stonewall*, 32; CSW diary, July 19, 1862, Winder Papers.

52. CSW diary, July 30, August 5, 6, 7, 8, 1862, Winder Papers; Howard, *Recollections*, 162–63.

53. Howard, *Recollections*, 165–69; E. A. Moore in undated contemporary newspaper clipping from *Lexington (Va.) Gazette*, photocopy in author's possession; E. A. Moore, *The Story of a Cannoneer under Stonewall Jackson* (Lynchburg, Va.: J. P. Bell, 1910), 97–98; John F. O'Brien to Edward Winder, October 16, 1862, Winder Papers; Hotchkiss, *Make Me A Map*, 66; Elizabeth Phoebe Key Howard to Charles Howard, September 1862, Elizabeth Phoebe Key Howard Papers, MHS; Robert K. Krick, *Stonewall Jackson at Cedar Mountain* (Chapel Hill: University of North Carolina Press, 1990), 76–77. In his memoir Howard wrote that President Jefferson Davis told him many years later that CSW "was just about to be made a major-general" before his death. This is a tiresome claim seen in the case of nearly every officer from the rank of colonel upward. If CSW had lived through Second Manassas and Sharpsburg, he likely would have been promoted—but probably not before that time.

54. Moore, *Cannoneer under Stonewall*, 98; Elizabeth Phoebe Key Howard to Charles Howard, September 1862, Howard Papers; John F. O'Brien to Edward Winder, October 16, 1862, Winder Papers; Howard, *Recollections*, 170–71, 306. Ned Moore noted with quiet irony that CSW had issued firm orders before the battle that men were not to leave their posts to help the wounded. When Moore saw CSW struck, he just turned and resumed his own place with his battery. CSW's opera glass was dented when he fell but was salvaged by his staff.

55. Howard, *Recollections*, 174; *Richmond Daily Whig*, August 18, 1862; *Richmond Daily Enquirer*, August 18, 1862; *Richmond Dispatch*, August 18, 19, 1862; Wallace, *Guide to Virginia Military Organizations*, 232. Nine months later the corpse of Stonewall Jackson lay in the Old Senate Chamber at the capitol, the same room where CSW was in August. According to McHenry Howard, CSW was interred at Hollywood Cemetery in the vault of someone named Davis, who charged an exorbitant price. A June 27, 1865, letter from J. Peterkin to James Howard (Howard Papers) says that the general was buried near President James Monroe in the most prominent section of that famous cemetery.

56. After CSW's death his widow claimed $1371.70 in back pay from the government (CSW's CSR, M331, roll 271, NA).

57. A. S. Pendleton to his mother, November 15, 1862, in William Nelson Pendleton Papers, Southern Historical Collection, University of North Carolina, Chapel Hill; G. Moxley Sorrel, *Recollections of a Confederate Staff Officer* (New York: Neale, 1917), 96;

James Cooper Nisbet, *Four Years on the Firing Line* (Chattanooga, Tenn.: Imperial Press, [1911?]), 134; John H. Worsham, *One of Jackson's Foot Cavalry: His Experience and What He Saw during the War, 1861–1865* (New York: Neale, 1912), 115; C. A. Fonerden, *A Brief History of the Military Career of Carpenter's Battery* (New Market, Va.: Henkel, 1911), 22; Mary Anna Jackson, *Memoirs of "Stonewall" Jackson* (Louisville, Ky.: Prentice Press, Courier-Journal Job Printing Co., 1895), 312; Casler, *Four Years in the Stonewall Brigade,* 102–4. CSW's personal staff seemed sincerely fond of him. John F. O'Brien wrote of his chief, "Not a braver, cooler, purer, more patriotic gentleman has fallen in this war than he" (John F. O'Brien to Edward Winder, October 16, 1862, Winder Papers). McHenry Howard, also of CSW's staff, praised his general in nearly embarrassing terms, both in his *Recollections* and in a postwar letter to CSW's widow; see McHenry Howard to Mrs. CSW, July 29, 1865, Winder Papers. Although historians rightly hold Howard's recollections in high esteem, it is my opinion that Howard's remarks about CSW's virtues (and especially his popularity) were selective and not entirely frank.

58. W. H. Winder to Gertrude P. Winder, August 16, 1862, Winder Papers; Douglas, *I Rode with Stonewall,* 126. The only other Marylander prominent enough to warrant consideration was Raphael Semmes, who moved to Alabama long before the war and is not always associated with his native state. His famous naval exploits, though singular, cannot trump CSW's legacy of having commanded the Stonewall Brigade in one of the most celebrated campaigns of the Civil War.

A. CASH KOENIGER

Prejudices and Partialities

THE GARNETT CONTROVERSY REVISITED

Liberty Mills, Virginia, is today a tranquil intersection of two country roads, situated on the right bank of the Rapidan River a few miles from the town of Orange in the rolling, red clay hills of Virginia's Piedmont. It can yet be found on the Gordonsville Quadrangle of the U.S. Geological Survey's topographic maps. But the place has been forgotten by the U.S. Postal Service, the official state road map of the Virginia Department of Transportation, and almost everybody else. There is nothing there to suggest that on this unlikely Orange County back road occurred one of the most famous and probably most unjust court-martial proceedings of the American Civil War. For here, on August 6, 1862, virtually on the eve of the battle of Cedar Mountain, at the headquarters of Maj. Gen. Richard S. Ewell, the two-day trial of Brig. Gen. Richard Brooke Garnett began.

Gen. Thomas J. "Stonewall" Jackson had never liked this brigadier, who handled Jackson's former duties as commander of the Stonewall Brigade for less than four months. Garnett was a Tidewater aristocrat, born in Essex County, Virginia, on the lower Rappahannock River, a man very different in background and temperament from the mountain-bred yeoman who would become his commanding officer and nemesis. He had finished at West Point in 1841, five years before Jackson, and had spent most of a twenty-year military career prior to the Civil War stationed at various points on the western frontier.[1]

The Confederate War Department assigned Garnett to the Stonewall Brigade because Jackson declined to recommend any of its regimental colonels for the job, believing that none was fit. Jackson immediately decided that Garnett also failed to meet his standards. He complained that Garnett lacked sufficient sternness in dealing with his men—the same reservation he had held concerning the regimental colonels. Years later a veteran of the Stonewall Brigade expressed the opinion that "Old Jack," after leaving his former command, wanted it put through its paces with an extra-heavy hand. "We had to pay dearly for our reputation," Pvt. John O. Casler of the 33rd Virginia observed, "for whenever there was any extra hard duty to be performed, Gen. Jackson always sent his old brigade to that post of duty for fear the other brigades under his command would think and say that he favored his old command."[2]

On the frigid Romney expedition in December 1861 and January 1862, Jackson reprimanded his new brigadier for allowing the Stonewall Brigade to fall out on a march—in eighteen-degree weather—long enough to cook a quick meal. Garnett's explanation that the men had not eaten in more than thirty hours and could not persevere further without food did not impress Jackson favorably. "I never found anything impossible with this brigade," he retorted.[3]

Within days Jackson wrote to Secretary of War Judah P. Benjamin about the need to replace Garnett. "General G. is not qualified to command a Brigade," he stated. "I do not feel safe in bringing it [the Stonewall Brigade] into actions under the present commander; as he has satisfied me that he is not able to meet emergencies even in the proper management of his Brigade in camp and on the march."[4]

The troops of the Stonewall Brigade, while initially displeased that an outsider had been brought in as their commander, came to hold a different view from that of Jackson. They soon realized, as Sgt. Thomas Gold of the 2nd Virginia said long after the war, that Garnett "looked upon them as men and fellow soldiers, not machines or dogs to be ordered and kicked around at his fancy." Affection and respect quickly developed between Garnett and his men.[5]

When the War Department failed to act on Jackson's request, the general took matters into his own hands. At the battle of Kernstown on March 23,

Confederate artist William L. Sheppard titled this drawing of miserable soldiers marching in the Romney campaign "Following Stonewall." Gen. W. W. Loring, another of Jackson's subordinates, shared Garnett's outrage at the brutal pace dictated by their commander. Editor's collection.

1862, he suffered his only tactical defeat. It was not a well-conceived battle. The Confederates attacked on the basis of faulty intelligence—cavalry chief Turner Ashby had reported four regiments of Federals when in fact there were three brigades. Outnumbered two to one, Jackson's weary soldiers had reached the field after covering nearly fifty miles during two days of forced marching. And Jackson confided absolutely nothing to his brigade commanders, including Richard B. Garnett, about his battle plan. Late in the day many soldiers in the Stonewall Brigade ran out of ammunition. Ignorant of Jackson's tactical blueprint, Garnett decided on the strength of his own judgment to withdraw his command from the field, touching off a general retreat despite Jackson's personal effort to rally the men.

The Confederates had done about as well at Kernstown as reasonably could be expected in the circumstances. The Stonewall Brigade had been in a hopeless situation. By quitting the field, Garnett had saved his artillery and his men. This decision had held down the number of casualties, but Jackson's overall loss still totaled 25 percent of his soldiers and two field pieces. Furious over the outcome of the battle, the Confederate commander would not accept defeat. He fixed his anger and blame for the reverse on Garnett. For Jackson, running out of ammunition was not a sufficient reason to abandon the struggle. "Go back and give them the bayonet," he had shouted at one of the retreating Confederates.[6]

On April 1, while encamped at Rude's Hill between Mount Jackson and New Market, Jackson relieved Garnett of command and placed him under arrest, charging him with improper conduct—neglect of duty—on the field. Taken to Harrisonburg, Garnett did not learn the specific accusations against him for several days.[7]

Stonewall Jackson spent much of the next three weeks—and off and on, part of the next four months—preparing a case for court-martial, to the consternation of nearly everyone else in his army, who thought Garnett had acted reasonably, prudently, and honorably. "Their regret at the loss of General Garnett was so great and their anger at his removal so intense and universal that their conduct amounted almost to insubordination," Jackson's staff officer Henry Kyd Douglas wrote of the Stonewall Brigade. Douglas added that Brig. Gen. Charles S. Winder, Garnett's replacement, "was received in sulky and resentful silence, and for nearly three weeks General Jackson was permitted to ride past his old command without hearing a shout." Likewise Gen. Richard Taylor remembered, "I have never met officer

This fanciful engraving celebrated the climactic Union assault at Kernstown. *Frank Leslie's Illustrated Newspaper*, April 26, 1862.

or soldier, present at Kernstown, who failed to condemn the harsh treatment of Garnett after that action." Winder's own staff officer McHenry Howard recorded that on one occasion the new brigade commander was even hissed by his troops, and that for a time the brigade's field officers expressed resentment over Garnett's treatment by refusing to call at Winder's headquarters.[8]

In May 1862, following the battle of McDowell, Jackson inquired of Col. Andrew Jackson "Jack" Grigsby, one of the regimental commanders in the Stonewall Brigade, whether the troops could not have stood against the fire for just five minutes more at Kernstown. "No sir," the colonel of the 27th Virginia replied, "they could not have stood a damned second longer." Jackson similarly questioned the other colonels of the Stonewall Brigade; their replies also were negative. This information, clearly not what Jackson wanted to hear, in no way deterred him from pressing his case. Why were five minutes such a major concern? At the court-martial he would testify that in his judgment, if Garnett's brigade had held on for five more minutes, the beleaguered Confederates would have been reinforced by other units in process of moving up. They would then have held their ground, and the battle soon would have ended with darkness.[9]

This episode brought out a trait of Jackson's often overlooked by his admirers. There is, to be sure, much to admire in his character and record, but like everyone, Jackson had his darker side. He possessed a strong quarrelsome

The Garnett Controversy Revisited

and vindictive streak and seldom dealt fairly with people he disliked—and an alarmingly large number of people fit that description. Exactly how he missed the New Testament's emphasis on forgiveness, as much as he read his Bible, one can only speculate, but clearly the seventy-times-seven formula was not a major part of his faith.

Jackson had a pronounced tendency to find fault, which resulted in a long history of acrimonious disagreement with other officers. One often reads that Jackson was a hard taskmaster to his junior officers, but his career in the regular army had come to an end in the early 1850s because of conflict with a superior. On duty as second in command and post quartermaster at Fort Meade, Florida, Jackson first fell out with his commanding officer, Capt. William Henry French, over which of the two had authority to oversee a construction project then in progress at the fort (the two later would count each other as enemies in more violent circumstances at such places as White Oak Swamp, Sharpsburg, and Fredericksburg). Jackson sought a transfer. While waiting for that, he began to "cut" French; that is, he refused to speak to him except in the line of official duty.

After several months of such tension, in April 1851 Lieutenant Jackson began to question enlisted men in an effort to collect evidence about a romantic affair he believed to be going on between the married Captain French and a female domestic employed by his family. When French learned of this unauthorized investigation into his personal life, he had Jackson arrested. Each man filed formal charges alleging conduct unbecoming an officer and gentleman on the other's part. A detailed account of Jackson's specifications and the hearsay and circumstantial evidence he offered in their support looks petty and contentious at best.

The dispute eventually came to the attention of Winfield Scott, general in chief of the army. After reviewing the evidence, as well as the already rendered thoughts of Gen. David Twiggs in New Orleans, Scott directed his adjutant general to write as follows:

> He [Scott] directs me to express his regret, that there is exhibited by these papers, conduct on the part of both Maj. French and Maj. Jackson [each had been a brevet major in the Mexican War] which require [*sic*] to be noticed. It was certainly a mistaken sense of duty, which led Lieutenant Jackson to examine privately, the soldiers of the company as to alleged moral conduct, on the part of their captain. Even if such ill-

conduct by becoming a matter of public scandal, is a proper subject for investigation by a Military Tribunal, this mode of seeking, or collecting testimony is highly objectionable. It is well calculated to originate scandal where none already existed, to bring into contempt the officer who is made the subject of it, and is highly prejudicial to good order and discipline. Nor, after an attentive examination, is it perceived, that the circumstances set forth in the additional specifications presented by Lieut. Jackson against Captain French, (whenever they are not so vaguely expressed as to make it impossible to investigate them,) contain anything which would support the grave charges they are intended to establish.

French was reprimanded as well, not for his alleged amorous activities but for the undignified nature of his response to Jackson's accusations.[10]

The controversy did no credit to either Jackson or French. There was no trial, and Jackson eventually succeeded in getting his leave and then in resigning from U.S. service. He was appointed professor of natural and experimental science and instructor of artillery at the Virginia Military Institute (VMI), with the rank of major in the Virginia militia, apparently without the superintendent and board of visitors ever learning of the Florida imbroglio.

Jackson soon established an up-and-down, and frequently strained, relationship with VMI superintendent Francis H. Smith, who found that his new professor "lacked the tact required in getting along with his classes." He also lacked the tact for getting along with Colonel Smith, with whom he refused at times to speak except when necessary in the line of duty, just as he had done with Major French. Jackson resigned as a director of the Rockbridge Bible Society because of a disagreement with Smith, and he took to writing curt notes to the superintendent, of which the following is but one surviving example: "Colonel, Feeling that your verbal reprimand of me on Tuesday last was unmerited, I respectfully request that you will communicate the same to me in writing." Smith did respond in writing, but only to state that the remarks in question were not intended as a reprimand. For ten years Smith demonstrated impressive patience in dealing with the prickly Jackson, whom he quietly and loyally defended against charges of incompetence by both cadets and parents.[11]

As a Civil War commander, Jackson was strikingly prone to judge harshly, quarrel with, and frequently arrest subordinate officers other than Garnett. The following, in chronological order of the incidents, probably represents only a partial count of individuals Stonewall Jackson either placed under arrest or preferred charges against:[12]

Col. William Gilham was Jackson's friend and former business partner, VMI colleague, and barracks roommate. Jackson charged him with "neglect of duty" over failure to capture a railroad depot at Bath, Virginia. Gilham left the service before the charges had been filed, and they were eventually dropped.

Jackson charged Brig. Gen. W. W. Loring with "neglect of duty" and "conduct subversive of good order and military discipline" over a myriad of disputes during the Romney campaign. The Confederate War Department shelved the charges.

Jackson arrested Col. Zephaniah T. Conner for losing Front Royal and large amounts of captured stores to a surprise attack by the Federals during the Valley campaign. This case was about to go to trial, also at Liberty Mills in August 1862, when Conner resigned from the service.

All five regimental commanders of Brig. Gen. Maxcy Gregg's South Carolina brigade were placed under arrest because their troops, uncomfortable on a rainy night, had torn down a fence for firewood against Jackson's orders near Fauquier Springs (also called the Fauquier White Sulphur Springs) during the Second Manassas campaign. They were released upon agreeing to pay for the fence.

Also in the Second Manassas campaign, an unidentified brigadier failed to leave a soldier behind at a crossroads to notify the next brigade in column of the proper road to take. Awakened near Bristoe by staff officer Alexander S. "Sandie" Pendleton and told that this mistake had occurred in contravention to his orders, with the result that troops had marched down the wrong road, Jackson replied, "Put him under arrest and prefer charges." Then Jackson went back to sleep. The episode's disposition is unclear.

Maj. Gen. A. P. Hill was arrested at the beginning of the Maryland campaign after angrily protesting to Jackson that he (Jackson) had issued direct orders to the brigadiers in his (Hill's) Light Division in Hill's own presence. Jackson filed charges of "neglect of duty" over Hill's lateness in having his division ready to march that same afternoon of September 4, 1862. Restored temporarily to command in Maryland, Hill saved the day for the Confederacy at Antietam by the timely arrival of his troops, after closing the surrender at Harpers Ferry and marching hard to reach the field. Hill subsequently filed countercharges against Jackson, whom he described to Maj.

Gen. James E. B. "Jeb" Stuart as "that crazy old Presbyterian fool." Both men looked forward to Hill's court-martial proceeding, which Hill expected would exonerate him and hoped would be the precursor to Jackson's own court-martial. Robert E. Lee, who wished to avoid either eventuality, pigeon-holed the papers and tried to mollify the officers. Both parties in the dispute still hoped for an eventual showdown right up to the time of Chancellorsville. One might wonder whether Jackson really thought he could wreck the military career of Ambrose Powell Hill without damaging the cause of the Confederacy, and whether he cared.

Jackson had Capt. William T. Poague of the Rockbridge Artillery and "quite a number of other [battery] commanders," Poague later recounted, placed under arrest after they permitted soldiers "to ride on [gun] carriages or caissons" while fording the Potomac River into Maryland on September 5, 1862. They were released and ordered to resume battery command after they left Frederick, Maryland.

During the Antietam campaign, Jackson also arrested Brig. Gen. William E. Starke for refusing to parade a Louisiana brigade through the streets of Frederick in order to permit an accusing townsman to identify individuals who allegedly had insulted certain ladies. Starke was held for several days, during which time, with Hill still in confinement, two of Jackson's three division commanders found themselves under arrest. Eventually the "Louisiana" miscreants turned out to be from the Stonewall Brigade instead. Starke was released, but Jackson never apologized for the mix-up. At the battle of Antietam, Starke suffered a mortal wound while leading a charge out of the West Woods.

Edward Porter Alexander, who served as Lee's chief of ordnance during the Maryland campaign, later wrote about the period during which Alexander Lawton functioned as Jackson's only division commander not under arrest. As brothers-in-law as well as comrades, Lawton and Alexander undoubtedly had discussed Jackson's behavior. "It seems that Gen. Jackson, at times, was something of a martinet—& this was one of his times," observed Alexander. Perhaps with tongue in cheek, he went on to say that Lawton himself "was in hourly fear lest Jackson might perhaps catch one of his men somewhere in the rear up an apple tree & send an aid ahead & tell Lawton to consider himself in arrest." Lawton escaped unscathed through the rest of the campaign, concluded Alexander, "& was one of the few of Jackson's generals with whom there was never the least unpleasantness."[13]

Jackson displayed his penchant for arresting officers on yet another occasion during the Maryland campaign, in this instance with two colonels of Maxcy Gregg's brigade (unless they were new to command since Fauquier Springs, these unfortunates thus had run afoul of Jackson for the second time). The pair transgressed by allowing troops en route to Harpers Ferry to break ranks to pick apples along the road. Gregg had begun to tire of such intercession by Jackson, describing Stonewall in a letter as "tyrannical & unjust." Subsequently the South Carolina brigadier filed charges of his own against Jackson, which were dropped at the request of Robert E. Lee. One of the offenders, Col. Dixon Barnes of the 12th South Carolina, like Starke died at Antietam.

Daniel Heyward Hamilton, colonel of the 1st South Carolina, joined the roster of accused derelict officers in Gregg's ever-offending brigade. In the words of historian James I. Robertson Jr., Hamilton was arrested in camp at Bunker Hill because he "failed to have his men fire muskets as promptly as the general wished."

An unnamed noncommissioned artillery officer probably holds the distinction of being the last man Jackson arrested. As the battle of Chancellorsville unfolded late on the afternoon of May 1, 1863, Jackson noticed a Confederate sergeant wearing a U.S.-issue rubber poncho. "Where did that man get that coat?" Stonewall demanded of Porter Alexander, who by this point in the war commanded a battalion of artillery. "From a row of knapsacks left by a regiment down the road there," replied Alexander, who had "looked on without objection" when the man picked up the coat. "Put him immediately under close arrest for stopping to plunder on the battlefield," Jackson said. This would be the last such order given by Jackson, who fell in a volley of North Carolina bullets the following night.[14]

In addition to the extraordinarily large number of arrests, Jackson endured strained relations with other officers. Some of these individuals sought transfers, tried or threatened to resign, or did resign over what they perceived to be Jackson's insults and unfairness. Jackson sought to remove others in this group over what he saw as their ill discipline or incompetence. A complete list would be difficult to compile, but it would include, at the least, Col. James W. Allen, a graduate of VMI who was killed at Gaines's Mill; Turner Ashby, the mercurial cavalry leader killed during the 1862 Valley campaign; Col. Arthur C. Cummings, who left the Confederate army in 1862; Brig. Gen. Arnold Elzey, who participated in the 1862 Valley campaign and was badly

wounded during the Seven Days; Maj. Gen. Richard S. Ewell, who alternated between admiration and befuddlement in his dealings with Jackson; Lt.
Col. Oliver R. Funsten, an officer who served with the 7th Virginia Cavalry
and the 17th Virginia Cavalry Battalion; Brig. Gen. Maxcy Gregg, whose
colonels, as already noted, seemed unusually adept at provoking Jackson;
Col. Andrew Jackson Grigsby of the 27th Virginia Infantry, whose notorious
swearing offended Jackson; John Harman, Jackson's efficient and profane
quartermaster; Brig. Gen. William B. Taliaferro, who served under Jackson
for much of 1862; Richard Taylor, whose brilliant portrait of Jackson in his
memoir *Destruction and Reconstruction* influenced generations of readers; and
Brig. Gen. Charles S. Winder, whom Jackson eventually came to value.

Some of the men who ran afoul of Jackson were incompetents or trans-
gressors who fully deserved censure. But such a pattern of personnel relations
begins at some point to tell us more about Jackson than about the men he
arrested, and what it conveys is a less-than-attractive dimension of his personality and a less-than-effective style of managing people.

Jackson's devout piety and unquestionable brilliance as a commander
should not obscure his human imperfections. He was difficult to please. He so
lacked tact as to be clumsy or even inept in personal relations. He was easily
angered and slow to forgive—in the unlikely event that he forgave at all. If he
did not like someone's performance, which happened often, he seldom took
the transgressing party aside for constructive criticism—or any criticism at all.
He usually did not ask for an explanation and rarely wanted to hear the other
side of the story. His typical solution was to place the unfortunate offender
under arrest.

A range of people found it difficult to work with Jackson. As Capt. Andrew
Wardlaw of the 14th South Carolina wrote home to his wife, "I must admit
that it is much pleasanter to read about Stonewall & his exploits than to serve
under him & perform those exploits." Sandie Pendleton of Jackson's staff was
one of the small number, most of whom were notable for their pronounced
faith in God, who did enjoy good relations with the general. But notwithstanding the signal recognition with which Jackson had honored his son, Brig.
Gen. William Nelson Pendleton, himself a man of the cloth, understood that
judging and relating to people constituted a major problem for Jackson. "It is
in such matters that Jackson makes mistakes," Pendleton privately wrote.
"His prejudices and partialities mislead him as to the merits or demerits of
individuals."[15]

Jackson may have acquired a litigious or irascible streak from his Uncle Cummins Jackson. A father or older brother figure to his young nephew, the uncle was a notoriously prolific filer of lawsuits in Lewis County, Virginia. Or perhaps this element of Stonewall's personality was a mask, donned unconsciously by a man painfully shy and insecure in dealing with people. Perhaps it was in some measure a sternness inspired by the Old Testament, an inclination to judge and punish wrongdoers for their sins. Whatever its origins, Jackson's severity clearly lessened his attractiveness and effectiveness.

One might wonder whether such a quarrelsome and tactless individual could have successfully moved up another step to the highest level of command. Robert E. Lee, who did command at that level, never found it necessary to arrest anyone, though during the Seven Days, if his mind had worked like Jackson's, he might have arrested the persistently tardy "Hero of the Valley." "When a man makes a mistake, I call him to my tent, talk to him, and use the authority of my position to make him do the right thing the next time," Lee once said of his own approach to erring subordinate officers. But such was not Stonewall Jackson's way.[16]

What became of General Garnett, whose misfortunes have served as a vehicle in this essay to take us to important questions about Jackson himself? His trial proved anything but a triumph for Jackson, then or now. The court records, including transcripts of testimony, are like most such documents detailed and tedious, as only legal maneuverings and language can be.[17] To cut to the essence: in the words of James I. Robertson Jr., "His seven specifications against Garnett ranged from inaccurate to niggling," or as Robert K. Krick has put it, they were "either patently absurd, greatly exaggerated, or inaccurate."[18]

The three surviving regimental colonels of the Stonewall Brigade—Arthur Cummings, John Echols, and Andrew Grigsby—had filed letters of deposition in support of the accused. Jackson himself testified. Garnett personally cross-examined him, emphasizing Jackson's own mistakes in the battle. Jackson denied making various statements Garnett recollected. In his copy of the trial transcript, which survives in the Museum of the Confederacy, Garnett wrote in the margin, "lie," "lie," "lie," beside Jackson's sworn statements.[19]

Sandie Pendleton took the stand on the second day, providing testimony in support of Jackson. But Pendleton himself had written home the night before the trial began that he believed Jackson's case and cause to be lost.[20]

Only Jackson and Pendleton testified at Garnett's court-martial. In an almost surreal, "saved by the bell" scenario, a courier interrupted the trial around noon on August 7 with news that a portion of Maj. Gen. John Pope's Federal Army of Virginia was detached at Culpeper and advancing south. Jackson relished precisely this sort of tactical situation. He suspended the proceedings and prepared to march to what would be greater glories—at Cedar Mountain, Bristoe Station, Manassas Junction, and Second Manassas.

The trial of Richard B. Garnett would never be resumed. Within a month R. E. Lee ordered Garnett's return to brigade command, but in Pickett's division of Longstreet's corps. Pragmatists or cynics could argue that Garnett had gotten a strange kind of break. Had he not run afoul of Jackson, he might have died in place of Winder at the head of a division at Cedar Mountain.

In the end it did not matter. Garnett fell instead at Gettysburg, heroically, in the vanguard of Pickett's Charge. Recovering from an injury, unable to walk and barely able to sit on a horse, he easily could have avoided duty on that July afternoon, but he was resolved to lead his men.[21] He became the second General Garnett to lay down his life for the Confederacy. The first, his cousin Robert Selden Garnett, had been killed in western Virginia in the summer of 1861, the first general officer on either side to perish in the war.

In a postscript to what can truly be called a sad life, Richard Garnett's body was never identified. Scavengers probably stripped him of his sword and other souvenirs. Long after the war, the sword turned up in a Baltimore pawnshop and today can be viewed at the Museum of the Confederacy. Garnett lay in all likelihood in a mass grave somewhere on the Pennsylvania battlefield, from which he was probably disinterred and reburied, with others, in Richmond's Hollywood Cemetery. There a monument to his memory was erected in 1991.[22]

Before he died, Garnett showed that he could forgive. As Jackson's body lay in state at the governor's mansion in Richmond, General Garnett paid his respects. With tears in his eyes, he drew Jackson's staff officers Sandie Pendleton and Henry Kyd Douglas aside after taking a last earthly look at the fallen warrior. "You know of the unfortunate breach between General Jackson and myself," he said. "I can never forget it, nor cease to regret it. But I wish here to assure you that no one can lament his death more sincerely than I do. I believe he did me great injustice, but I believe also he acted from the purest motives. He is dead. Who can fill his place!" Pendleton asked if Garnett would be a pallbearer at the Richmond memorial service the next day; the general agreed.[23]

Although long identified as a photograph of Richard Brooke Garnett, this image was pronounced by collateral members of the family to be "an authentic likeness of Robt. S. Garnett, and not Richd. B. Garnett, of whom there is no picture in existence." Francis Trevelyan Miller, ed., *The Photographic History of the Civil War*, 10 vols. (New York: Review of Reviews, 1911), 10:152.

Maj. John Warwick Daniel was one of Jackson's own, having begun a colorful, varied, and thrice-wounded Civil War career in Company C, 27th Virginia Infantry, Stonewall Brigade. Left crippled for life by the last of his wounds, sustained in the Wilderness, he would become, in the late 19th century, "The Lame Lion of Lynchburg," a gifted lawyer, author, orator, U.S. senator, and leading devotee of the cult of the Lost Cause. After the war he expressed his reverence for his former chieftain in these words:

The world has never known a sublimer man than Jackson. His character was stainless; his soul was meek; his courage was dauntless; his energy was irrepressible; his ambition was chastened; his religion was pure; his patriotism was fervent; his mind was vigorous; his heart was charitable; he was valorous of his convictions; he was shrinkingly modest; he was grandly audacious; of his soldiers he was the idol; of his country he was the hope; of war he was the master; his genius was transcendent; his deeds were wonderful. To serve his God and his country he lived; serving and loving them he died. His manliness and his godliness were alike preeminent, and the memory of him will never die.[24]

With most of this tribute Garnett, good man that he was, doubtless would have agreed. He had some reason to dissent from the passage about the charitable heart. But perhaps he would have agreed with it all.

NOTES

1. James I. Robertson Jr., *Stonewall Jackson: The Man, the Soldier, the Legend* (New York: Macmillan, 1997), 297; Ezra J. Warner, *Generals in Gray: Lives of the Confederate Commanders* (Baton Rouge: Louisiana State University Press, 1959), 99; Robert K. Krick, "Armistead and Garnett: The Parallel Lives of Two Virginia Soldiers," in *The Third Day at Gettysburg and Beyond*, ed. Gary W. Gallagher (Chapel Hill: University of North Carolina Press, 1994), 93–111; John E. Pierce, "The Civil War Career of Richard Brooke Garnett: A Quest for Vindication" (M.A. thesis, Virginia Polytechnic Institute, 1969), 1–11; Walter Harrison, *Pickett's Men: A Fragment of War History* (New York: D. Van Nostrand, 1870), 18–19.

2. Robertson, *Stonewall Jackson*, 296–97; John O. Casler, *Four Years in the Stonewall Brigade* (Guthrie, Okla.: State Capital Printing, 1893), 66.

3. G. F. R. Henderson, *Stonewall Jackson and the American Civil War*, 2 vols. (London: Longmans, Green, 1905), 1:190.

4. Jackson to Benjamin, January 10, 1862, quoted in Robertson, *Stonewall Jackson*, 310.

5. Thomas D. Gold, *History of Clarke County, Virginia, and Its Connection with the War between the States* (Berryville, Va.: n.p., 1914), 210.

6. John H. Worsham, *One of Jackson's Foot Cavalry: His Experience and What He Saw during the War, 1861–1865* (New York: Neale, 1912), 68. For a full-length treatment of Kernstown, see Gary L. Ecelbarger, *"We Are in for It!": The First Battle of Kernstown* (Shippensburg, Pa.: White Mane, 1997).

7. W. G. Bean, *Stonewall's Man: Sandie Pendleton* (Chapel Hill: University of North Carolina Press, 1959), 58–59.

8. Henry Kyd Douglas, *I Rode with Stonewall* (Chapel Hill: University of North Carolina Press, 1940), 37; Richard Taylor, *Destruction and Reconstruction: Personal Experiences of the Late War* (New York: Appleton, 1879), 79; McHenry Howard, *Recollections of a Maryland Confederate Soldier and Staff Officer under Johnston, Jackson, and Lee* (Baltimore: Williams and Wilkins, 1914), 83. Elaborated Howard, "All the field officers, certainly the colonels [of the Stonewall Brigade], were resenting strongly the arrest of General Garnett—Winder's predecessor—for withdrawing the brigade when out of ammunition at Kernstown on March 23, and I believe the feeling was shared largely by the men" (Howard, *Recollections*, 81).

9. Thomas H. Williamson note, April 14, 1881, and transcript of Jackson's testimony, Garnett Papers, Museum of the Confederacy, Richmond, Va.; William Thomas Poague, *Gunner with Stonewall: Reminiscences of William Thomas Poague, a Memoir Written for His Children in 1903*, ed. Monroe F. Cockrell (Jackson, Tenn.: McCowat-Mercer, 1957), 20. The idea that a few more minutes of tenacity would have saved the day for the Confederates had been expressed in northern newspaper accounts of Kernstown read by Jackson and his staff. See Bean, *Stonewall's Man*, 60; Sandie Pendleton to his mother, April 3, 1862, quoted in W. G. Bean, ed., "The Valley Campaign of 1862 as Revealed in Letters of Sandie Pendleton," *Virginia Magazine of History and Biography* 78 (July 1970): 344.

10. Quoted in Byron Farwell, *Stonewall: A Biography of General Thomas J. Jackson* (New York: Norton, 1992), 84. Detailed accounts of the Jackson-French imbroglio can be found in ibid., 75–85, and Robertson, *Stonewall Jackson*, 98–109.

11. Robertson, *Stonewall Jackson*, 125–26, 141–42, 156, 170, 184.

12. The incidents compiled in the following paragraphs, with the exception of the arrest of Poague and others for the September 5, 1862, infractions, are treated in detail by Jackson's biographers. See ibid., 321, 325, 418, 521, 545, 551, 585, 589–90, 594–95, 625, 627–28, 639, 679–80, 693, 709, 895 n 45; Farwell, *Stonewall*, 210, 220–21, 301, 378, 395–96, 398, 416–17, 421–22, 448, 458, 485–86. On arrests resulting from the events of September 5, see Poague, *Gunner with Stonewall*, 41–43. The episode in the Second Manassas campaign involving the unidentified brigadier who failed to leave a soldier at the crossroads may not have happened—or at least some of the details may be confused. Robertson recounts it in *Stonewall Jackson*, 551, citing William Willis Blackford, *War Years with Jeb Stuart* (New York: Scribner's, 1945), 111–12. The incident allegedly occurred on

August 26, 1862; however, Pendleton was sick and at home in Lexington, Virginia, from August 15 to September 9, 1862. See Bean, *Stonewall's Man*, 72–73.

13. Edward Porter Alexander, *Fighting for the Confederacy: The Personal Recollections of General Edward Porter Alexander*, ed. Gary W. Gallagher (Chapel Hill: University of North Carolina Press, 1989), 141.

14. Ibid., 199. Alexander explained what happened after Jackson gave the order to arrest the sergeant: "The next afternoon, when we expected to go very soon into a severe action, I let myself be persuaded by Capt. [Pichegru] Woolfolk to take the responsibility of returning the sergeant to duty as he was an excellent gunner. All of this was very unmilitary, & I have often wondered to this day what would have happened to me had Jackson lived."

15. Wardlaw quoted in Robertson, *Stonewall Jackson*, 628; Pendleton quoted in Bean, *Stonewall's Man*, 79.

16. Quoted in Douglas Southall Freeman, *R. E. Lee: A Biography*, 4 vols. (New York: Scribner's, 1934–35), 3:331.

17. For the best published analysis of the trial, see Robert K. Krick, "The Army of Northern Virginia's Most Notorious Court Martial: Jackson Vs. Garnett," in *The Smoothbore Volley That Doomed the Confederacy: The Death of Stonewall Jackson and Other Chapters on the Army of Northern Virginia* (Baton Rouge: Louisiana State University Press, 2001), 42–56. Surviving primary sources are in the Garnett Papers.

18. Robertson, *Stonewall Jackson*, 521; Robert K. Krick, *Stonewall Jackson at Cedar Mountain* (Chapel Hill: University of North Carolina Press, 1990), 14.

19. Garnett Papers.

20. Pendleton to his mother, August 5, 1862, in William N. Pendleton Papers, Southern Historical Collection, Wilson Library, University of North Carolina, Chapel Hill.

21. Walter Harrison, professing close personal association with Garnett in Pickett's command, wrote soon after the war that "his peculiar sensitiveness suffered under this supposed imputation at Kernstown, and he was ever thereafter anxious to expose himself, even unnecessarily, and to wipe out effectually by some great distinction in action, what he felt to be an unmerited slur upon his military reputation" (Harrison, *Pickett's Men*, 20).

22. Krick, "Armistead and Garnett," 122–23.

23. Douglas, *I Rode with Stonewall*, 38.

24. John W. Daniel, "Character of Stonewall Jackson," in *Speeches and Orations of John Warwick Daniel*, comp. Edward M. Daniel (Lynchburg, Va.: J. P. Bell, 1911), 41.

BIBLIOGRAPHIC ESSAY

Readers interested in the 1862 Shenandoah Valley campaign can choose from a rich array of titles. In addition to those listed in this brief overview, they should consult the notes accompanying the essays in this collection for pertinent published items and manuscript collections.

The best source for printed primary material on the 1862 Valley campaign is U.S. War Department, *The War of the Rebellion: A Compilation of the Official Records of the Union and Confederate Armies*, 127 vols., index, and atlas (Washington, D.C.: GPO, 1880–1901), ser. 1, vol. 12, pts. 1–3. These volumes contain more than 2,750 pages of official reports, correspondence, and other documents relating to military events in Virginia between mid-March and early September 1862. Parts 1 and 3 are most useful for the Valley campaign. Volume 2 of part 1 of *Supplement to the Official Records of the Union and Confederate Armies*, ed. Janet B. Hewett and others, 100 vols. (Wilmington, N.C.: Broadfoot, 1994–2000), also contains a small amount of relevant material. Anyone interested in particular military units should consult the volumes in part 2 of the *Supplement*, which reprint "Record of Events" information from the National Archives that includes facts about personnel and movements.

Several published collections of testimony from participants shed light on the campaign. The most convenient of these is Editors of Time-Life Books, *Voices of the Civil War: Shenandoah 1862* ([Alexandria, Va.]: Time-Life Books, [1997]), which contains a good selection of Union and Confederate material as well as excellent illustrations (many of which are contemporary sketches). For Confederate accounts, see *Southern Historical Society Papers*, ed. J. William Jones and others, 52 vols. (1876–1959; reprint, with 3-vol. index, Wilmington, N.C.: Broadfoot, 1990–92), and *Confederate Veteran*, 40 vols. (1893–1932; reprint, with 3-vol. index, Wilmington, N.C.: Broadfoot, 1984–86). Federal material can be found in the *Papers* of the Military Order of the Loyal Legion of the United States, 66 vols. and 3-vol. index (Wilmington, N.C.: Broadfoot, 1991–96). Abraham Lincoln's correspondence, which reveals how closely he followed events in the Valley, is in volume 5 of *The Collected Works of Abraham Lincoln*, ed. Roy P. Basler, 9 vols. (New Brunswick, N.J.: Rutgers University Press, 1953–55), and in *The Collected Works of Abraham Lincoln: Supplement, 1832–1865*, also edited by Basler (Westport, Conn.: Greenwood, 1974). Additional useful evidence from a Federal perspective is in volumes 1 and 6 of *Papers of the Military Historical Society of Massachusetts*, 14 vols. (1895–1918; reprint in 15 vols. with a general index, Wilmington, N.C.: Broadfoot, 1989–90). Although probably the most often cited collection of Civil War military reminiscences, Robert Underwood Johnson and Clarence Clough Buel, eds., *Battles and Leaders of the Civil War*, 4 vols. (New York: Century, 1887–88), allocates just thirty-five pages to the 1862 Valley campaign.

No one has written an in-depth history of the campaign that allots equal space to Confederate and Union elements of the story. The best overall study is Robert G. Tanner, *Stonewall in the Valley: Thomas J. "Stonewall" Jackson's Shenandoah Valley Campaign, Spring 1862* (1976; rev. ed., Mechanicsburg, Pa.: Stackpole, 1996), which, as its title suggests, focuses on the Confederates. Competently researched and well written, Tanner's book provides tactical and strategic details and offers generally balanced assessments of leaders. The most influential older title is William Allan, *History of the Campaign of Gen. T. J. (Stonewall) Jackson in the Shenandoah Valley of Virginia. From November 4, 1861, to June 17, 1862* (1880; reprint, Dayton, Ohio: Morningside, 1987). A member of Jackson's staff, Allan produced a careful and informative, if somewhat plodding, narrative that centers on the Confederate Army of the Valley and its enigmatic chief. For a brisk, engaging, shorter text supported by scores of illustrations, see Champ Clark and the Editors of Time-Life Books, *Decoying the Yanks: Jackson's Valley Campaign* (Alexandria, Va.: Time-Life Books, 1984). John W. Wayland, *Stonewall Jackson's Way: Route, Method, Achievement* (Verona, Va.: McClure, 1940), which devotes considerable attention to the 1862 Valley campaign, combines a sound text and dozens of late 19th- and early 20th-century photographs that show the Valley much as it looked during the Civil War.

Five books with a broader emphasis deserve consultation by readers exploring the 1862 Valley campaign. Laura Virginia Hale, *Four Valiant Years in the Lower Shenandoah Valley, 1861–1865* (Strasburg, Va.: Shenandoah Publishing, 1968), the work of an energetic collector of local history, brings together a wealth of descriptive anecdotes about the Confederate soldiers and civilians who lived and campaigned in the lower Valley. Sanford C. Kellogg, a U.S. Army officer, devotes two chapters to Jackson's campaign in *The Shenandoah Valley and Virginia, 1861–1865* (New York: Neale, 1903). Michael G. Mahon, whose overall argument suggests that the Valley did not serve as a major producer of food and fodder for Confederate armies after the early part of the war, spends one chapter on 1862 in *The Shenandoah Valley, 1861–1865: The Destruction of the Granary of the Confederacy* (Mechanicsburg, Pa.: Stackpole, 1999). Roger U. Delauter Jr. also dwells at some length on 1862 in *Winchester in the Civil War* (Lynchburg, Va.: H. E. Howard, 1992), as does Edward H. Phillips in *The Lower Shenandoah Valley in the Civil War: The Impact of War upon the Civilian Population and upon Civil Institutions* (Lynchburg, Va.: H. E. Howard, 1993).

Five of the campaign's six principal engagements have been the subject of at least one monograph (only Front Royal, smallest of the six, has not). By far the best of these is Robert K. Krick, *Conquering the Valley: Stonewall Jackson at Port Republic* (New York: Morrow, 1996). Contrary to the title's implication, Krick covers both Cross Keys and Port Republic, bringing to his task great depth of research and attention to tactical detail and character development—but relatively little interest in Jackson's opponents. Other tactical studies include Gary L. Ecelbarger, *"We Are in for It!": The First Battle of Kernstown* (Shippensburg, Pa.: White Mane, 1997), a dependable examination of the campaign's opening clash; Brandon H. Beck and Charles S. Grunder, *The First Battle of Winchester: May 25, 1862* (Lynchburg, Va.: H. E. Howard, 1992), a very brief account that nonetheless serves as a useful introduction to the subject; and Richard L. Armstrong, *The Battle of McDowell: March 11–May 18, 1862* (Lynchburg, Va.: H. E. Howard, 1990), another short book that probably offers as much information as most readers would want about Jackson's unremarkable victory in the Allegheny highlands.

Few military figures in U.S. history have attracted more interpreters than Stonewall Jackson, and all of the major biographies linger on the Valley campaign. G. F. R. Henderson, *Stonewall Jackson and the American Civil War*, 2 vols. (London: Longmans, Green, 1898), stood for decades as the definitive work. Henderson corresponded with former Confederate officers and drew on available published sources to craft his exhaustive, highly favorable account. Two important biographies appeared in the late 1950s, Frank E. Vandiver, *Mighty Stonewall* (New York: McGraw-Hill, 1957) and Lenoir Chambers, *Stonewall Jackson*, 2 vols. (New York: Morrow, 1959). Vandiver wrote with enormous flair and sometimes criticized Jackson quite sharply, while Chambers provided more detail and deliberately sought to disentangle the real Jackson from the legendary Confederate hero. The most recent biography, James I. Robertson Jr.'s massive *Stonewall Jackson: The Man, the Soldier, the Legend* (New York: Macmillan, 1997), rests on an impressive base of research in manuscripts and printed materials and, while admiring of its subject, does not shrink from pointing out some of Jackson's military errors and personal failings. For superb biographies of two of Jackson's key lieutenants in the Valley, see T. Michael Parrish, *Richard Taylor: Soldier Prince of Dixie* (Chapel Hill: University of North Carolina Press, 1992), and Donald C. Pfanz, *Richard S. Ewell: A Soldier's Life* (Chapel Hill: University of North Carolina Press, 1998). Volume 2 of Douglas Southall Freeman, *Lee's Lieutenants: A Study in Command*, 3 vols. (New York: Charles Scribner's Sons, 1942–44), examines Jackson and his subordinates in an engaging and perceptive fashion.

As a group, the Federal commanders in the Valley have received only a fraction of the attention lavished on Jackson. Irvin McDowell commanded U.S. armies through much of the first year of the war but awaits his first biographer. James Shields and Robert H. Milroy, admittedly less important officers, similarly have not been the subject of biographies. Two books on John Charles Frémont are noteworthy. Allan Nevins, *Frémont: Pathmarker of the West* (1955; reprint, Lincoln: University of Nebraska Press, 1992), chronicles in workmanlike fashion "The Pathfinder's" unsuccessful career in the Valley, while Andrew Rolle, *John Charles Frémont: Character as Destiny* (Norman: University of Oklahoma Press, 1991), employs a psychological approach that highlights the general's recklessness, trouble with superiors, and ultimate failure as a commander. There is also a brace of titles on Nathaniel P. Banks. The more recent one, James G. Hollandsworth, *Pretense of Glory: The Life of General Nathaniel P. Banks* (Baton Rouge: Louisiana State University Press, 1998), finds almost nothing to praise about Banks's military leadership. Fred Harvey

Harrington, *Fighting Politician: Major General N. P. Banks* (Philadelphia: University of Pennsylvania Press, 1948), a well-researched but somewhat dull effort, similarly presents Banks as a far from gifted soldier whose failures in the Valley represented just one of many unfortunate episodes in his Civil War career.

Civil War literature is especially rich in reminiscences, diaries, and collections of letters. For the 1862 Valley campaign, Confederate sources of these types far outnumber their Federal counterparts. Two justly can be called classics. Jedediah Hotchkiss, *Make Me a Map of the Valley: The Civil War Journal of Stonewall Jackson's Topographer*, ed. Archie P. McDonald (Dallas: Southern Methodist University Press, 1973), offers an unparalleled view from Confederate headquarters. As Jackson's indispensable cartographer, Hotchkiss played a critical role during the campaign, and his journal includes innumerable observations about movements, weather, topography, and other topics. Richard Taylor, who commanded a Louisiana brigade in the Army of the Valley, created an unforgettable portrait of Jackson, as well as of Richard S. Ewell, in *Destruction and Reconstruction: Personal Experiences of the Late War* (New York: Appleton, 1879).

Among other revealing titles are Charles R. Adams Jr., ed., *A Post of Honor: The Pryor Letters, 1861–63. Letters from Capt. S. G. Pryor, Twelfth Georgia Regiment, and His Wife, Penelope Tyson Pryor* (Fort Valley, Ga.: Garret Publications, 1989), a set of correspondence as rich in observation as it is idiosyncratic in grammar and spelling; John O. Casler, *Four Years in the Stonewall Brigade* (1893; reprint, Dayton, Ohio: Morningside, 1971), a highly entertaining but not always trustworthy memoir by a member of the 33rd Virginia Infantry of the Stonewall Brigade; and McHenry Howard, *Recollections of a Maryland Confederate Soldier and Staff Officer under Johnston, Jackson, and Lee* (Baltimore: Williams and Wilkins, 1914), one of the more quotable Confederate reminiscences. Margaretta Barton Colt, *Defend the Valley: A Shenandoah Family in the Civil War* (New York: Orion, 1994), is an unusually well executed compilation of various kinds of testimony from several individuals that includes a long section on the 1862 campaign.

On the Union side, David Hunter Strother [Porte Crayon, pseud.], *A Virginia Yankee in the Civil War: The Diaries of David Hunter Strother*, ed. Cecil D. Eby Jr. (Chapel Hill: University of North Carolina Press, 1961), illuminates the campaign from the perspective of a member of Nathaniel P. Banks's staff. Secretary of the Treasury Salmon P. Chase took an active interest in Irvin McDowell's activities, as evidenced by various documents in Salmon P. Chase, *The Salmon P. Chase Papers*, ed. John Niven and others, 5 vols. (Kent, Ohio: Kent State University Press, 1993–98). For the observations of a soldier with John C. Frémont, see Oscar D. Ladley, *Hearth and Knapsack: The Ladley Letters, 1857–1880*, ed. Carl M. Becker and Ritchie Thomas (Athens: Ohio University Press, 1988).

Civilian observers left a rich legacy of evidence. Cornelia Peake McDonald, *A Woman's Civil War: A Diary, with Reminiscences of the War, from March 1862*, ed. Minrose C. Gwin (1935; Madison: University of Wisconsin Press, 1992), traces the ebb and flow of morale and expectations in Winchester. Readers should be warned, however, that the editor's introduction does little to enhance McDonald's wonderful diary. Lucy Rebecca Buck, *Sad*

Earth, Sweet Heaven: The Diary of Lucy Rebecca Buck during the War between the States, ed. Dr. William P. Buck (Birmingham, Ala.: Cornerstone, 1973; reprinted as *Shadows on My Heart: The Civil War Diary of Lucy Rebecca Buck of Virginia*, ed. Elizabeth R. Baer [Athens: University of Georgia Press, 1997]), rivals McDonald as a valuable account by a woman, while Thomas A. Ashby, *The Valley Campaigns: Being the Reminiscences of a Non-Combatant While Between the Lines in the Shenandoah Valley During the War of the States* (New York: Neale, 1914), includes a number of memorable passages.

Four other general works offer worthwhile perspectives on the 1862 Valley campaign. Herman Hattaway and Archer Jones, *How the North Won: A Military History of the Civil War* (Urbana: University of Illinois Press, 1983), relates events in the Valley to the larger strategic picture, as does volume 1 of Kenneth P. Williams, *Lincoln Finds a General*, 5 vols. (New York: Macmillan, 1949–59). Bruce Catton, *Terrible Swift Sword* (Garden City, N.Y.: Doubleday, 1963), which is volume 2 of the 3-volume "Centennial History of the Civil War," showcases the author's literary gifts and sound historical sense. Finally, the first volume of Shelby Foote, *The Civil War: A Narrative*, 3 vols. (New York: Random House, 1958–74), traces the campaign in memorable prose.

JONATHAN M. BERKEY, a doctoral candidate in history at Pennsylvania State University and contributor to a book of essays on Unionism in the Confederacy, is completing a study of the lower Shenandoah Valley during the Civil War.

KEITH S. BOHANNON, a member of the Department of History at the State University of West Georgia, teaches courses on the Civil War and on the history of Georgia. He is the author of *The Giles, Alleghany, and Jackson Artillery* and a number of essays and articles and coeditor of *Campaigning with "Old Stonewall": Confederate Captain Ujanirtus Allen's Letters to His Wife*.

PETER S. CARMICHAEL is a member of the Department of History at the University of North Carolina at Greensboro. The author of *Lee's Young Artillerist: William R. J. Pegram*, as well as several essays and articles in popular and scholarly journals, he is completing a study of Virginia slaveholders' sons and the formation of southern identity in the late antebellum years.

GARY W. GALLAGHER is the John L. Nau III Professor in the History of the American Civil War at the University of Virginia and editor of seven previous titles in the Military Campaigns of the Civil War series. His books include *The Confederate War* and *Lee and His Army in Confederate History*.

A. CASH KOENIGER is professor of history at the Virginia Military Institute. His previous publications include articles in the *Journal of American History*, the *Journal of Southern History*, the *Journal of Military History*, and the *South Atlantic Quarterly*.

ROBERT E. L. KRICK, a Richmond-based historian, was reared on the Chancellorsville battlefield. He is the author of *The Fortieth Virginia Infantry*, *Staff Officers in Gray: A Biographical Register of the Staff Officers in the Army of Northern Virginia*, and a number of essays and articles.

ROBERT K. KRICK grew up in California but has lived and worked on the Virginia battlefields for more than thirty years. He has authored dozens of articles and twelve books, including *Conquering the Valley: Stonewall Jackson at Port Republic* and

The Smoothbore Volley that Doomed the Confederacy: The Death of Stonewall Jackson and Other Chapters on the Army of Northern Virginia.

WILLIAM J. MILLER, editor of *Civil War: The Magazine of the Civil War Society* for several years, is the author of *The Training of an Army: Camp Curtin and the North's Civil War* and *Mapping for Stonewall: The Civil War Service of Jed Hotchkiss*, editor and coauthor of the 3-volume *The Peninsula Campaign: Yorktown to the Seven Days*, and editor of a forthcoming volume of Jedediah Hotchkiss's Civil War letters.

Bedinger, Carrie, 107

Bedinger, Virginia, 112

Bel Air (Va. home), 89–90, 107

Belgian muskets, 60

Bell, Andrew J., 136

Bellingham, Wash., 185

Benicia, Calif., 184

Benjamin, Judah P., 27–28, 220

Benton, Thomas H., 46

Berkeley County, Va., 95

Big Sandy Valley (Va.), 65

Biskey, Louis, 68–69

Blackford, William W., 234

Bladensburg, battle of, 179

Blair, Francis P., 47, 80–81

Blakemore, Letitia A., 97, 100

Blamphin, Charles, 36

Blandford, Mark H., 118

Blenker, Louis, 59–60, 66, 68–69, 89

Bolivar Heights, Va., 199–200

Boltz, John H., 151–52

Boston, Mass., 184

Boston Daily Advertiser, xvii

Boteler, Alexander R., 27–28, 154, 157, 164

Boyd, Belle, 97

Brawner's Farm, battle of, 208

Bridgewater, Va., 123

Bristoe Station, Va., 226, 231

Brooke, Benjamin F., 96

Brown, G. Campbell, 131

Brown, John (slave), 92

Brown, William F., 130

Brown's Gap, Va., 75

Buchanan, Franklin, 179–80, 208

Buchanan, Robert, 204

Buck, Lucy R., 89–90, 107, 128, 240–41

Buck, Marcus B., 90–91, 93, 108

Buck, William M., 107

Bucking (disciplinary measure), 206

Bunker Hill, Va., 15, 200, 228

California, 45, 182, 184

Camp Alleghany, Va., 118–19

Camp Bartow, Va., 118

Campbell, Mrs. John, 99

Camp Washington, Va., 153

Candy, Charles, 91, 100

Cape Hatteras, N.C., 182

Carroll, Samuel S., 76–78

Casey, Silas, 185

Caskie, William H., 145, 168

Casler, John O., 88, 197, 200, 206, 210, 220, 240

Castle Pinckney (Charleston Harbor, S.C.), 191

Casualties, xxi, 49, 61, 105–6, 123, 130, 139, 202, 204, 222

Cedar Mountain, battle of, xx, 206–9, 219, 231

Centreville, Va., 14, 64

Chambersburg (Pa.) Times, 103

Chancellorsville, battle of, 208, 228

Chandler, John G., 182–83

Charleston, S.C., 178, 191–93

Charleston Courier, xiv

Charleston Mercury, xv

Charlestown, Va., 15, 70, 91–92, 103, 106, 128, 130, 167, 199

Charlottesville, Va., 75, 78, 161

Chase, Charles S., 97

Chase, Julia, 97, 105

Chase, Salmon P., 8, 12, 22–23

Chesapeake & Ohio Canal, 87

Chesnut, Mary B., 144

Chester Gap, Va., 54, 64

Chicago Tribune, xvi

Chilton, Robert H., 134

Civilians: impact of military operations upon, xix, 28, 86–114

Clark (Union colonel), 94

Clark, John P., 93, 106

Clark, John S., 99–100

Fort Donelson, Tenn., 3
Fort Hamilton, N.Y., 181, 195
Fort Henry, Tenn., 3
Fortifications, 53
Fort Meade, Fla., 224
Fort Monroe, Va., 185
Fort Sumter, S.C., 178, 191, 195, 209
Fort Vancouver, Wash., 185
Fort Walla Walla, Wash., 186–89
Four Lakes, battle of, 189, 209
Frank Leslie's Illustrated Newspaper, 46, 48, 54, 69, 105, 223
Franklin, Va., 11, 61–63, 66–68, 79, 198
Frederick, Md., 6, 97, 227
Frederick County, Va., 88, 93
Fredericksburg, Va., xii, 4, 11, 14, 28, 31, 53, 62, 65, 72, 79, 127, 133, 224
Frederick the Great, 30
Freeman, Douglas S., 32, 41, 239
Freeman, Eli, 42
Frémont, Jesse Benton (Mrs. John C.), 46, 58
Frémont, John C., xii–xviii, 4, 8, 10–11, 14–19, 22–23, 76–80, 87–88, 119, 160, 197; generalship assessed, 43–49, 51, 58–71, 80–81, 239
Fremont, Sewall L., 183
French, William H., 224–25
Front Royal, battles of, xiii–xiv, xvi, xviii–xix, 8, 10, 12, 18, 28, 33, 55–57, 63–66, 72, 104, 127–35, 198–99, 226
Front Royal, Va., xi–xii, 15–17, 36, 45, 51, 53–54, 74–75, 78–79, 89–93, 97, 102, 107–8, 144, 167
Fulkerson, Samuel V., 27, 33
Funsten, Oliver R., 157, 229
Furlow, William L., 118, 125–27, 129, 135, 140

Gaines's Mill, battle of, ix, 33, 203–5, 209, 228

Garland, Samuel, 195
Garnett, Richard B., xx, 32, 41, 195–96, 219–35
Garnett, Robert S., 231–32
Gates, William, 183–84, 212
Gay, Edward S., 208
Geary, John W., 6, 12, 15, 21–22, 54, 64, 72, 98, 151
Georgia Military Institute, 118
Georgia troops: 1st Infantry, 27; 12th Infantry, xix, 115–42; 21st Infantry, 30, 104
Germans. *See* Europeans
Gettysburg, battle of, 208, 231; Jackson's absence at decried, 30
Gilham, William, 226
Gold, Thomas D., 220
Gordon, George H., 55–57
Gordonsville, Va., 52–53, 75, 219
Gorgas, Josiah, 192
Grant, Ulysses S., 6, 20, 47, 189
Greenbrier River, battle of, 118, 123, 137–38
Gregg, David McM., 213
Gregg, Maxcy, 226, 228–29
Greggs, M. L., 92
Grigsby, Andrew J., 223, 229–30
Grimes, James W., 8
Guyandotte Valley (Va.), 65

Hagerstown, Md., 97–98
Hall, Ralf M., 92
Hall, Silas, 92
Halleck, Henry W., 3
Hamilton, Daniel H., 228
Hampshire County, Va., 150
Hancock, Md., 27
Hanging Rock, Va., 150
Harman, John A., 89, 131, 157–58, 229
Harpers Ferry, Va., xii, xvi–xvii, 4, 7–8, 12, 14, 16–18, 32, 44–45, 65, 79, 87, 91, 98, 108, 151, 199–201, 209, 226

Salem, Va., 59

Sanders, Miles, 92

Sanders, Tom E., 136

San Diego, Calif., 184

San Francisco (steamer), 182–84, 191, 209, 212

San Francisco, Calif., 184, 190

Savage's Station, Va., 204

Savannah Republican, xv

Saxton, Rufus, 14, 17, 21, 65

Schenck, Robert C., 61

Scott, Andrew V. B., 39

Scott, Irby G., 130

Scott, Reuben A., 97

Scott, Winfield, 47, 184, 224–25

Seminole Wars, 116, 179

Semmes, Raphael, 218

Seven Days, battles of, ix–xi, xiv, xx, 4, 18–19, 80–81, 133, 203–5, 228, 230

Seven Pines, battle of, 18, 34

Seward, William H., 8, 98

Sharpsburg, battle and campaign of, 208, 224, 226–28

Shaw, Robert G., 154

Shenandoah River, xi, 18, 75–76, 87, 155–56

Shenandoah Valley (Va.): 1864 campaign in, xx–xxi, 6, 109; Federal military command in, 3–23, 43–85; geography and description of, xi–xi, 58, 68, 87, 163

Shepherdstown, Va., 93, 97–98, 107, 111, 154, 166

Sheppard, Willliam L., 221

Sheridan, Philip H., xix, 109

Sherman, William T., xix

Sherwood, Asa E., 120

Shields, James, xiii–xvi, xviii, 12, 15–18, 53, 62, 65, 71, 88, 91, 99, 127–30, 199, 202; generalship assessed, 43–45, 49–50, 71–81

Shiloh, battle of, x, 3

Simms (Union quartermaster), 31

Sitlington's Hill (Va.), 119–22, 138–39, 198

Skoch, George F., xxi

Slaves, 8, 12, 64, 87, 91–95, 98, 101, 103–4, 108–9, 125, 127, 135, 147–50, 163, 169

Smead, Abner, 116

Smith, Francis H., 225

Smith, George C., 117

Smith, Isaac N., 96

Smith, William, 212

Smoothbore muskets, 120, 186, 192

Snake River, 186–88

Sorrel, G. Moxley, 210

South Carolina troops: 1st Infantry, 228; 6th Infantry, 192–94, 205, 215; 12th Infantry, 228; 14th Infantry, 229

Southern Illustrated News, 145, 166, 168

The South Reports the Civil War, 136

Southwest Virginia & Tennessee Railroad, 59, 62

Sperry, Kate, 94–95, 101

Spokane Indians, 186, 189

Spokane Plains, battle of, 189

Spokane River, 186–89

Stanardsville, Va., 53, 74–78

Stanton, Edwin M., 4, 7–8, 11, 15, 44, 52–54, 60, 64, 66, 72, 79–81

Starke, William E., 227–28

Staunton, Va., xii, 51, 60–61, 65, 80, 87, 96–97, 119, 124

Steiger, T. Albert, 66–67

Steptoe, Edward J., 186–88

Steptoe Butte, battle of, 187–88, 199, 209

Steuart, George H., 195

Stewart, Thomas J., 120

Stonewall Cemetery (Winchester, Va.), 167

Straggling, 205–6

Strasburg, Va., xi–xiii, xvi, 12, 14, 16–18, 45, 50, 53–57, 62, 69–70, 74, 79, 87, 96, 158, 200, 209

Strayer, Clara V., 89, 104

Strayer, John, 108
Striden, Elizabeth, 92
Strong, George T., 7–8
Strother, David H., 56–57, 91, 99, 101–3, 154
Stuart, James E. B., 149, 170–71, 227
Suckley, George, 69
Sumner, Charles, 8
Sumter Republican, 124–25
Swift Run Gap, Va., 53, 74, 88, 97

Talbot County, Md., 179, 190
Taliaferro, William B., 27, 31–33, 39, 229
Tanner, Robert G., xvii, 7, 20, 172, 238
Taylor, Oliver H. P., 213
Taylor, Richard, 31–33, 41, 197, 199, 201, 222–23, 229, 239–40
Taylor's Hotel (Winchester, Va.), 130–31
Texas, 149
Thomas, Henry W., 135–36
Thomas, J. William, 106
Thoroughfare Gap, Va., xii, 16, 64
Three Bells (steamer), 183
Toombs, Robert A., 29
Tracy, Albert, 60, 66, 69
Trimble, Isaac R., 32–33
Trueheart, Charles W., 7, 166
Trumbull, Lyman, 8
Turner, Joseph A., 124
Twiggs, David E., 224
Tyler, Erastus B., 77–78

United States Military Academy, 56, 116, 118, 154, 179–81, 185, 195, 208, 212
United States troops (Regulars): Buchanan's Brigade, 204; 3rd Artillery, 181–84; 4th Artillery, 181; 9th Infantry, 184–89

Valley Turnpike, xii, 55, 75, 200–201
Vermont, 34

Vicksburg, Miss., xiv
Virginia, CSS, 4
Virginia Central Railroad, xii, 208
Virginia Historical Society, ix
Virginia Military Institute, 198, 225–26, 228
Virginia troops: Public Guard, 208; 7th Militia Brigade, 163; Stonewall Brigade, xx, 28, 88, 106, 195–210, 218, 220–23, 227, 233; Charlottesville Artillery, 29; Rockbridge Artillery, 197, 227; Rice's Battery, 127, 130; 7th Cavalry, 152, 154, 229; 17th Cavalry Battalion, 229; 2nd Infantry, 42, 196, 204, 220; 4th Infantry, 29, 196; 5th Infantry, 196, 202; 11th Infantry, 29; 21st Infantry, 210; 23rd Infantry, 27; 27th Infantry, 28, 196, 200, 202, 216, 223, 229, 233; 33rd Infantry, 96, 196, 200, 206, 220; 37th Infantry, 27; 48th Infantry, 103, 128; 52nd Infantry, 106; 55th Infantry, 29
Vizetelly, Frank, 35

Walla Walla, Wash., 186–89
Wardlaw, Andrew B., 229
War of 1812, 179
Warren, Edward T. H., 155
Warrenton, Va., 14, 64
Washington, D.C., xii, xvi, 6–8, 10–11, 14, 20, 45, 50–52, 64–65, 80, 87, 179
Washington, George (slave), 92
Washington Territory, 185–90, 199
Wayland, John Walter, 96, 238
Wayland, John Wesley, 96
Waynesboro, Va., xii, 77
Wearing of the Gray, 151
West, Beckwith, 128
West Point. *See* United States Military Academy
West View, Va., 61, 119
Wheeling, Va., 48, 58–59